# One Woman's Walk

# One Woman's Walk
## From Land's End to John O'Groats

*by*
## Shirley Rippin

**Shirley Rippin**
*in association with*
**Logaston Press**

LOGASTON PRESS
Little Logaston, Logaston, Woonton,
Almeley, Herefordshire HR3 6QH


First published by Logaston Press 1998
Copyright © Shirley Rippin 1998

ISBN 1 873827 45 8


Set in Times by Logaston Press
and printed in Great Britain by
The Cromwell Press, Trowbridge

*In memory of my mother*

# The Length of Britain Walk

### 1

Twelve hundred miles (or thereabouts)
And not a pair of boots worn out.
A million things you've seen and done,
All made walking so much fun.
Green 'roads' that you can freely roam,
The great outdoors your 'mobile home'.
So many friends, so many tales,
Since first you nervously left Wales,
And trod through Cornwall, full of flowers,
(Your seven league boots ate up the hours).
Through Devon, Somerset and then -
The Severn Bridge and home again.
From ancient Glastonbury's streets,
To modem engineering feats.

### 2

Now a week long, work forced break,
And most impatiently you wait.
Then off on routes now so well known,
With history writ in every stone
On Offa's ridgeway, trod each day,
By dozens travelling the Way.
Then into England, via Chirk.
A massive stretch of sheer hard work
Still lies ahead, but every day
You grow more confident of the way.
You fall in love with Pennine scenes,
Its lonely panoramic greens.
Three glorious weeks and then one day,
Another barrier in the way.
Historic Hadrian's Wall looms high,
And Scotland beckons by and by.

*Barbara Beardsmore*

### 3

But first a day of relaxations,
As you stand between two nations,
And realise just what you've done,
And (of course) what's still to come.
Of the rest we know but little.
But you know every jot and tittle
Of each lonely hill and glen,
Populated not by men,
But curlews, eagles, stag and grouse.
This is better than any house.
Calm lochs reflect cruel hills,
With tumbling crystal Scottish rills.
All too soon (and before time),
John O'Groats is on the sign.
Success has sent the senses reeling,
Anti-climax is the feeling.

### 4

What a change from humdrum life
As cook and cleaner, mother, wife.
You've been master of your fate,
Time not waiting at the gate.
Rucksack moulded to your back,
Feet in rhythm with the track.
The next campsite up ahead,
Your tent is better than any bed.
You've even slept with other men,
(I bet you won't do that again!)
But all good things come to an end,
You must come back to us, my friend.
There's a lot of normal living,
This is the advice I'm giving,
Unwind with a second honeymoon,
But don't forget to come back soon.
Eagerly all await the talk -
About the LENGTH OF
BRITAIN WALK.

# Contents

# Acknowledgements

To achieve my ambition and complete this walk I am indebted to many people without whose help and support it would not have been possible. Some helped in material ways, others gave up their time to provide physical encouragement by walking with me and there were those who simply by believing I could do it, gave me the confidence to have a go.

I am indebted to: the late Glyn Jones of the Map Shop Abergavenny for supplying many of my maps; Longtown Outdoor Education Centre, Herefordshire, for advising on camping foods and tents and for their supportive interest throughout; Frances Kenward who, in the wake of fears and worries in the planning stage and during the pre-walk panic attacks, gave me the benefit of her own experiences as a lone walker; and my good friend Barbara Beardsmore, so confident of my success that she extracted a promise of a talk and slide show in the village hall when I returned. With her enthusiasm and encouragement and unfailing faith in my ability how could I dare give up?

My heartfelt thanks go to Walter and Diana Hearne in Cornwall and my cousin Helen in Bridgwater who provided accommodation *en route*; and to Ben Andrews who not only provided bed and board, but turned out to walk with me in torrential rain in the Pennines: to all those individuals mentioned in the text who offered lifts, dried washing, provided refreshments or un-scheduled campsites and helped in countless other ways to make my journey a successful one. The names of most are unknown. Others have had their names changed.

I am grateful to: Vicky Muter for giving up a day to walk with me in Wales and for her help and advice in writing this book; Rosemary Russell for the many hours spent reading and correcting the final product; and Andrew Johnson for taking on the task of taking the manuscript through to the final product.

And most of all I thank my family. My son Robin who walked from Bridgwater to the Severn Bridge giving me valuable support in an area through which I would not have been comfortable walking alone—and suffering extreme pain in the process. My daughter Helen for her company through the Peak District and Southern Pennines. My Uncle, Colin Crump, for providing the necessary support through the campsite-free area between Chirk and Mow Cop, a job he fulfilled with good humour and competence leaving me free of worry for 50 miles. And last, but not least, to my husband Michael; for putting up with the long winter months of planning; for taking on the extra work I would normally do; for always being on the end of the phone and for keeping my bank balance topped up. But most of all for giving up his time to drive several thousand miles in delivering me to the start, collecting me from the end, coming up to the Pennines twice and providing car support between Edinburgh and Glasgow.

Without such a supportive family my walk would have been far more difficult to achieve and far less pleasurable. To them all I am truly grateful.

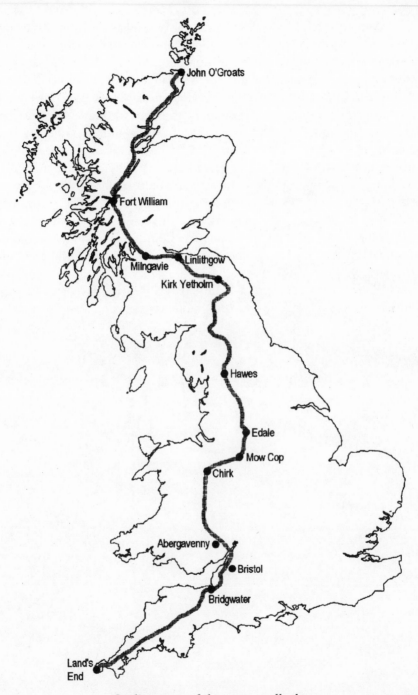

*Outline map of the route walked*

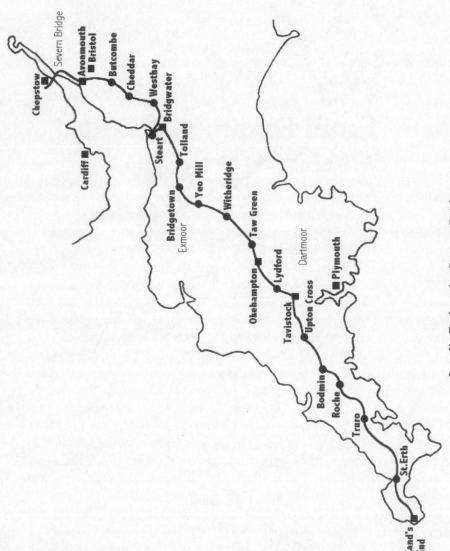

*Land's End to the Severn Bridge*

# 1
# From Dream to Reality

"Mum, you can't!" my eldest daughter said emphatically when I announced my intention of walking from Land's End to John O'Groats, "It just isn't safe." And when she found that no amount of persuasion was going to change my mind, bombarded me with dire warnings not to talk to strangers and on no account to accept lifts.

But for me, it was to be the fulfilment of a lifetime's ambition. Since 1960 when the Russian-born Dr.Barbara Moore had made the headlines walking from John O' Groats to Land's End in 22 days, the idea had been at the back of my mind. I was eighteen at the time and had followed her progress avidly on our family's newly acquired television, full of overwhelming admiration that a lady of her age was capable of doing such a marathon walk. Now, at a similar age, with my own family grown up and my present lifestyle flexible, I saw the opportunity to make the dream a reality.

I had another reason to go too. Agoraphobia. For half my life I have suffered in varying degrees from both this and depression and have only in recent years made significant headway in overcoming my fears. Many forms of travel filled me with dread. As did most social occasions and public places. Only in the wide open spaces of the hills, alone, was I completely at ease. But to undertake a thousand mile journey on foot and be prepared to face any eventuality—and cope with it—would be a testing experience. It was not the physical effort of walking that bothered me. It was whether I was mentally able to do it. I believed that I could. And, strengthened by the desire to fulfil a dream—I knew I had to do it.

1

With this lack of confidence, it was never my intention to go the whole way alone. Several likely candidates were approached but the initial interest expressed produced no firm commitments, only a vague promise that fell through for a genuine reason. But after two years of thorough planning there was no way I was going to allow a little thing like walking alone, put me off. If I waited for other people, I might wait forever. Some inner feeling told me it was 'now or never.' Also, my mother, who had died the previous year after a long fight against cancer, had known of my dream. She loved travelling herself and had been full of enthusiasm and encouragement. My inheritance from her, though not large, was sufficient to finance the trip and I felt that it was something she would have wanted me to do—a parting gift that I would always treasure in her memory.

My love of wild desolate landscapes dictated that wherever possible the route would be in upland, open country. Also, from the point of view of personal safety I wanted to avoid main roads and large towns, using national trails and recognised public footpaths. From a personal point of view, I had no hesitation in planning to walk north. My husband's home was in Cornwall. I had lived there for several years when we were first married and knew the county well. There would be no great adventure in ending at Land's End. By walking north, I would be walking always into the unknown and it would be getting wilder and better all the time.

From preliminary enquiries I had discovered there was no established route for the End to End. People choose their routes to suit their mode of travel or the time available. Some choose the shortest way. Others have eccentric agendas, such as visiting an alphabetical list of towns! Most walkers devised their own routes from around four hundred long distance paths and a network of public rights of way.

I planned to camp for the entire trip. It was the cheapest accommodation and I love the freedom of camping. So, at the end of each day there had to be a campsite. Gradually the outline of my journey began to take shape. There were sections that were obvious. The Pennine Way and the West Highland Way were two Long Distance Paths I had always wanted to walk. But in other areas there were many possible options. Should I cross the Severn Bridge into Wales and follow the Offa's Dyke Path? I could then call in at home in the Black Mountains on the way North and turn off somewhere near Chirk making my way to the Pennines through Cheshire. Would a more easterly route through the Cotswolds and Midlands be more interesting? The end of the Pennine Way and start of the West Highland Way are on opposite sides of Scotland. Perhaps I should consider a westerly route through the Lake District? In the end, I drew up three routes. Worked out the milage and time needed for each, then 'sat' on the proposals for several months before hatching a decision.

Once the decision was made, there followed three months of intensive planning. Night after night I pored over maps and guide books, working out each day's route in meticulous detail. My walk was for enjoyment. Time was unlimited. I was not setting out to break any records. I wanted time for visits and leisurely activities and above all to pursue my interest of recording and studying wild flowers. As I can achieve fifteen miles comfortably in a day, this distance and the availability and location of a campsite determined the length of each day. Finding and linking public rights of way in a direct route to a suitable destination was not always easy and inevitably some days turned out to be much longer than others.

As each section of the journey was finalised, it was drawn on the maps with a highlighting pen, so that there could be no mistaking where I should be going. This effectively dispatched with the need for detailed route notes. My basic schedule was simple: the date, starting and finishing points, milage and campsite, and a few useful additions such as availability of shop, café or telephone. The finished schedule was then given to my husband, Michael and to several friends who wanted to keep tabs on me. My copy I carried with me adhering to it faithfully unless forced to make changes, when for instance, a campsite had been closed, or the weather cut short a day.

By March my schedule was complete. I had decided on a starting date which would accommodate various pre-arranged commitments. I began methodically assembling my kit. What did I need? What could I do without? I checked and rechecked food, clothes and first aid, posted maps off to strategically placed friends and relations ready for collection *en route*, and started to worry.

I had been apprehensive all along. Now as the days grew longer and the calendar turned from May to June, I was on the verge of panic. I became paranoid about all the things that might go wrong. What would I do if I was taken ill or twisted an ankle? I remembered seeing a television programme where a jogger was stung by a bee and suffered a severe allergic reaction when there was no-one near to help him. I worried about what might happen to a women walking alone and wasn't helped by well meaning friends who asked me what I would do "if this" or "if that" should happen. Walking in certain places had always worried me. I never felt at

3

ease on golf courses. They always seemed to be surrounded by a thick belt of trees and bushes and there were so many men around. I was apprehensive about dense woodland and canal towpaths, especially in built-up areas. If you were unfortunate enough to be attacked in any of these places, dragged off into the undergrowth or pushed in the water, no-one would ever know. My mind ran riot with lurid scenarios. I lay awake at night turning over these thoughts and repeatedly checking all the things I had to remember.

There was little more to do except prepare myself mentally and impatiently await the arrival of June 8th.

# 2
# Travels in the West Country
## Land's End to Bridgwater

When you wait for an important event in your life, the last few weeks seem to drag by. Then suddenly you are on a runaway bus! The final week slips by in no time at all. To me it was like waiting for the birth of a child. You want the big day to come quickly. You look forward to it, while at the same time you dread it and know it is inevitable.

Friends and relations rang to wish me luck. Others who didn't know where I was going, looked in disbelief when I casually mentioned that I would be away for a few weeks walking from Land's End to John O'Groats. "Not actually ALL the way?" they would say, still not believing, "Not WALKING all the way." One acquaintance in an aside to my son said gloomily, "It's quite sad when your mother reaches 50 and starts to go mad." Perhaps I was mad. But I was going to be mad my way, doing something I really wanted to do and although I was scared of what the future held I was also eager to get started.

At last the big day arrived. The Land Rover was packed and ready to go—and so that I could start early on the morning of June 8th, a Saturday—we travelled down overnight. With virtually no traffic on the motorway we drove all the way to Truro before stopping for a few hours sleep in a layby. By 6.30 we were eating breakfast in the deserted car park at Land's End. There were no tourists; no signs of life at the hotel; no photographer to take 'starting pictures' at the famous signpost, in fact, there was not even a signpost! And the toilets were locked. All in all, it was an inauspicious start.

5

I posed for photographs beside a boat firmly moored on dry land in the childrens' play area. Then, while Michael went back to the Land Rover to catch up on sleep, I set off along the cliffs, for the first few miles of my marathon journey; my first priority being to find somewhere for a pee. So far so good. It was 7.30 and I'd started on the right day. I had one of our dogs for company, a Sheltie named Fern. Like most dogs he loves going for walks, but little did he know he was going to walk 50 miles in the next couple of days. Michael was staying over the weekend to see that all was well and I wanted to walk as far as possible while I had a vehicle at my disposal—putting off the evil moment when I must carry the rucksack. I hoped to reach Truro before this was necessary.

### A flowery start

It was a glorious morning. Clear blue skies; the sun already warming the chilly morning air. Below the cliffs, the deep blue swell of the Atlantic rose and fell in benign mood, sluicing lacy cascades of spray over treacherous granite. White surf frothed around the offshore reefs of the Longships Lighthouse. Wild flowers painted the cliff tops in a riotous palette of colour; yellow vetches and bird's-foot trefoil adding bright splashes to the softer pink and white carpets of thrift and sea campions and the tiny pale blue spring squills.

This was to be my only coastal walking until the north of Scotland. A mere two miles of the North Cornwall Coastal Footpath. Although many End-to-Enders use this path, I calculated that to walk its entirety would add an extra 100 miles to the route through the West Country and discarded the idea at an early stage of the planning. It's tough too. Statistics quote more feet of ascent per mile here than on the Pennine Way. Also, I wasn't at all sure I wanted to walk beside the sea for days on end. I had heard of more than one walker who had abandoned the coastal path and turned inland because they couldn't stand the continual sound of the sea and the wind blowing always in the same ear.

Nevertheless I was sorry to leave so soon. Life was beginning to stir. At Sennen Cove, early surfers were gathering on the beach. Locals were out exercising dogs. Naturalised magenta gladiola and brilliant blue borage added exotic colour to the grass fringed sand dunes bordering Whitesand Bay. The beach, smooth, still damp from the receding tide was as yet unsullied by the tramp of human feet. Whistfully, I turned my back on the sea and with the sound of surf and seagulls lingering in the air, turned inland towards Land's End Aerodrome.

The Penwith Peninsular, this most westerly part of Cornwall has a wealth of ancient settlements. Tumuli, hut circles, crosses and standing stones litter the countryside. Fields are 'hedged' with massive boulders placed there centuries ago when these granite uplands were cleared for cultivation. As I approached the ancient settlement of Carn Brea and looked back to the coast, the first planes of the day were leaving for the Isles of Scilly. A gorse-covered moorland track, teeming with butterflies led directly to another settlement at Carn Euny; a beautifully preserved group of Iron Age dwellings clustered round a central underground 'fogou', the Cornish word for cave, whose original purpose is still uncertain. Nearby, St. Euny Holy Well was an oasis in a wilderness of rampant June undergrowth. Lovingly tended roses bloomed beside the granite steps leading down to the spring and someone had cleared away the nettles and brambles which threatened to engulf it. Ancient paths and narrow lanes twisted and turned between the farms and villages of Sancreed, Sellan, Tremithick Cross and Madron as I made my way in the general direction of Penzance.

I could not have chosen a better time of the year to start. In June, Cornwall is at its best. The air is heavy with the heady fragrance of bluebells. Nowhere else has lanes like Cornwall, deep set between high banks which in early summer are a patriotic blaze of red, white and blue. Bluebells, taller and larger flowered than anywhere else I know, mingle with red campions and the dainty white flowers of stitchwort and another of Cornwall's specialities, the triangular-stalked garlic. I passed the time counting bells on bluebells. My record was 32.

As the hours passed and the sun climbed higher, temperatures soared—although there was a refreshing breeze which I appreciated even if the dog didn't. Each time he reached the Land Rover, he thought the walk was finished and threw himself on the floor, closed his eyes and was out for the count in seconds, only to be woken up again after I had quenched my thirst and briefed Michael on the next stop.

At Chysauster, another early settlement high up on the granite moorland of Guval Downs, we stopped for longer and spent an hour looking round before I took to the lanes again for the ultimate destination of the day, St. Erth. Here, in the middle of the narrowest part of Cornwall we could drive to either coast. The south won. Marazion has always been a family favourite and a visit to Cornwall wouldn't be the same without watching the sun go down in the beautiful setting of Mount's Bay. That evening we sat on the sea front eating pizzas and watching basking sharks swimming off shore on the incoming tide.

### *Getting into my stride*

Day two began with a complete change of weather. Totally overcast, cooler and looking very much like rain. Two peacocks roosting high in trees somewhere close to our tents mewed raucously late into the night and started again at the crack of dawn, ensuring I was on the road by 7.30am. I had done 24 miles the previous day and was anxious to get in another long day.

Leaving the rugged granite uplands of Penwith, lanes and bridleways took me through countryside characteristic of inland, lesser known Cornwall. An area where horticulture and mining, the industries on which Cornwall historically depended for its economy have left their mark on the landscape. Tiny fields, many less than an acre and sheltered from the ferocious salt-laden winds by high hedges, were full of broccoli and parsley. Years ago violets, anemones and a much wider range of crops were grown in these parts and dispatched by rail to Covent Garden. Now it's all monoculture and articulated road freight to supermarkets. Fields of daffodils, the flowers now over, looked untidy and neglected, the blue-green leaves drooping and withering in the aftermath of harvest. Desolate wastelands marked the sites of once thriving mines; tall chimney stacks and empty shells of Engine Houses were the only remains of the great steam powered Cornish Beam Engines. Everything that can be is made of granite: massive gateposts, stiles and for what must be unique to Cornwall, the construction of cattle grids.

Wayside curiosities abound. It's one of the things I love about walking. You see so much more than people who travel everywhere by car. Where else but in Cornwall would you find a road sign depicting pixies at work. I passed a topiary tractor parked outside a farm gate. It looked an extraordinarily clever feat of gardening until I realised it was a real tractor, totally overgrown with carefully trained and neatly clipped ivy. At another farm an old fashioned water pump made entirely of natural wood looked perfectly authentic but was a complete fake. The water trickling from the outlet was discreetly piped through a bit of modern plastic hose. A chapel bore a sign proclaiming it to be Teetotal whilst a vintage railway carriage in beautiful condition, was someone's home! The term 'green wellies' took on a whole new meaning when I spied a pair hanging outside a cottage door, stuffed with plants.

For us, Cornwall is a second home. Michael grew up there and even after we married and left the county, we had continued to spend holidays and most Christmases with his father. We had visited most places but one I had read about and never seen, was Gwennap Pit and I had included this in my route. The natural amphitheatre thought to have been formed by the collapse of mine workings beneath, is 50 feet deep and located high on a hill nearer the village of Carharrack than Gwennap. It was used for the first time in 1762 when John Wesley was forced to find a sheltered place for the thousands of tinners who had come to hear him preach. Its suitability for such a gathering was immediately recognised and Wesley addressed enormous congregations there a further 18 times. Estimates of the size of the crowds vary from 20 to 30 thousand and are not exaggerated. With people standing outside the pit, it could indeed have held that many. The 13 concentric turf-covered rings of seating seen today were constructed when the pit was remodelled at a much later date.

We found it impressive. We could see why Wesley had found it such a suitable preaching place. It had been raining most of the morning. I was cold and wet. The wind howled across the top of the hill and we were thankful to descend to the relative calm of the centre of the pit. In the homely little visitor centre full of Wesley memorabilia the lady on duty told us that the Pit was used regularly for fundraising events—and if we were interested, there was a Male Voice Choir Concert that night. With both Welsh and Cornish interests how could we miss such an opportunity? We bought tickets there and then—even though we had no idea where we would spend the night.

It turned out to be on the outskirts of Truro. Not far to drive back to Gwennap. However the weather had steadily deteriorated all afternoon. At short notice the concert venue was switched to Carharrack Methodist Church with an audience smaller than the 50 strong choir. We were disappointed. An open air concert in that marvellous amphitheatre would have been a unique occasion and a wonderful memory to take with me as I plodded north. However, the church was a good second best. The Four Lanes Male Choir gave their all in rousing choruses delivered with great enthusiasm. We had a small voice recorder in the Land Rover, totally unsuitable for such a purpose and the reproduction was far from good, but it reminds us of that delightful damp evening in Cornwall.

*With my rucksack on my back*

Land's End is about 45 miles from Truro. Not a bad distance for two days. I was pleased with my progress. It was my training period. I didn't have time for any before I left, and hoped these first few days would be enough to 'walk in' my feet and legs. They soon became conditioned to the daily tramp, but I knew from past experience that the first days of carrying the rucksack would be hard. I wanted to start carrying it before Michael left, in case there were any problems. So, at Truro I shouldered my load.

It weighed 38lbs. and although this was just within the limits of the quarter of one's body weight recommended for backpackers, it was more than I usually carried. Keeping the weight down is a problem for solo backpackers. Two of you can distribute the gear between you. Alone you have to manage the lot. My rucksack was far too heavy but there was nothing I could heave out to reduce it.

Everything I carried, even my clothes, had been chosen with weight in mind. My tent, specially purchased for the trip weighed only $3^{1}/_{2}$lbs. and was one of the lightest on the market. To keep cooking equipment to a minimum, I had ditched half of the compact nesting aluminium pans, taking only one and a small kettle. I had just one all purpose plastic bowl on the basis that you can use a bowl for soup, cereal or anything you like, but you can only use a plate as a plate. Then there was my sleeping bag, first aid kit, torch, stove, light shoes to wear in the evenings, dozens of small but essential items such as the whistle, compass, extra films, spare batteries, personal items and about 5lbs. of food—and the mobile phone which I was probably only taking as far as the Severn Bridge.

But at the start of every journey everything—from gas to tooth-paste—is full. Packed to capacity, at that weight, I could not put it on. As long as Michael was there he could give me a helping hand. After he had gone, I had to rely on a stile, wall, gate or bank, to lodge it up high while I wriggled into it. The ease with which I could put it on was a very reliable guide to weight. At 36lbs. I could just about do it. At 35lbs. it was no trouble. If it was dead easy, then I knew I was running out of food and gas. Later, as I became more accustomed to it being part of my body, I could cope whatever the weight and thought nothing of it. However I was always able to roughly assess its weight and this was useful to know—a few pounds can make a lot of difference on a tough or long day. I could organise food purchases and adjust the weight accordingly.

Truro was the first and last town of any size I would encounter for a long time. Once free of its busy streets my path took me through Bishop's Wood nature reserve, a maze of waymarked paths and rides. I tried to memorize the layout from the information board and managed to find the ancient hill fort and derelict Gunpowder Mill on my way. The dog still plodded faithfully beside me, though I think he was beginning to realise that he was walking for walking's sake, and for the most part looked thoroughly bored perking up only when he met a Labrador bitch!

Then came the moment I dreaded. It was time for Michael to leave. All the fears of the last few weeks flooded into my mind. Would I be lonely, scared, ill, unable to cope? What would I do if I broke an ankle, encountered unwanted company or had dreadful weather? I'd done less than 60 miles and there were nearly 200 more to the Severn Bridge—and that was just the beginning. It suddenly seemed a very long way and a completely crazy thing to be doing.

The dog put back in the Land Rover looked as dejected as I felt. I'm sure he knew his walk was over and he wouldn't see me again for weeks. Michael wished me luck, gave me a hug and we parted. It was a tearful moment. I watched the Land Rover until it was out of sight and felt very much alone. I told myself it was not for long. I was visiting friends near Bodmin and a cousin in Bridgwater. I would take each day as it came.

### Sampling Cornish weather

I was going to camp near Roche, where I wanted to see a tiny ancient chapel. The farm I was looking for wasn't marked on the map—and I couldn't find it. And I couldn't find anyone to ask directions from either. An alternative campsite at first didn't look promising but the farmer's wife, a lively young Irish girl made me most welcome and introduced me to the only other occupant of the site, a lady living permanently in a caravan. We soon found we had a common interest in wild flowers and I enjoyed hearing at first hand about the local specialities, particularly the royal fern, *Osmunda regalis* which I had noticed growing in the hedgerows. This is a rarity in most parts of Britain, but here is not uncommon and is apparently on the increase.

It was a windy night. I spent half the night listening to the noisy flapping of the tent and wondering if it would blow down. I woke to a damp morning—neither mist nor drizzle; what the Cornish term 'mizzle'. The countryside was veiled in a wet haze. All morning I saw only a postman, parked up a deserted track reading a newspaper, a farmer and a handful of cars. I estimated I was walking at two miles an hour which surprised me as my pack was so much heavier than normal. From time to time, the 'mizzle' became proper rain, at one time so torrential I stopped to shelter in the corner of a field under some trees. It was dry enough there to get the stove out and brew some tea—my first hot drink of the day. It had been far too gusty first thing to light the stove and I had made do with a cold drink for breakfast.

I arrived in Bodmin at lunchtime and took shelter in a phone box. Underneath my waterproofs I was still basically dry, but a few more hours of driving rain would change this. I had only done ten miles, but with the weather as it was, I decided to call it a day. The map showed a convenient campsite about a mile away. I shopped for milk, extra films and a news-paper and spotted a fish and chip café on the opposite side of the road. A hot meal in the dry instantly appealed. I made it last a good hour before venturing out again to face the deluge.

Far from passing over, the rain became heavier. At the campsite, I went to book in. I'd seen my reflection in a window and knew I looked like a drowned rat. My hair was soaked. Water trickled down my face and poured from my clothes making a puddle on the office floor. The warden took one look at me, and said, "You're not one of those John O'Groatsers are you?"

"Yes I am." I replied, " I expect you think I'm mad!"

"No! I don't think you're mad. What charity are you doing it for?"

"I'm not. I'm doing it for fun."

"Oh well! In that case you are mad!" He spoke in a resigned way as if he actually thought I was mad, then pulling on a cagoule said, "You'd better have my special wet backpacker's pitch."

This was under a group of trees next to the toilet block. Once the tent was up I peeled off my wet clothes and crawled into my sleeping bag to warm up. The rest of the afternoon was spent reading the newspaper until the rain eased enough to sort things out properly. By evening I was able to hang my wet clothes on the lower branches of the trees and use the redun-dant newspaper to mop up the tent and stuff my boots. Down the road bell ringers practised in Bodmin Church. It was lovely to hear them again. I had forgotten how keen the Cornish are on their bellringing. When we lived there our house had been across the green from the church and we grew accustomed to the weekly practise night.

Overnight the rain died out. I awoke to a perfect morning—but discovered the down side of the wet backpacker pitch. Beneath the trees no sun penetrated to dry out the tent. I had to pack it up wet. I donated my remaining milk to a passing dog, then using quiet field footpaths made for Cardinham. The air had that special clarity you often find in Cornwall. The countryside looked fresh and clean. Colours were brighter. Detail sharper. Looking back I could see the white conical 'mountains' of china clay waste at St. Austell and Roche; a lunar landscape that had been hidden by mist the previous day when I had actually passed them.

Cardinham Woods, like Bishop's Wood had a confusing number of waymarked trails but none actually went to the village. It was not even marked on the plan. The woods were eerily quiet making me feel nervous and vulnerable and there was little of interest except a wacky picnic area where the seats were brightly painted tree stumps with carved faces. More by luck than judgement I did reach Cardinham. Then I was offered a very dubious lift to somewhere I didn't want to go by a slick, dark-suited gent who seemed to know the area no better than me. I declined and was relieved that he did not persist. Michael had given me a personal alarm, but I doubted its usefulness. In most of the places I would be walking, no-one would hear an alarm. Unless I carried it round my neck all the time, it was not easily accessible and I had enough things round my neck without adding more.

### *A close encounter on Bodmin Moor*

Lunch was a lazy affair on Goonzion Downs, an outlying area of Bodmin Moor. I lounged barefooted in long grass—my boots and socks, still wet from the previous day, draped over clumps of heather to dry in the warm sunshine. It annoyed me that I should have wet feet just from a day's road walking. But I was not wearing leather boots. Apart from brief sorties onto the Moors, there was nowhere in the West Country heavy walking boots were essential, so I'd bought cheap fabric boots to wear until I returned to Wales. I had been doubtful whether they would be waterproof. Now I knew they weren't. In rain or long wet grass, I might as well have been walking in bare feet.

The narrow twisting lanes of Cornwall are so complex and efficient, there is hardly any need for public footpaths, but this does lead to a lot of road walking. The occasional tractor or postvan passes; the odd car; usually driven by a woman—rural wives going shopping, running errands for the farm or taking children to school. Nationwide, Britain experiences noticeable rural rush-hours. Between 8 and 9 in the morning and 3.30 and 4.30 in the afternoon, cars overflowing with children, school minibuses, huge coaches, private taxis, farm Land Rovers, children on bicycles, all converge on narrow lanes and otherwise quiet roads. Suddenly, you become aware you are jumping into the hedge every minute. Then the penny drops. The kids are going home from school.

In the picturesque moorland village of St. Neot's I stopped in the churchyard to admire the rhododendrons—an exotic extravaganza of crimson, pink and white more suited to the Chelsea Flower Show than a country church. I passed Golitha Falls, a popular beauty spot on the River Fowey—overvisited and spoilt by a large carpark and woodland worn bare

13

of undergrowth by the tramp of countless feet. Further upstream, on a barren empty expanse of moor, King Arthur's sword Excalibur reputedly lies at the bottom of Dozmary pool. The lane I'd been following ended at Golitha and joined an unclassified road which led on to Bodmin Moor—an insignificant yellow road according to the map and I was not expecting the amount of traffic it carried. Cornish roads are definitely not made for walkers. You need to keep your wits about you all the time! There are no verges. Steep banks rise from the edge of the road and underneath their floriferous clothing is a very solid granite wall. Impossible to jump up if you need to get off the road. In June, the hedges had yet to be cut. Grass, bluebells, cow parsley and a multitude of other plants grew long as hay. For safety I tried to stand where I could be clearly seen or waited in a gateway for traffic to pass. If it seemed the safer thing to do, I'd disregard the 'walking-facing-oncoming-traffic' rule and cross to the other side.

As I approached the Moor I had the biggest scare of the entire 1,200 miles. There was frequent traffic in both directions. I took precautions, but on one blind bend I could do nothing. I could hear a car approaching and by the engine note, very fast indeed. I was close to the bend. A car coming from the opposite direction prevented me from crossing over and would reach the bend at the same time as the other. The hedge towered steeply and solidly way above my head. All I could do was lie flat against it pressing my rucksack into the vegetation. A sleek white sporty saloon, shot past, sweeping the overhanging grasses as it went and brushing the loose cloth of my trousers. I doubt whether the driver ever saw me. I was badly shaken. With knees turning to jelly, it took me the next mile to recover.

Once on the open moor, I walked freely, well away from the road, though still in sight of it. Bodmin Moor is a dreary unexciting place even on a fine day, though Daphne Du Maurier found inspiration here for her novel Jamaica Inn. Like the Penwith peninsula, it is rich in antiquities. I passed King Doniert's stone—two chunks of granite bearing a Latin inscription which translated reads 'Doniert ordered this [cross] for the good of his soul.' Doniert was a Cornish King who drowned in 878 AD. Further on are three stone circles known as the Hurlers—reputedly these are the players of an ancient ball game, turned to stone for daring to play on the Sabbath. Two coach-loads of excited children on a school trip hurled themselves round the circle apparently without the need of a ball.

Though Bodmin Moor lacks the number and variety of tors so characteristic of Dartmoor, the rocky prominence overlooking the Hurlers deservedly warrants the name of Cheesewring. A precariously balanced mass of weathered rock formations towering above worked-out quarries and the stark ruins of mine buildings. It looked as if a push would send it toppling.

On this clear, fine day, the views were superb. The vast urban sprawl of Plymouth and the coast to the south; the high dark outline of Dartmoor filling the horizon more than 20 miles away to the east and nearer, the village and square-towered church of St. Clears. Ahead, the high television mast on Caradon Hill was my landmark. Just below the mast, at a farm whose boundaries border the moor, lived old friends. I was looking forward to seeing them again.

Cornish hospitality is always warm and involves eating lots of home cooking. Rich fruit cakes, enormous pasties made with cream, and daily doses of clotted cream with almost anything. Diana always was a wonderful cook. A generous supper of both macaroni cheese and beef curry was finished off with another of Cornwall's specialities, Saffron cake—a bright yellow bread-like cake heavily impregnated with currants. In the warm evening sun I hung my tent out to dry and aired my sleeping bag. It was only the fifth day, but I already had a small pile of washing which I did outside in the garden in an old tin bath, Diana currently having no washing machine. Later, we settled down in the kitchen round the Aga, catching up on four years' news and putting the world to rights until well after midnight.

### Visiting old haunts

I was invited to stop an extra night—as long as I didn't mind falling in with the usual weekly routine. As next day was market day—the day every local farmer goes to town whether or not he is buying or selling, this meant a trip to Liskeard. There I was left to my own devices to wander round the stalls and up and down the steep streets. I felt sorry for the pensioners of Liskeard! While all the most important shops are at the bottom of steep hills, the banks and Post Office are at the top. Whatever you need involves a climb!

That evening Diana took me to look at old haunts; my father- in-law's small holding, now modernised and almost unrecognisable; the house we had lived in when we were first married, and the church where my husband's parents are buried. So many memories. So many familiar scenes. I almost felt homesick.

I was worried about the next day's journey. It was more than 20 miles—the longest distance since I had been alone and I felt that unless I

15

left unsociably early, I would be trying to do a long walk in a short day. After struggling with my conscience overnight, I decided to cut the 20 miles to 13 by walking to Callington, catching a bus to Tavistock and then completing the remaining seven miles to Lydford on foot.

As expected, I was late leaving. However I hadn't gone far before I encountered a friend of Diana's fetching her morning paper. She guessed immediately who I was and in response to my enquiries about bus times, said "I'm going to Callington to get petrol. I'll give you a lift."

I loved Pat at once and felt quite at ease with her. She was a lady of impulses and exuded a tremendous love of life. As we drove into Callington, by a circuitous route, she suddenly said, "I haven't been to Tavistock for ages. Why don't I take you all the way and get my petrol there?" I mumbled something about not putting her to any trouble, and said I really didn't mind going by bus, but she wouldn't be put off saying she liked unexpected things happening. It made life more exciting. We got on like the proverbial house on fire and nattered non-stop all the way.

Once in Tavistock, after strolling along the River Tavy Pat pointed me in the direction of Brent Tor and went off to do some shopping. The road I took enabled me to rejoin my original cross-country route and was a safe one—wide enough for traffic to pass easily and with verges. About four miles from Tavistock I met a sprightly elderly lady carrying a large empty shopping bag. She greeted me cheerfully, "You look as if you're going a long way! And your bag looks heavier than mine!" Like me, she didn't drive and said she walked to Tavistock every week to do her shopping— ten miles there and back, though often someone stopped and gave her a lift.

Pleasant lanes, lush and green and overgrown with flowers provided lovely walking and led gradually towards Dartmoor. Ahead was Brent Tor, a high isolated hill with a church on top. The 12th Century church dedicated to St. Michael can be seen for miles around and is worth the climb. Services are still held there, though I suspect it gets far more curious tourists than congregation. I stopped to eat croissants and strawberry jam in a pretty valley where the course of the old mainline railway crosses the moor. Then I was on the moor myself, where ponies, many with a foal at foot grazing the short springy turf, were my only company. Distant Tors and the rolling expanses of empty wilderness looked benign on this hot and breezeless day. In a totally treeless landscape, there was no shade and I was almost out of water. I was glad I had shortened the day to a more manageable distance.

## *Dartmoor*

Lydford Gorge is a spectacular part of the Lyd Valley where the river, though small, plunges over a sill into a deep gorge. This extends through luxuriant woodland for another one and a half miles. A complete circuit of the gorge is three miles and visitors may enter at either end. By entering at the lower end and following the compulsory one way system, I saw the best of the gorge in half the distance. Many years ago, before the National Trust took over, Michael and I used to come here for free. But that was a long time ago. I had forgotten how pretty it was. The heavily wooded gorge gets narrower and more dramatic at each step, the river tumbling over boulders into deep pools, rushing in an endless race through water-worn rocky clefts. Masses of bright pink purslane clothed the banks to the water's edge and in both the deep shade beneath the trees and the nooks and crannies of water-splashed rocks, mosses and ferns grew luxuriantly in almost rain forest conditions. The riverside path, cut into solid rock, was wet and slippery and in the steepest and narrowest places the metal handrail was vital. At the head of the Gorge is the Devil's Cauldron, an immense circular 'pot' carved out of solid rock. There is no room for people to pass along the rocky ledge leading to it—on one side is a wall of rock, on the other a sheer drop into the swirling waters of the cauldron. A sign warns those of a nervous disposition to go no further—the path ends with a fragile looking bridge from which you can look down into the 'pot'. The path was very narrow. My rucksack was wider than I was. I made do with 30 year-old memories.

Lydford lies on the fringe of the moor, within the bounds of the National Park, and was once an important Saxon town. It's a charming place with a fascinating history and is still much as it was when King Alfred laid out his fortified town on the site of a much earlier settlement. At one time it was home to the local mint. The castle was used as a prison for centuries, right up to the time that the new 'Dartmoor' prison was established at Princetown.

I was up early next morning and soon on the moor—looking for letter-boxes. I had caught the letterboxing bug when doing the Two Moor's Way the previous year. For the uninitiated there are letterboxes hidden all over Dartmoor. These are not letterboxes from which you can send your mail, but small army ammunition boxes or plastic pill pots which can be found by deciphering clues, working out compass bearings or plain hard work looking under rocks and searching every gully and crevice. Each contains a rubber stamp with the name of the box, and a book for the finder to stamp with their personal stamp. The object is to collect the stamps from boxes in your own book. As there is now an official club, thousands to find and a thick catalogue of clues, letterboxing is one of Dartmoor's most popular pursuits. Anyone can put out a box. The first was put out in 1854, in an extremely inaccessible spot. It was an interesting challenge—to leave a note on some remote part of the moor and see how long it was before another person found it. Now many are put out for charity, money being raised by the sale of clue sheets. However, it is a regulated 'sport'. All boxes must be registered with the National Park and can be left out for only a limited time, to avoid overuse of areas where they are located. You could never accidentally stumble on one. They are so well hidden that even with clues they can be elusive. I searched for about an hour and found none.

For such a fine summer's day, it was ferociously windy. On the high tors I could hardly stand up. Even on the lower, clitter-strewn slopes it was a struggle to make any headway. But it was exhilarating. The sky was deep blue, the air clear. The view was almost aerial; distant Bodmin Moor with Caradon television mast clearly visible; the Tamar Valley; Tavistock; the patchwork fields and scattered villages of north Devon. And Dartmoor. Not the featureless blanket bogs of the central moor but grassy hillsides sweeping up to meet a skyline crowned by Tors. Eroded outcrops of granite whose distinctive shapes have given rise to fanciful names. Here, well worn tracks lead—who knows where? A cairn or ancient settlement. In hidden valleys, crystal streams cascade between massive boulders. Hawthorns and hollies, stunted by the constant nibblings of sheep, strive to grow.

Much of this area is a military zone. Prominent red flags on the tors warn the public when firing is taking place. Widely scattered, a few cattle grazed, but no person was in sight. I was alone; indulging my love of solitude. When I reached Meldon Reservoir I was invigorated and in high spirits. Head-height, golden flowered gorse bushes swept down to the water's edge. I took off my rucksack to ease my shoulders and sat on a boulder listening to the larks singing—so high in the sky they could barely be seen. From Meldon, the footpath was closed owing to overhead repairs on the viaduct. A complicated map showed the re-routed path, but details drawn out of context on a small section of a very large scale map are difficult to equate to your own one inch map. What I *could* see, was that the detour was considerably longer than the footpath it was replacing. I came across two soldiers leaning on the bonnet of their Land Rover in a wood. They would surely know the way I reasoned—the army are supposed to be good at that sort of thing. But they looked blankly at the map and shook their heads. They couldn't work out the diversion either.

Meldon has been quarried extensively in the past, and is still quarried today. Some of the old workings are now flooded and the reason for the soldiers' presence soon became apparent. Six mini-bus loads of Devon Army Cadet Force youngsters were canoeing or tearing round in a motor-powered rescue dinghy. By this time I had come round in a circle and was nearly back where I had started, passing under the viaduct for the second time. Delicately engineered in iron and spanning the valley on lofty lattice-work trestles it was shrouded in wooden shuttering and polythene. Beneath it I met two walkers and asked them if I was going in the right direction. "It doesn't matter" they said. "It's Saturday. The footpath is only closed during the week while they're working. You could have gone straight through."

### On the trail of Tarka the Otter

Okehampton Castle, set amongst dark trees in the bottom of a valley, is a gloomy place and is haunted. I didn't stop. Soon I was back up on the Moor at Belstone, a pretty moorland village with uncomfortable granite stocks on the village green. I sat on a bench in the shade of trees marvel-ling at the fickle moods of the British weather. It was now suffocatingly airless.

In Okehampton I had picked up the Tarka Trail, a long distance path developed by Devon County Council to promote conservation, and loosely based on Henry Williamson's book "Tarka the Otter". It starts and finishes at Barnstaple, wandering through North Devon for 181 miles and was of no great use to me except as a convenient path for just a few miles. But it was poorly marked. Signposts bearing the Otter paw print were few and far between. With difficulty I reached Sticklepath and South Tawton where hopes of an ice-cream and cold drink were dashed. Everywhere was closed. It was late afternoon. I had done 14 miles and both available camp-sites were still some way off. A woman in her front garden called out "Hello! Are you going to the new Camping Barn?" She had heard that a camping barn had just opened in the village hall at Taw Green, only two miles along the road. This seemed perfect. But when I arrived, the 'iron clad' village hall was firmly locked. It *was* going to be a 'barn', but work on the conversion had not yet started.

I had no intention of walking any further. I asked at the first likely looking farm for some water, always a good 'opener', and then if there was a small corner of a field I could use to camp. A frail old lady invited me in and offered tea in the charming sitting room of her Devonshire longhouse. At one end was a huge fireplace. Oak beams made the room seem dark, yet sun shafting in from small windows glowed on age old furniture. Pictures and ornaments covered every wall and surface. She would, she said, have to ask her son, and at the moment he was doing the milking. She was at least 85, so her son had to be around 60. While we waited she kept up a lively conversation. Although she had spent her entire life on a farm, she was a vegetarian. She could never get used to the sad look in the cow's eyes when they went to market.

The son showed me into the garden, nicely secluded and sheltered by shrubs and roses, but unfortunately with no outside tap or outside toilet. These were at the far end of the house. As it meant asking at the back door, I managed without. I had only dehydrated food to cook that night too, and could have done with unlimited access to water. And after such a hot day, I could have drunk a gallon of tea. The old lady gave me a large jug but I didn't like to ask for more and economised with what I had. Once it was clear I was there to stay, a black dog took up residence outside my tent and provided company for the remainder of the evening. This often happens on farms and brings mixed blessings. The company is great, but there's a tendency for food to go missing and 'calling cards' to be left on the corner of the tent!

### The consequences of getting lost

The Tarka Trail took me as far as North Tawton. Then I had to find my way east for about seven miles to link with the Two Moors Way. This was primarily a rural landscape; picturesque villages; cob and thatch farms; cottage gardens at their summer best. But occasionally agri-business intrudes. I found myself at one point walking between high chainlink security fences beside a monstrous modern cheese factory. In appearance, it could have been a chemical plant. Large settling tanks—similar to those of a sewage farm—were full of sour smelling white slurry.

An elderly lady in Zeal Monochorum misdirected me after giving me her own life history and that of half the village. "I know where you want to go" she said, " I used to take a short cut down there when I was a child." But we were not talking about the same footpath. Following her advice I went through a muddy farmyard where a burly farmer called out "You'll never get through the river in they boots!" What river? There shouldn't be a river. Further down the overgrown track, there was a river and the farmer was right, I couldn't get across. I had come some way from the village and didn't want to go back, least of all so that the farmer could say "I told you so." I was determined to cross somehow.

The water was deep—easily up to my knees. My map indicated it was the River Yeo. It was not wide, but the water was fast flowing over a bed of sharp jagged rocks. Not the best river for crossing with bare feet. I looked round for extra rocks to make stepping stones. There was nothing on the bank. I felt in the riverbed to find enough flat less jagged ones to make a firm footing—but still well under water. It was easier to take my trousers off than roll up the legs and I threw them, my boots, socks, map case and other loose items over. Then I ferried over my camera and water bottle before making the last precarious bare foot journey with the rucksack. The whole exercise took three-quarters of an hour. It would have been far quicker to have gone back. I vowed I'd be more cautious next time I took local advice.

On the Two Moor's Way I lost my way crossing large undulating fields. Having done the route before I hadn't bothered with the guide book. But it wasn't as easy as I thought. There were so many waymarked paths I couldn't work out which *was* the Two Moor's Way. I wasted valuable time getting back on course, then only a mile or two later I mislaid the path again ending up on the wrong side of a farmhouse—in a field instead of the farmyard. I was spotted by the eagle-eyed farmer's wife who came out and, in a very friendly manner, put me right. I apologised and asked if she could fill up my water bottle. "Would you like a cup of tea as well" she offered. This proved to be far more than a cup of tea. It was shearing day and it was teatime. The vast kitchen was packed with hunky young lads from neighbouring farms, all there to help out. An enormous table filled one end of the room, groaning under the weight of a feast fit for a wedding. And being Devon, there was a preponderance of rich cakes, jam, cream and scones. I was invited to help myself.

I was bombarded with questions. Faces registered open disbelief when they heard I was walking to Scotland. The farmer's wife and her daughter were shocked and concerned. They could not understand why I was doing it. Wasn't I scared or worried about being on my own. Both said they would never walk *anywhere* on their own.

Three hours later, I staggered wearily up the lane to a farm at Witheridge where I had stayed the previous year. Now the place was totally deserted. Doors locked. No signs of life. Not even a barking dog. I considered pitching the tent without asking but thought perhaps the farm had changed hands. So, I trekked back to the last farm I had passed and asked if I might stay there. The farmer, who told me that the other farmer always went Sheep Dog Trialing on a Sunday, said all his fields either had stock in or were shut up for hay. All he could offer was a gateway to a hayfield. The ground was like concrete and knobbly. There was a cold water tap in the yard and rather surprisingly, a hot tap too so I was able to have a strip down wash behind a hedge in my collapsible bowl. Weighing only a few ounces, this folds up flat, takes up little room—and can be used to carry water in. When amenities are absent it is indispensable. After 19 miles of frustrations and delays, I would have liked someone to talk to, but could get no signal on the mobile phone. I went to my hard, knobbly bed hoping that next day would be more straightforward.

### Sun, snails and antlers

The next day was very hot—the hottest day so far. I rested every half hour in the shade—under scant trees on Knowstone Common where orchids grew over large areas and again in the cool sunless sanctuary of Knowstone Church. The altar and lectern cloths were beautifully made of brilliantly coloured satin patchwork, giving the effect of stained glass. Knowstone is mentioned in the Domesday Book. The village is little more than a row of white-painted cottages with uneven thatched roofs. Shrubs and flowers growing at the base of the walls spilled over onto the road. Everything was small—the church, the cottages; one so tiny, it is named 'Little cottage'. The landlord of the thatch-roofed Mason's Arms filled up my water bottle.

Progress in the heat, was slow—a bare mile an hour and it was late afternoon when I walked down the hill to Yeo Mill. All afternoon I had been mentally listing the things I was going to buy. But the only shop there is so small that stock consists mainly of an assortment of single tins—and everything in the largest size. I ended up with far too much; a litre of orange juice, a large tin of oranges—the only fruit they had, large tins of evaporated milk, potatoes, minced beef and creamed rice (my alternative breakfast), and a pint of fresh milk. My brain must have been addled by the heat to suppose I was going to eat all that!

Yeo Mill lies in the valley of the River Yeo. Level pastures border the river, but then the fields rise steeply to the boundary of Exmoor. The village is a hotch-potch of old and new. A row of council houses; an ugly village hall surrounded by tarmac and a farm that used to be a coaching inn. Outside the Post Office, an early petrol pump, restored and painted bright red had a netball basket tied on top. The campsite, which I had to myself, was a field doubling as the village football pitch. It had only a cold water tap. Toilets were in the village hall.

The following morning, the grass was heavy with dew. When I left, well before 8am, the countryside was still shrouded in a wet mist. The sun glowed moon-like behind a veil of low cloud. Swallows swooped low over the football pitch in pursuit of insects.

I had coined the phrase for myself of being 'Up with the snails'. Starting out as early as I usually did, hundreds of snails would be still grazing along the bottoms of hedges and along the verges of metalled roads. So many, that sometimes it was difficult to avoid walking on them. As the sun rose, they disappeared back into the grass. Shattered shells indicated the traffic casualties. This early, bird-song filled the air, though the songs of larks and yellowhammers often accompanied me all day long. And if bluebells were the flower of Cornwall, then gorse was the flower of Devon. Later, as I crossed the boundary into Somerset, ticking off with some satisfaction my second county, I reflected that my abiding memories of Devon would be of sunshine, green lanes, gorse and larks.

Exmoor is less harsh than the rock strewn expanses of Dartmoor. The open moorland was dotted with the white lollipop shapes of full blossomed hawthorns and the emerging fronds of young bracken.

At Hawkridge the owner of the intriguing Antler Shop was opening up and sweeping out his workshop. He called out good morning and was obviously in the mood for a chat.

"How do you find the antlers?" I asked.

"By looking in the right places," he replied. "I know where the deer rest and feed—and where they will shed their antlers."

"You must need a lot of patience and lot of luck," I observed.

"You'd be surprised," he said, "I've often stood watching deer, when visitors have walked by without knowing they were there. Antlers aren't so easy to find these days though. Too many people are looking for them. It's not like it used to be. I used to make a living. Now I just eke out my pension."

The walls of the workshop were festooned in antlers of every size. I asked the price. Large full size stag's antlers mounted on wood, just right for the baronial hall, cost around £90, while smaller, less impressive sets were about £40. I made my excuses and said I couldn't really carry one, to which he replied that he had sold some once to a walker who had tied them to his rucksack.

23

Soon after this, I met a pretty dark-haired young woman who was visiting home territory. She loved both Dartmoor and Exmoor and while still at school had taken part in the Dartmoor Ten Tors Challenge. The weather had been so hot they had been airlifted to safety suffering from sunstroke and heat exhaustion. The Ten Tors Challenge always takes place at the same time of the year and only a few weeks before starting my walk this year's participants had again been airlifted from the moor—this time to escape blizzards and appallingly cold conditions.

We swapped notes on walking experiences and both agreed that as lone women walkers we are very much aware that we may be putting ourselves at risk. In order to enjoy a pastime that we love, we have to take this risk. We cannot let fear of possible 'sticky' situations hang over us like a dark cloud, spoiling our pleasure in walking. She observed that she felt far safer walking alone in Devon than catching a tube at night in London where she worked. No doubt all of us have our own way of overcoming worries. In my case I found reassurance in constantly reminding myself that if this was 'my village' or this 'my local woodland walk,' I would feel quite comfortable knowing that the people I met would be kindly friends and neighbours—and that any village or wood was no different to my own. I had nothing to worry about.

Having said that, I am still aware that people may not always be what they seem and always quickly try and assess anyone I meet, popping them into convenient mental pigeon holes. The genuine walkers, whether they be long distance, Sunday ramblers or youngsters on expeditions, are easily spotted, as are those intent on some outdoor activity; birdwatching, climbing, fishing or sketching. I'm suspicious of anyone not engaged in an obvious pursuit and not looking dressed for the situation, whatever that may be. My policy then is: act cool; keep my distance; engage in conversation if necessary but divulge little and try to draw out information from them. At the same time I am ready with an escape plan: I am being met by a back-up car, or I have to divert to a farm for B and B. In all my years of walking, I've never had a really difficult situation arise, but I know others who have, so it is just as well to be prepared.

### Exmoor antiquities

At Tarr Steps, Exmoor's famous clapper bridge which reputedly dates from prehistoric times, I stopped only to record the dainty flowered Star of Bethlehem growing near the carpark. Then I left the northbound Two Moor's Way, and struck eastward across the moor. It was a day for talking.

I met a couple who spontaneously engaged in conversation. They had just dropped off their son at Minehead to do the South West Coastal Path—about 520 miles to Poole in Dorset. They suggested I should go and see the Caractacus Stone. I had never heard of it and it was off my route, but I was always willing to go out of my way to see anything interesting. An inscribed standing stone protected from the elements by a tiny building, it wasn't even a memorial to Caractacus—just someone claiming kinship to him. Captured in its little stone prison, it was hardly worth a photograph. The freshly shed skin of a grass snake which I found nearby was far more exciting. I folded it carefully between the folds of the map to keep as a souvenir.

The weather was altogether more tolerable. Sunny but nowhere near as hot. I didn't walk, I strolled—reluctant to leave the moor for Bridgetown and the Caravan Club site on the banks of the River Exe. I wasn't at all sure they would take a camper but the warden said he would never turn away a backpacker, though campers in cars he would not accept. It was a pleasant site beside a white-painted watermill. Discreetly quiet with smart caravans and an air of retired gentility. Even the toilets were approached by flowery borders. As a travel stained backpacker I felt conspicuous as I pitched my tent a few feet from the river. To reach the shower block I had to walk the full length of the site and couldn't help wondering what people thought when they saw me going to shower with a towel the size of a flannel draped over my arm and my complete washing kit in a little bag which would pass as a purse!

The mobile phone was useless in this deep valley, so I went to find a callbox. A group of local children hanging over the parapets of the bridge fishing for eels were anxious to show off their skills at enticing eels with bits of cheese. The eels, about 18 inches long and clearly visible in the shallow water beneath the bridge didn't appear to be taking too much notice.

### Alone—but not alone

The next 14 miles was all on little used footpaths. I had chosen bridleways whenever I could; these were less likely to be obstructed and were usually better signposted. My chosen route was across the grain of the country; constantly up and down and hardly a soul all day, except the occasional farmer on a tractor far away in a distant field. Everyone was busy hay-making. Everywhere, acres and acres of hay. Hedgerows were pink with campions amongst which fluttered hundreds of tiny brown butterflies.

Somehow I missed the turn to Wimbleball Reservoir but I just could not be bothered to retrace my steps and decided to revise my route. Northerly winds and cooler weather had been forecast, but it was still boiling hot.

It was perhaps just as well that the countryside was deserted. All day I had been inconvenienced by an uncontrollable urge to spend a penny. With irritating frequency I had to take off the rucksack, check the coast was clear and drop my pants—only to find it was quite un-necessary. But I didn't dare ignore the signals for fear of wetting myself. At first I worried I might have picked up some infection but then decided it was more likely to be caused by drinking too many highly concentrated fluids in the evenings and insufficient water during the day. That evening I made a positive effort to drink gallons of water and thankfully had no repeat of the problem.

In choosing my route through Somerset, I avoided towns. I had assumed that the many villages would have a small shop or Post Office. I had not appreciated how rural the area was. Withiel Florey with its delightful white-painted church, a farm and a handful of cottages, was typical of many. None had a shop, a school or even a pub. I had very little food left. My eleventh day and my last-ditch-reserves were running out. Lunch consisted of two slices of three day-old Saffron cake, a packet of Lucozade tablets and a Cheese Dip Snack pack. At this stage I was not worried. With several more villages to go through I expected to find somewhere to buy something.

For several miles across endless fields, meticulous map reading was essential. I was aiming for Clatworthy Reservoir where there is a permissive footpath on a nature trail. It was a long, lonely walk and for some reason I became overwhelmingly concerned for my safety. It worried me that I had seen no-one all day. I was in an extremely isolated area and no-one knew I was there. I had to go through some steep, rough woodland where there was a high risk of tripping over tree roots or slipping on damp rocks. I worried that I might fall or twist an ankle, or even knock myself unconscious. As I had neither seen or spoken to anyone all day, no-one would be able to recall seeing which way I had gone. In fact, no-one knew where I was heading, so no-one would even know I hadn't arrived and report me missing. All these thoughts were chasing through my head and I couldn't get rid of them. I was becoming more and more anxious and neurotic.

By the time I reached the peaceful waters of the reservoir I was a nervous wreck. This was the only time on the entire journey when being on my own really affected me. There were other occasions when I felt very much alone, but not lonely. This may sound a contradiction, but there is a difference. At Clatworthy I first became aware of what I later thought of as my 'guardian walkers'. I find that when I am alone for such long periods I tend to speak out loud. By that, I don't mean the exclamations of annoyance or frustration when I sat on my sandwiches or put my foot in a cowpat. I mean proper talking, saying what was in my head. It was while stumbling through the unfrequented woods surrounding the reservoir that the lines of a childhood prayer came into my head:

> Matthew, Mark, Luke and John,
> Bless the bed that I lie on.
> There are four corners to my bed.
> There are four angels round it spread.
> One to watch. One to pray.
> Two to carry my soul away.'

I called for my guardian angels. At least, what I actually said was "Come on people. Where are you?" Immediately I felt calmer with a sense of security that everything would be alright. Even stranger was the feeling that someone, or something, watched over me. After that, whenever I became aware of my isolated vulnerability, whenever a day felt long, or I was weary, when my pack was too heavy or the weather dispiriting, I only had to say, "Come on people.Where are you?" and I would sense an almost tangible, warm presence and be absolutely certain that my 'guardian walkers' were with me.

### The depths of deserted Somerset

The reservoir was actually a very pretty place, surrounded by deciduous woodland and not despoiled by man's leisure activities. Hundreds of geese were gathered on the banks taking *en masse* to the water at my unexpected arrival. Flowers in great variety flourished in the long grass and in damper hollows there were masses of orchids. But lovely as it was, it was with great relief that I climbed up through the woods to Clatworthy village. I was dismayed to find it too had no shop. The next village Brompton Ralph did, but it was half day closing and I was too late, so there went my last chance of food. I already knew that Tolland, where I intended to camp, had no shop.

All these villages were deserted. It was not until I reached Tolland in the evening that I met and spoke to the first person of the day—a tweedy lady looking for her cat. Tolland is just a hamlet and not the sort of place where you would expect to find a campsite. But I was looking for a Camping Club Hideaway Site—which means you can't find it unless you are a Camping Club Member and know where to look. An enquiry at a farm directed me "Back up the road in the field behind the barn." I paid my dues, (a bit much I thought for a cold water tap in a hayfield) and was told that no-one would be around in the morning as they were off on their summer holidays. I put up my tent round the back of the barn and surveyed my remaining rations. All I could allow myself for supper was a packet of noodles and half a packet of instant custard.

Tolland has nothing except the farm, a couple of houses and a church—but it did have a telephone so I was able to ring home. To pass the time, I wandered along to the church which had massive ornate wrought iron gates set between impressive gateposts more suitable for a country mansion than a country church. Set in the gates are the words 'ENTER INTO THIS GATE WITH THANKSGIVING'. From the outside the church is not as impressive as its gates. The churchyard was a classic conservation project. Notices indicated conservation areas. Paths were cut in unmown areas. Other areas were being cut in different stages of growth. The overall impression was of neatness alongside controlled wilderness. One of the best 'managed' churchyards I had seen.

### A wet birthday—and no food

As darkness fell there were distant rumbles of thunder. A full scale thunderstorm persisted most of the night. I was woken at intervals more by light flickering through the thin sides of the tent than by the thunder. It was still raining hard at 6am. A wretched morning. June 20th and my birthday. So I had a birthday lie in. Flaming June is not what it is cracked up to be. It nearly always rains on my birthday.

All I had for breakfast was the remaining half packet of instant custard and a muesli bar, which was at least warm and filling. Then I ferried my gear to the barn for packing, watched by half a dozen curious calves.

An overgrown green lane with hay length grass was very wet after the previous night's rain. Within minutes my boots and socks were soaked, as were my trousers up to my thighs. It was still raining, though not heavily and I decided to stick to proper metalled roads for the rest of the day—or at least as long as it rained. At the first opportunity I stopped in the comparative dryness of an oak tree and rummaged in my rucksack for dry socks and polythene bags to wear inside my boots as over-socks. I could only find one, but at least I had one dry foot which felt much more comfortable and reduced the risk of blisters on that foot at least. I was beginning to regret my decision to use cheap, non-waterproof boots for the West Country.

As I trudged along wet lanes towards the Quantocks the rain became heavier and steadier. I was intrigued to hear the whistle of a steam engine and consulting the map discovered this was coming from the West Somerset Railway. I've had a soft spot for steam ever since teenage days of trainspotting on Birmingham's New Street Station. Only a slight detour was needed to reach Crowcombe Heathfield Station. It was unmanned but had a timetable pinned up and I was in luck. A 'steamer' was due in 20 minutes. I roamed round the immaculate station with its many artefacts and railway memorabilia. When the train arrived, the engine was at the rear. The carriages drew to a halt beside the platform, but the engine was still outside the station. It stopped so briefly I barely caught a glimpse of the engine.

### In the steps of Samuel Taylor Coleridge

There had been no let up in the rain all morning, though this was only the second wet day since leaving Land's End. I retraced my steps to Crowcombe village in the hope of finding food. Just a dream. There was no shop. Wet and hungry I began to make the steep climb up on to the Quantocks. A blister began to develop on my wet foot.

A thick mist hung over the tops of the hills. I was soaked already without more long grass and bracken and abandoned ideas of a pleasant cross-country walk. Instead I chose roads all the way to Nether Stowey. From Crowcombe the road leading up onto the Quantocks is exceptionally steep. It was no more than a mile but it took me a long time and half way up I stopped and ate my lunch in the shelter of beech trees. A meagre meal. All I had left was the crumbling remains of a packet of ryvita and a tiny pot of jam.

I had never been to the Quantocks before and was looking forward to hills after days of fields and lanes. On reaching the top, the mist was as thick as ever. I was disappointed. Where were my views? I had expected to see the Somerset levels; Bridgwater; the Bristol Channel and the distant Mendips. But on each side of the unfenced road I could see barely a hundred yards. Cresting the hill were beech-woods criss-crossed with bridleways. After this, tree-covered heathland merged into mist. Tall moorland grasses sagged under a silvery shroud of moisture. It was a drab and dismal scene. A party of soggy teenagers engulfed in cagoules slouched by looking dejected. I knew how they felt.

Samuel Taylor Coleridge lived near here. He was a walker too—sometimes walking 40 miles in a day. He spent much of his time wandering over the Quantocks in the company of William and Dorothy Wordsworth—exploring streams and making observations on nature. He lived what today we would call a life of self sufficiency, in a tiny thatched cottage in Nether Stowey and it was here that he wrote the Rime of the Ancient Mariner. The village lies at the foot of the Quantocks. As I passed the remains of the castle and reached the first houses, the rain finally ceased. Then, like a nomad finding an oasis in a desert, I went into the first shop which sold food, buying on impulse things I fancied—and sat outside devouring them.

My cousin, a teacher, lived only a mile or two away. I left a message on her answerphone, telling her I had arrived and browsed round the shops. More shops than I had seen in a week. While waiting to be served in the greengrocers, someone tapped me on the shoulder and said, "Are you Helen's cousin Shirley?" I shouldn't have been surprised. Helen has loads of friends and a big rucksack is a give away. Having received my message, she phoned a friend who happened to live next door to the greengrocer. I was promptly whisked next door for coffee while we waited her arrival.

Helen's home is on the Severn Estuary. At the back of her old farm-house the sea is so close you can here the waves breaking on the beach. At the front, the broad estuary of the River Parrett sweeps in huge bends from Bridgwater to its mouth on the Severn. That night we had a party. Unaware of my birthday, she had organised a 'bring a plate' supper for a group of walking friends—a lively crowd of 50-something women who abandon their husbands and children once a year for a weekend walking and youth-hostelling. They were all in high spirits and after a wet and arduous day it was a convivial and appropriate way to celebrate my birthday.

# 3
# Somerset Delights
## Bridgwater to the Severn Bridge

Midsummer's Day on the Severn Estuary. Any ideas I might have had of sitting with my feet up recuperating, evaporated as Helen appeared and disappeared between work and ferrying children around with cheerful shouts of, "Oh. Can you feed the chickens?" "Would you mind hanging the washing out?" and finally "I don't suppose you'd have time to dig the veggie patch?" This was a disaster zone, already planted once but decimated by the resident rabbits who had eaten all the vegetables and left the weeds. The sun blazed mercilessly from a cloudless sky and in the hot dry heat the garden, sheltered from the salt-laden winds of the estuary by high hedges, was like an oven. It took me all day to turn the ravaged plot into a tidy allotment, re-sown and labelled ready for the next batch of rabbits.

That evening we walked along the beach to watch the Midsummer Solstice, the dark outline of Hinkley Point Power Station silhouetted against the red flush on the horizon as the sun set in explosive glory over the coast of Wales. Pen y Fan, the highest point of the Brecon Beacons is unmistakable from Helen's and on a clear day the hills of our own Black Mountains can be seen. From home, I can see the Severn Estuary and the hills of the Quantocks. We joke that we can wave to each other.

My stopover at Steart was longer than planned as I offered to chicken-sit and holiday cottage-mind while Helen went off with her boys for the weekend. And my younger son Robin had been in touch to say he would walk with me all the way to Chepstow. He would join me at the weekend—but couldn't say exactly when.

Once the holiday cottage tenants were safely installed, I was free to follow the Parrett Trail upstream towards Bridgwater. Within the Bridgwater Bay National Nature Reserve, the Parrett Estuary is part of the Severn Estuary Special Protection Area. Extensive areas of saltmarsh and mudflats are home to hundreds of wading birds, flocks of widgeon, teal and shelduck and there is a diverse range of maritime and saltmarsh plants. With all this to explore, my progress up river was slow and took all afternoon. It was still sunny but a fresh breeze kept the temperature down to a more reasonable level than the previous day.

### A 'nice way to go'

Robin eventually arrived from Dorset and we prepared for an early start on Monday morning. We had 17 miles to cover, quite a long way for Robin's first day. As an agricultural contractor, the furthest he normally walks in a day is from his car to his tractor. So, as I had already walked most of the way up the Parrett, we gratefully accepted Helen's offer of a lift to Bridgwater.

At 8am we were deposited with bulging rucksacks at the sea lock of the Bridgwater and Taunton Canal. We set off along the towpath intent on walking the canal for only a short way before transferring to the River Parrett and then cutting across to the King's Sedgemoor Drain. This was not my original route, but one suggested as being "a nice way to go" by someone living locally. It did appear to be an interesting route, but this person had evidently only walked the separate sections of canal, river and drain and never tried linking the three together. After three miles, having exchanged the canal for the Parrett, we realised too late that there was no way of crossing the river—still tidal and running in a deep, muddy channel. Close scrutiny of the map confirmed our fears and was verified by several fishermen and a cyclist. The only crossing, unless we went miles upstream, was back in Bridgwater. This was a frustrating delay after an early start and I kicked myself for not checking the route first. Not for the first time did I regret taking local information on trust. It was no doubt an innocent mistake. So many people rely on cars, they forget the needs of walkers. To drive to the bridge would take only minutes. It wouldn't occur to them that a walker would take perhaps two hours. So, having left Bridgwater at 8.15, by 11am we were back again only a mile from where we started.

We crossed the river via a railway footbridge on a path that took us immediately underneath the M5. This was an interesting experience. A large bridge or flyover effectively becomes a vast shed and all sorts of things may be stored there. This one was used by a farmer for storing hay and a local bus company for parking coaches. Looking up, under a seemingly fragile structure of concrete, it's un-nerving to think of the volume of traffic you know is roaring overhead. I never drive over a motorway bridge now without visualising how little is between me and the ground—and wondering what secrets are hidden below.

### Drains, ditches and peat

It was early afternoon by the time we finally reached the King's Sedgemoor Drain; a broad straight artificial river; one of the largest of the region's complex system of drainage channels. These innumerable ditches and straightened rivers support a wide variety of wildlife and the fields they drain support the dairy herds producing milk for Somerset's best known commodity, Cheddar Cheese. It was still breezy and the water rippled and glittered in the sun as we sat on the banks munching croissants and cheese. Swans drifted lazily with the current, amongst patches of both yellow and white waterlilies. We passed the pumping station museum at Westonzoyland which we had planned to visit, but because of the morning's delays we hadn't time and hastened on to the pretty village of Catcott. As my rule is never to pass a shop without topping up either supplies or stomach, we pigged-out on fruit drinks, peaches and cakes before crossing lush, cow populated fields towards Canada Farm Nature Reserve.

We were now in the heart of the Somerset Levels, included on my route as being somewhere I had always wanted to see. An area of flooded meres, withy beds, reed-fringed drainage ditches green with duckweed and flower-rich hay meadows. Straight, narrow roads run in ordered geometrical patterns with drainage ditches on each side, controlled by a system of sluices. In the damp woodland of Canada Farm, where leather waste from a shoe factory was used to stabilise the soft peaty tracks, the reserve's warden came upon us lounging by the wayside eating pork pies. I had already made his acquaintance as he was also the warden of the Bridgwater Bay Reserve. Another Robin—and able to provide a solution to the dilemma we had over visiting the Peat Moor Visitor Centre. We didn't want to miss it, but we were now so late we knew it would be closed by the time we arrived. Our intended campsite was much further on—too far to consider coming back. Robin solved the problem by telling us of another less than a mile away which would enable us go to the Visitor Centre next day. He offered to take us in his Land Rover but like the good walkers we were, we felt morally obliged to decline!

Despite the fact that much of the Levels are designated as an Environmentally Sensitive Area, great quantities of peat are still being removed for the garden trade, though we were told this was all done under a strict management régime. Some of the workings can be seen from the road; the surface peat being rotovated by tractors, scraped up by mechanical diggers and dumped in vast heaps—like coal tips in mining areas—to await screening and bagging. I had no idea of the scale of the Somerset peat industry until I saw this for myself.

### A glimpse of ancient Somerset

Our farm campsite was basic but adequate and we had it to ourselves. A converted building housed an ingenious shower cubicle made from garden panels, but so well done it was hard to tell. The same building also housed the farm's heating system. It was beautifully warm. We left our boots, socks and towels in there overnight. It was Robin's ideal farm. Hi-tech modern tractor driver he may be, but in his heart he prefers the vintage stuff and this farmer collected all manner of things, specialising in old cheese presses. The assortment of farming bygones tucked away in every corner were right up his street.

It was a chilly evening. We turned in early, glad of the warmth of our sleeping bags. Next morning we were ready with rucksacks packed long before the Peat Moor Visitor Centre opened at 10am. The farmer suggested we left our packs and picked them up later, so rather than doing nothing, we walked along to the Centre, even though we had at least half an hour to wait. However, three young men who were energetically ripping the office apart for a refit, obligingly let us in well before opening time.

The Centre manages to pack a surprising amount into a small area with a fascinating reconstruction of an Iron Age Settlement. Round huts, thatched with reed are furnished with the tools and belongings of an Iron Age family while wattle shelters protect the work areas of the potter, carpenter and smith. The museum's curator proudly removed the tarpaulins from their recently completed 'dug-out' canoe, made from a single oak tree in the traditional manner, a replica of one found locally preserved in the peat. When we retrieved our packs, we learnt from the farmer that it was his father that had made the discovery of the original canoe. We walked with some trepidation along replica sections of the various prehistoric tracks found in the Levels. The best known, the Sweet Track, we had passed the previous day in the Canada Farm reserve where the water levels have to be kept high enough to prevent it drying out and deteriorating.

An hour passed quickly and could easily have been stretched to two, but we had to get to Cheddar by evening. It was almost lunchtime when we left the farm and we supplemented our basic diet with extra items from a village shop. Bridleways, field paths and quiet lanes took us past more flooded reed beds and flowery meads and a path along the banks of the diminutive River Axe took us in the general direction of the Mendips. From geological information at the Visitor Centre we now knew that the Somerset Levels had been formed when the massive river valley between the Quantocks and the Mendips, originally below sea level, had filled up over several thousand years with the sediments washed off both. As the sea level fell the marshes built up forming the deep peats of the moors and levels that we see today. Drainage, begun way back in Roman times, has continued ever since. The whole area is only between 4 and 7m. above sea level and the River Axe, we observed, had no perceptible flow at all, apparently dropping less than a foot in a mile. Higher ground becomes very noticeable in such a flat area. One prominent hill we used as a landmark proved to be only 76m. high. The rivers were as clear as the bogs of Dartmoor and full of water flora; distinctive arrowheads, waterlilies, bulrushes and along the banks hundreds of dazzling bright blue damsel flies fluttered low over the water.

During the morning it drizzled off and on and became increasingly more oppressive as the day wore on. In the sweltering humidity of late afternoon thunderclouds gathered ominously over the Mendips. Tractors were flying around everywhere in a frenzy of hay and silage making. Robin was having to reconsider his thoughts on Somerset. He often works around Glastonbury and from the tractor driver's point of view, thought it was flat and boring. Now, as a walker he saw it with different eyes and found it was much more interesting than he had previously thought.

## Crossing the Mendips

The Cheddar campsite was far too trendy for us, but it had to do. Tents were pitched between caravans, on the banks of a small river with a stone crocodile lurking in its depths and a herd of sculptured deer standing rigidly nearby. By evening the sultry weather had passed and the air became clearer. We treated ourselves to chips and wandered along the road through the bottom of the gorge, peering through the closed turnstiles of the show caves.

The following day was less than 11 miles, mostly across the Mendips and next morning we climbed the steep bridlepath to the top of the Gorge to follow the cliff top Gorge Walk. The limestone cliffs of Cheddar Gorge are

450ft. high and are some of the most dramatic in Britain. Because of its unique geology, endangered animals and rare flowers, the whole gorge is a Site of Special Scientific Interest, which was the reason for including it on my route. I hoped to see Cheddar Pinks which grow nowhere else but on these cliffs and although I had driven through the gorge many times and visited the caves when the children were small, I had never been up on the top.

Before starting the Gorge Walk, we climbed Pavey's Tower, a Victorian lookout tower constructed entirely of iron. From the top a stupendous view unfolds back across the Somerset Levels towards the Quantocks. Much nearer, the towns of Cheddar and Axbridge converge on the circular expanse of water which is Cheddar Lake, and looking towards the Mendips there is the deep gash of the Gorge and the stark white scars of the vast controversial quarries. Around the viewing platform, cast into the ironwork are the distances to various towns in Britain which strangely, for a Victorian edifice, are in kilometres. Edinburgh, I noted, was 522 kilometres, though this actually meant very little as I had no idea what that was in miles.

The Gorge Walk follows the edge of the cliffs and has the most spectacular views. Anyone afraid of heights would be well advised not to walk too near the edge. Information boards point out geological features and we could hardly tear ourselves away, stopping every few yards to gaze down some sheer rock face at the tiny cars on the road far below. We watched a peregrine falcon being mobbed by a crow as it defended its nest and I got very excited when I found my first Cheddar Pinks. Robin was appalled when I suggested he held my feet while I hung over the edge to take photographs, but these were after all some of Britain's rarest plants. The Victorians made them rarer, by avidly collecting them to take home to their gardens. I was not going to reduce their number by picking any, but I was not going to miss the opportunity of a photograph either. Nowhere did we see any signs warning us to keep away from the edge and we have only found out since that the limestone of these cliffs is highly likely to crumble and give way. Fatal accidents are not uncommon and we now realise we should have been more careful and are lucky to be alive.

There were many other lime-loving plants: yellow rockroses especially and pink valerian, making the cliffs of Cheddar better than any cultivated rock garden. The mile along the top of the Gorge took so long, it was more of a crawl than a walk. We were reluctant to leave, but there was more to come. The descent from the top brought us to Black Rock Quarry Nature Reserve. Still on limestone this has fossils, a dry river and a blow hole, where underground water escapes from the caves below at certain times. The waters of the non-existent river leach down through the lime-stone to the lower levels of the caves below and the footpath follows its dry, winding course through a deep valley. Here, in the past, the limestone cliffs were quarried. Now masses of rockroses cascade over rocky outcrops in sunny abandon. There were several people about, following the nature trail or walking the West Mendip Way. I left Robin for a few minutes while I disappeared into some bushes for a pit-stop and it didn't take him long to take advantage of mother's absence. When I came back he was chatting up a couple of girls.

Leaving Black Rock Quarry Nature Reserve, we were immediately into another, this time the Long Wood Reserve, an ancient broadleaved wood that has survived since the thirteenth century. After this we became hopelessly confused crossing large fields with no indication as to where the seasonally overgrown stiles might be. When we eventually emerged onto a narrow lane, we were not where we were supposed to be and had to re-route ourselves to the summit of Beacon Batch, for which we were heading. We were now on the highest point of the Mendips and from here it was all downhill to a road, a layby and a very welcome icecream van — which we naturally patronised.

## Last stop before Bristol

Since leaving Cheddar we had followed two waymarked paths, the West Mendip Way and the Limestone Link, but coming down off the Mendips we were back to lanes. At the Post Office in Blagdon, I withdrew enough cash to see us home, and bought enough food to keep us, or rather Robin, going. He refuels on pork pies and Mars Bars at every shop we pass.

Blagdon, dominated by its tall towered church, is picturesquely located on the side of a hill overlooking Blagdon Lake, a reservoir storing water for Bristol. The old steam powered pumping engines are open to the public, but we found to our disappointment it was closing day. We crossed the dam and followed a path along the shore, where in the shallow water there were thousands of tiny fish. There were many water birds too and we sat on a bench, eating sandwiches and watching families of coots and moorhens amongst the reeds, the pretty red-headed coot youngsters trying desperately hard to keep up with mum.

The nearest place to Bristol that I could find a campsite was Butcombe and this was still more than ten miles from the city. It was in a field beside an inn and it did not look very promising. No-one in the pub seemed very sure that it even *was* a campsite and had no idea whom we should pay.

Hours later a farmer arrived in a Land Rover and collected five pounds—in return for which we had a cold water tap and a toilet with no light and no paper. Not that the folks at the inn weren't friendly, they just seemed rather surprised to actually get a camper and even more surprised to get back-packers. I suspected they thought I was a middle-aged loony with a toy-boy, but for all that they were able to offer the useful information that the Avon Walkway was a popular path and a good way to by-pass Bristol. This was welcome news as it was the most favoured of several ways I had considered to avoid the city. Trusting that for once local information would for right, we decided that this was the way we would go next day.

### *The longest day*

With Bristol Airport only a mile and a half along the road, the Bungalow Inn was not a peaceful spot. The runway is beside the road and we spent the evening watching the arrival and departure of planes. To our relief all this activity ceased at 11 o' clock. We had a peaceful night and by the time flying commenced next morning at 6, we had been up an hour. The tents were dry when we got up, but in the short time it took to take them down, it began to rain and they had to be packed away wet. Packing was done quickly and we were on the road by 7. We knew we had a very long day ahead. Even by opting for the Avon Gorge through Bristol, there were several alternative routes we could choose for the rest and I expected we would do well over 25 miles.

Surprisingly, and not visible to traffic driving down the A38, there is a sizable piece of common land next to the airport. This is Felton Common and from here lanes, closed to four wheeled traffic, form part of a network of cycle paths around Bristol and took us into Long Ashton. We phoned Michael to confirm our arrangements for the evening, and established from a girl riding a pony that Ashton Court was a Country Park and that the grounds were freely accessible to the public. We had been unsure about this but it meant we could go all the way to the Avon Gorge without using roads.

Roe Deer grazed in the Park. People exercised horses and dogs. Kids played. Joggers jogged and golfers practised their swings. A monster sculptured head with a brass toposcope fixed to its scalp gazes out from a hilltop overlooking the city. Greville Smythe, the one time owner of Ashton Court who also owned just about everything he could see from here, was a keen plant collector. Many of the trees, specifically the giant redwoods growing in the grounds today, were raised from seed he collected on his expeditions.

Ignoring signs to Clifton Suspension Bridge as we left the park, we descended the hill to join the river at Cumberland Basin. From here, the joint Avon Cycleway and Walkway follows the Avon Gorge using an old railway track along the south bank of the river for about five miles as far as Pill. It's an area well known to botanists with a number of rarities and a variety of alien species, many of them introduced to his country by means of shipping passing through Avonmouth docks. Recently it had been the scene of a localised environmental tragedy when, during the cleaning of the Suspension Bridge, much damage had been done by tons of toxic dust falling onto the plants. Many of the plants that grow here are specific to the Gorge. I kept my eyes peeled and notebook handy for anything unusual and even enthused Robin enough that he spotted one rarity that I hadn't noticed.

Gun shots being fired close by worried us for a time and we were relieved to find that it was only police marksmen whose firing range is located in one of the Gorge's disused quarries. Feeling that this was after all a very safe place to be, we stopped and unpacked the stove for a brew of tea. It was our first proper stop of the day and we had already done 14 miles. We needed a break. Robin was beginning to get pains in one leg and hip and the rain, never heavy, had nevertheless been continuous, alternating between drizzle and copious showers. The track was actually fairly sheltered and dry, running for most of the time through woodland close to the river bank. The tide was almost full out; the river, a mere muddy stream many feet below at the bottom of steep slimy mudbanks. Every so often flights of steps led down to navigation lights perched precariously near the water to guide vessels safely along the Avon's notorious winding approaches to the floating harbour.

The village of Pill, at one time of considerable importance, is now quite literally overlooked by the modern world. Gone is its railway, once going all the way to Portishead. Gone is the ferry, the lowest crossing point of the river for many years and no longer do the pilot cutters anchor here in its tidal creek. Across the marshy riverside wasteland the Avon Bridge, spanning far more than the width of the river, stands on lofty concrete pillars, carrying the relentless flow of M5 traffic to and from the West Country.

It was now drizzling more heavily than ever and we spotted a baker's shop with a 'Special Offer' sign in the window. 'Mug of tea and any doughnut for 60p.' How could we ignore that? Revitalised and warmed, we emerged into the rain again for the daunting prospect of walking across the motorway bridge. These bridges take far longer to walk across than you would think when you are used to driving over them. The pedestrian way is actually a service road wide enough to take a lorry. Traffic flow was heavy; lanes in both directions packed with vehicles hell bent on getting to journey's end; air foul with exhaust fumes and a permanent mist of surface spray reducing visibility. Enormous lorries thundered past, their drivers' faces never glancing sideways, eyes never seeing us. I commented to Robin, "Just look at them. They're all mad." Robin gave me a quizzical look. "No mum,", he said "It's you that's mad!"

There were extensive road works being carried out and an isolated portaloo, protected by a little circle of orange road cones, was strategically placed in the central reservation. We both agreed that if we worked there, we would not feel at all happy about using it. On the other hand, if you were at all constipated, sitting in the middle of a motorway might well do the trick!

On reaching the other side, we sheltered from the rain under a flyover, eating sausage rolls bought in Pill. Then, as I had finished my last film, we went firstly in search of a chemist in Avonmouth and then in search of the Severn Way. This is a long distance footpath which follows the River Severn from Tewkesbury for 66 miles along the east bank of the river as far as Avonmouth, and ends after a bit of a detour, at Pill. It was supposed to be my final off-road link to the Severn Bridge but was disappointing. We found signposts pointing to it but try as we might, we could find no passable foot-path. Twice we attempted to push our way through thigh-high grass and nettles but it was the brambles that really defeated us. It wasn't just one season's growth. These brambles hadn't been cut for years. They were tall as a man. We gave up. With no nice waymarked footpath to follow we had no alternative but to take to the road and dodge the traffic. Robin's hip and leg became increasingly painful. He found it almost impossible to walk. We stopped on a patch of wasteland, unpacked the stove again, drank more tea and rested for half an hour before setting off once more along verges which in places were only a few feet wide.

From Avonmouth it is eight miles to the Severn Bridge. The road has long straight stretches. It is fast and busy, carrying heavy lorries to the docks. Anyone who has ever walked beside a road like this will know that a fast moving lorry produces an air current that nearly sweeps you off your feet. Carrying a rucksack is even more hazardous as it is wider than the body. There is a danger that such huge vehicles thundering by will catch it and whip you into the road. While in Cornwall I heard of just such a case, in which the walker sustained injuries from which he later died.

Without going into more details, it is enough to say that those eight miles were not pleasant and neither of us would want to do them again. A lorry driver offered us a lift, but we declined on principle—and because

Robin was determined to get to the Severn Bridge even if he had to crawl, which he nearly was. Eventually we reached the stage where we walked for half a mile and stopped for a quarter of an hour and our progress was agonisingly slow. We tried Michael's mobile to tell him of Robin's problem and that we might be late, but could not make contact.

When we reached the Severn Bridge at the end of those dreadful eight miles we practically kissed its tarmac with relief. Then the awful realisation sank in. The bridge is two miles long. It would take an hour to cross and then there was a further mile and a half to our pick-up point at Chepstow. It was nine o'clock and the rain had returned. Our minds were dulled by fatigue. Our legs reluctant to move. Once on the bridge though, the novelty of the experience perked us up. With the new Second Severn Crossing taking the bulk of the traffic, the old bridge now carries hardly any and at that time of night was so quiet that when a vehicle did cross we immediately noticed the whole structure bouncing like a giant springboard. Robin hobbled painfully, dragging himself along using the handrail as support. Thankfully, although it was wet, there was only a light breeze. Anything more would have made it even more difficult for him.

Wooden pallets stacked with large cans of Severn Bridge white paint were dumped at intervals along the walkway. To keep Robin's spirits up, I suggested purloining one for a souvenir. He said he didn't like the colour. In any case, the police security cameras were probably watching us and neither of us wanted to carry it! As we reached the the half way point the rain at last ceased and we were rewarded with a radiant sunset over a stormy Wales, though I think by this time Robin was incapable of appreciating it. As soon as we arrived on the other side he sank to the ground. I left him sitting beside the road and went ahead to see if Michael was waiting. He wasn't. I tried the mobile again. No reply! It was now dark and I didn't fancy loitering on the side of a main road by myself so I went back to Robin. We sat by the roadside wondering what was the best thing to do. We had walked for 15 hours and had covered 28 miles, with an extra three miles for me. All we wanted to do was go home and go to bed.

Why was Michael so late? Should we phone for a taxi? Carry on walking? Ring friends or neighbours or sit it out for a bit longer? Thankfully, before panic and hypothermia set in, he arrived with acceptable excuses. In September, I was able to look back and say without hesitation that the longest and the worst day of the entire trip was the last day in the West Country. After 20 days and 250 miles I was back home in Wales—sincerely hoping that I would never have another day like it.

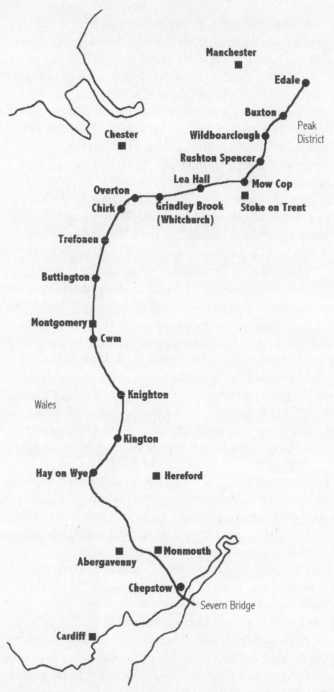

*Along Offa's Dyke and across Cheshire to the Pennine Way*

# 4

# Border Patrol

## Along Offa's Dyke to Chirk

In the eighth century, under the direction of Offa, King of Wessex, a massive dyke was constructed along the border between England and Wales. It was a considerable feat of engineering even by today's standards; a barrier not so much to keep the Welsh out, but more as a demarcation line to remind them of where they were supposed to be. And, it was built to last. Today it forms the basis of one of the oldest of Britain's Long Distance Paths; the Offa's Dyke Path. For 80 of its 190 miles, the path, which runs between Chepstow on the Bristol Channel and Prestatyn in North Wales, is actually on, beside or within sight of, the Dyke's surviving embankments.

As I have lived less than two miles from the Offa's Dyke Path for 20 years, this is familiar territory. I have walked sections nearest to home many times and the more distant stages three or four times. The whole length I did several years ago with Robin and Helen on a sponsored walk for our parish church. We left Prestatyn using borrowed rucksacks and heavy, ancient equipment and never thought we'd make it to the other end. It was a great adventure. We couldn't get over the fact that we could walk so far in such a relatively short time and I realised that if you can walk 200 miles, there's nothing to stop you carrying on and doing more. I had become hooked on long distance walking.

On Offa's Dyke I knew exactly what to expect. Unless I detoured there would be no new discoveries, no real challenge. Apart from the

Pennine Way, there can hardly be another path in the land that leads so directly north. In addition, it is well waymarked and almost entirely rural. If I still had qualms about walking alone, I knew that I would have a certain peace of mind walking a familiar route. Possibly a false sense of security as being in the wrong place at the wrong time can happen to anyone.

But by using the Offa's Dyke Path, I could come home, catch up on family and work. Although we live on a hill farm and keep sheep, our main business is landscape gardening and for three months other arrangements had been made for my work. But I had promised one person that when I arrived back in Wales I would make sure her garden was looking its best for a fête to be held there on the first Saturday in July. A lot to pack in in one week, and walk the intervening miles from Chepstow.

From Chepstow the path is hard-going—uphill and down dale through the thickly wooded Wye Valley. Offa's Dyke is well-defined in places and occasionally merges with the path. From the heights of the cliffs on the Gloucester side of the river there are aerial views of the sweeping curves of the river, Chepstow Castle and scenic Tintern Abbey. It gets easier from Monmouth where the path leaves the Wye to traverse the gentler countryside of Monmouthshire with the promising vista of the Black Mountains ahead getting closer all the time. Only when you reach these do you truly feel you are in Wales. This is the beginning of wilder country. The official route climbs up onto Hatteral Hill, the Black Mountains' prominent eastern ridge, and after a few miles becomes a badly eroded peaty highway through monotonous heather-clad moorland. In good weather there are fine views; in bad it's an inhospitable place. Home is on the adjacent ridge which is much more pleasant to walk with better terrain, more interesting scenery and a less bleak aspect. Both ridges terminate above Hay on Wye with far-reaching views north to the hills of mid-Wales.

As luck would have it, it was a wet week. There was panic amongst the organisers of the fête and a marquee was hired as a precaution. Would the venue be changed at the last minute to the village hall? In the short time available it was not easy to fit in the walking and I actually walked from home to Hay on Wye in reverse as it was pouring with rain. Then I didn't have to wait in Hay, cold and wet, to be collected.

I have walked this ridge in all its seasons and moods and don't ever remember it being as windy in summer as it was that day. The drenching rain in which I left Hay had cleared by the time I climbed up on to the ridge from the Gospel Pass but I was nearly blown back again by the force of a howling south-westerly. Home was directly into the wind. I had to keep my cagoule on and hood up to protect my ears from the noisy buffeting of the wind. The cagoule billowed out like a sail taking me in the opposite direction.

By the end of the week most jobs on my list had been ticked off. I couldn't spare the time to attend the fête, which did in the end take place in good weather. My rucksack was repacked along with enough maps to take me to the Peak District. My youngest daughter Helen was to join me somewhere in this region on July 17th when I expected to be north of Stoke on Trent. She would bring the next set of maps with her, but I took a couple extra to be on the safe side.

### The real adventure begins

As I left on the morning of July 8th, I really felt that the big adventure was just beginning. Land's End to the Severn Bridge had in a way been a trial run. I hadn't known how I would cope with being alone; whether it would worry me unduly and if my route would work. There had been added pressure knowing that I had to be back home in good time to get the promised work done. Now with almost a quarter of the journey behind me, I was no longer worried about 'going it alone' and barring accidents, I knew I could make the distance. I was fit and raring to go. Vicky, a friend and neighbour had agreed to accompany me from Hay on Wye to Kington and we left Hay in weather that looked more promising than it had done all the week—and was forecast to continue to improve. As we walked down the road from Hay Castle, passing the many second-hand bookshops for which Hay on Wye is famed, I turned my back on husband, family and home comforts for the next two months.

Despite the fact that we are neighbours, Vicky and I don't see each other that often and we had plenty to talk about. So much so that it wasn't long before we missed our path. Deep in discussion and with a tractor parked in a gateway hiding a signpost and stile, we went happily marching on in the wrong direction until it dawned on us that we should not be going downhill on a road, but uphill through a wood. It was a simple mistake and nothing to worry about but illustrates how easily it can happen. One of the things about walking alone is the lack of someone to confer with when things go wrong. Your fate is in your own hands. You have to make the final decision: which way to go, whether to press on in bad weather or, less critically, will the bread last until tomorrow or is it worth a long detour to get some? Often, two heads are better than one, the other person making a valid point you hadn't thought of. There were times when I would dearly have welcomed another opinion and times when I regretted changing my mind and wished I had stuck to an earlier decision.

It's a pleasant walk all the way from Hay to Kington, but to me the most enjoyable part is unquestionably along Hergest Ridge. Standing apart from the surrounding hills it enjoys superb views and once the top is attained, provides an easy two mile walk along a ridge traced by the patterns of history. The odd erratic boulder indicates that ice once covered the region; long ridges in the turf mark areas ploughed up for wartime food production, the circular track of the old racecourse cuts a swathe of green through the bracken and young Monkey Puzzle trees, natives of Chile, stretch their dark spikey branches skywards, looking oddly out of place on top of a Welsh mountain.

Kington is a quiet border town on the banks of the River Arrow. Half timbered buildings rub shoulders with nineteenth century architecture along a narrow high street. Elegant town houses and a spired church suggest a prosperous past. Vicky's husband was waiting as we came down off the hill and we parted in the garden of a house in the town—one of the unofficial campsites nurtured by the Offa's Dyke Association's good relationship with guest houses and farmers along the route. Many of these allow overnight camping in the garden, usually with the use of their own bathroom and toilet. I felt safest on these sites and sure of a warm welcome. Within minutes of arrival a pot of tea and plate of cake appears and the owners are happy to spare time for a chat. At Kington I was the only camper in the total privacy of an old walled garden with a picnic table at my disposal and my hosts, I learned, were the parents of one of our local vets. On hearing that I was an End to Ender, they told me that they had others from time to time. One elderly man who stayed there had shopping trolley wheels fixed to the top of his rucksack—in order to be able to pull as well as carry it!

### Sill in sight of home

The first time I walked Offa's Dyke, Robin managed to knock a large bottle of red sauce off a shelf in the supermarket here with his rucksack. I had to pay for it and learnt my lesson. I remove my rucksack in any supermarket now and ask if I can leave it at the till.

The simple task of shopping had in the past been one of the biggest hurdles in overcoming agoraphobia. Along with churches, theatres, public houses, restaurants and any type of public transport, any shop was a 'no-go' area. I would be filled with panic; unable to breath, sweating, feeling faint. I thought all eyes were on me. I would bolt for the door. Over many years these fears had been conquered. But slowly. Taking one step at a time. Even then, I still felt happier in any of these situations if I had someone with me. Walking Offa's Dyke before I'd had Robin and Helen. They were my 'props' though they weren't aware of it. Then I'd done other long distance paths with Helen. But we had never eaten out, gone in pubs or socialised. This walk was a test of my self confidence. At no previous time in my life could I have done it. Always at the back of my mind was the fear of a panic attack. Only now did I feel that I would be able to cope with every occasion. But I still had worries and had been grateful for Vicky's company. Now I was once more alone.

Over the next five days, Offa's Dyke was my companion. From Monmouth to Kington, the Path is in name only, Offa having constructed his frontier much further to the east in the direction of Hereford. The Dyke is rejoined at Kington and from there is followed closely, through countryside devoid of people, cars and commerce. Some of the happiest days of my journey were spent here and I was surprised to find how much I enjoyed re-walking familiar territory and how different it was walking it in the opposite direction. The weather could not have been better; blue skies, bright and sunny; a few cottonwool clouds and a stiff breeze. Most of the time I met no-one. A dumpy, grey-haired woman passed me one day. Head down, she scurried passed without speaking—like a frightened rabbit. By the size of her pack she must have been doing the whole path. I was gratified to see she carried two plastic carrier bags, as I often seem to end up doing this, much to the amusement of many of the male walkers who wouldn't be seen dead carrying 'shopping'. I made the brief acquaintance of a Dutch couple walking to Snowdon, but I never saw them again. There seemed, in general, to be a dearth of walkers.

After three days the Black Mountains were still visible on the southern horizon giving me my last glimpse of home. I strode out along the Dyke with high hilly countryside stretching endlessly in every direction. Nature seemed oblivious to my presence. I froze in my tracks to watch a green woodpecker searching for insects in a rotten tree stump just a few feet away, and sat under larch trees where skylarks fed unconcerned.

I quenched my thirst in a farmyard where an illustrated poem hangs above the tap, inviting walkers to 'imbibe the elixir'. It's 'cool and fresh and free'. Some days, with time not pressing, I'd unpack the stove and have tea with my lunch. Normally I just drank water. Often, the only signs of human life were a distant Land Rover, a farmer rounding up sheep on a farm bike, or a tractor working far away in a field. Many a time—and not just here—anywhere on my journey, I was conscious that, while all the world was rushing about its business with cars streaming into cities full of noise and pollution, Britain still has its peaceful havens of unspoilt countryside. Often I found my thoughts turning to the lines of the poem, Leisure, by William Henry Davies: "What is this life but full of care / We have no time to stand and stare?" Very true in modern times. But the lone walker has time to stand and stare. Alone in such surroundings you become acutely aware of everything around you; the slightest change in wind or weather; the presence of an animal; the sound of birds and the scent of flowers. Even the smell of other humans—deodorant, perfume, cigarette smoke, food and sweat, can linger long after another person has passed by.

Each area has its distinctive sounds too. In Cornwall it was the constant song of larks. In rural Devon, even on the wide open spaces of Dartmoor, it is difficult to get away from the sound of traffic. With major road links throughout the county, the dull roar of traffic could always be heard in the distance, sometimes up to six miles away. Later, in the Pennines there was always the curlew's plaintive call and the noisy cries of oystercatchers. Here through border country, it was yellowhammers with their persistent repetition of 'Little bit of bread an no cheese.'

### Knee-wrecking hills

The Dyke is at its best north of Knighton where it can be seen snaking ahead sometimes for several miles, often delineated by a dark line of trees crossing farmland, or as a grassy bank rounding a hillside. In places it is no more than a raised hummock across a field, intentionally razed by years of cultivations. At its highest, the best preserved sections stand 27ft. above the ditch bottom. Many miles are walked along the top, past ancient oaks and groves of Scots pines. The burrowings of rabbits and badgers cause far more erosion than the walkers and make walking quite a hazardous occupation at times. You need to keep your eyes on the ground and one of my constant niggling worries was that I should sprain an ankle or worse. In the event of a mishap, I had only my whistle to summon help. The chances of being able to use the mobile phone in areas likely to pose the threat of an accident were remote. Weighed against the disadvantages of extra weight, spare batteries and difficulties of recharging, I had abandoned this bit of technology.

Through the upland area of Clun Forest the path follows a notoriously tortuous course across the grain of the country. It's known as the 'switch-back'. No sooner have you sweated and panted to the top of one hill, than you are gritting your teeth against the agony of the pain in your knees as you descend the other side—only to repeat the experience on the next hill. It was just as well there was enough breeze around to keep the temperature at a reasonable level. One of the few people I met was on one of these hills. A television aerial repair man, struggling up through woods with tool bag and a coil of cable over his shoulder, trying to improve reception to an isolated cottage. We talked at length. Only later did I remember that I had two pairs of black panties hanging on the back of my rucksack to dry. Maybe that was why he stopped for so long!

One of the steepest descents is down to Churchtown; two cottages and a church at the bottom of a deep valley. On the opposite side of the valley a tractor was ploughing an unbelievably steep field. Clouds of dust hung over the field almost obscuring the tractor. I could hardly bare to watch each time it reached the top and began its next terrifying descent of the slope. The church, dedicated to St. John the Baptist, is Mainstone's parish church. It provided welcome shade and rest, though the place reeked of bat urine and everything was covered in droppings. No pew was fit to sit on. A large boulder reclines on the floor below the pulpit , a relic of the days when the young men of the parish proved their strength trying to lift it. I didn't bother to try; I tested my strength on my rucksack every morning. But I did buy a souvenir pen from this 'Church on the Dyke', a personal memento which served me all the way to the end.

From the summit of any of the hills it was easy to see why the Dyke was necessary. In each direction I was surrounded by countless hills. Not the rugged mountains of Snowdonia, nor the moorland wastes of the south, but gentler, rounded hills, some clothed in bracken or woodland. The deep valleys and complexity of the countryside were perfect for harbouring marauding parties and launching surprise attacks. Significantly, as an added deterrent to the wild hill-men, the ditch of the Dyke is on the Welsh side. At intervals, official trading gaps were constructed. They can still be seen, and there were strict rules of passage. Anyone caught breaking these rules was tried by a jury of twelve men. A method of bringing men to justice so successful we still use it today.

Tramping for miles along the Dyke I could also appreciate the sheer scale of the undertaking. How many men were needed to construct it? How long did it take them? Where on earth did they all come from? The population then was not great. How did they keep such a straight line? In fact they weren't infallible. At one point a sharp bend is thought to be where two gangs of workmen failed to meet. If this was the only mistake it was a tremendous achievement.

### Welsh Hospitality

On no other long distance path have I come across so many friendly and helpful people as those offering camping along Offa's Dyke. One night I stayed at a farm I had been to before. Then we had camped in a field. This time, perhaps because I was on my own, I was offered the lawn. Within five minutes the farmer produced a tray of tea and Bara Brith. At another, the farmer's wife had been on a shopping trip to buy a wedding outfit— two in fact, because she couldn't make up her mind and was hedging her bets on the weather. She kept popping out into the garden with a different outfit on, price tags dangling, giving me a fashion show and asking for my opinion. The farmer was still out haymaking. Later she told me that her husband and son didn't like either of the outfits. She was going to take them back!

At most sites, I washed a few clothes. Rather than wait until everything was grubby, I tried to wash one or two items whenever I had chance and something larger if the weather looked likely to dry it . T-shirts and trousers if still damp soon dried with wearing. But on most days I would have my towel or a pair of socks hung on my rucksack to dry. It was typical of the generosity of many border farmers that at both these farms, when my washing failed to dry overnight it was popped in the tumble dryer before I left.

The first time we walked the Dyke, we had briefly visited Montgomery by car and I thought it a delightful place. This time I intended making a detour to pay a longer visit. It was four miles extra to walk but it also gave me an opportunity to phone home which I hadn't done for two nights.

Montgomery is the smallest county town in Britain and to call it a town is something of a misnomer. I've seen larger villages. Its few shops are clustered round the ancient market square, dominated by the market hall and overlooked by the castle. This is an impressive sight perched high on its tree-covered, rocky prominence overlooking the Vale of Montgomery. A steep path leads up from the square and at the top there's a fine outlook along the line of the old Roman road towards Shrewsbury and the English border. No enemy could approach unseen. From the ramparts you can see where the Battle of Montgomery took place a few miles away. It was only the second week of July. Schools had not yet broken up and there were several parties of children picnicking, filling in questionnaires and clearly enjoying their day out. I tagged on to one of the groups taking advantage of their guided tour.

The dry moat and surrounds were bordered by wild roses, the pink flowered bushes carefully mown round and tended as if they were prize specimens. In these lovely surroundings I ate an early lunch before leaving the town by a B road. I had gone nearly a mile before I realised two things. First I was on the wrong B road and second, I had forgotten to phone. As there was no chance of phoning that night, this took priority, but I also had to find my way back onto the path. The quickest way to do that had no telephones. To find one I had to make another detour.

That afternoon was intensely hot—a humid draining heat. For all that I notched up 19 miles and still arrived at Buttington View by tea time. This was another farm site I had stayed at before and I was astonished to find that Doreen and Trevor Jones remembered me. Trevor produced a beautifully laid tray of tea, fresh scones and jam which I ate on a garden bench in the company of a black cat and the dog Butch. Buttington View has a delightfully cottagey garden, crammed with flowers and vegetables and several separate little lawns—each perfect for a single tent. There were no other campers and as the garden bench looked like being a useful camping accessory, I put my tent beside it.

Throughout my End to End walk I was continually amazed at the number of small co-incidences. The 'What a small world syndrome'. Meeting someone who knew an acquaintance, or, as in the Pennines, discovering that a farmer's wife had lived in the same small Worcestershire town as me back in the 'sixties'. That night, when Doreen offered to dry my towel and socks over the Rayburn, I found out that her daughter lived in the same village as a cousin of mine, and not only that but had the same christian name and their husbands worked at the same place.

Four men, booked in for the evening, were late arriving, causing consternation in the kitchen. How to keep the evening meal hot without spoiling it? They turned up eventually having done over 20 miles from Newcastle (a village near the Dyke not *the* Newcastle), and finding it hard going. They were two fathers and sons from near Malvern who were tackling their first long distance walk. By 9 it was raining heavily. Trevor bought a mug of coffee out to my tent. Would that all campsite operators were such lovely people and so genuinely interested in their guests and their welfare. Nothing was too much trouble. Before leaving, Doreen made me promise to send her a postcard from John O'Groats.

Next morning after a night of rain, the tent was soaked. Even with no rain, a tent is frequently wet with dew or condensation. I carried two camper's towels purely for the purpose of drying it off on wet mornings. As my tent is so small, it easily fits inside the rucksack and needs to be dry or everything else gets wet. A wipe over with the absorbent towels is usually sufficient if the sun hasn't dried it before I am ready to leave. On days when there is no option but to pack it wet, I pack the inner and groundsheet, generally relatively dry, in a polythene bag in the rucksack, and strap the wet flysheet top of my pack.

A backpacker's best friend is a polythene carrier bag. I usually had one good strong one tucked away ready for putting the tent in, and several others for damp washing, my towel, dirty clothes, my spare shoes if they were wet or dirty, carrying the daily rubbish until a bin was found, and as a useful 'sitter' if the ground was wet. Spare and unpackable food also ends up tied on the rucksack in a bag. I don't like being cluttered up with bags but at times it's the only way. Half a dozen bread rolls, for example, provided lunches for two days. In the rucksack they rapidly became pancakes but hung outside, they remained in a usable state.

### Jungle tactics on the towpath

From Buttington there is a respite from the hills. Offa, to save on manpower and un-necessary digging, wisely used the River Severn as his frontier and the path follows either the bank of the river or the towpath of the Montgomery Canal. Bill and Pete and their sons, (both young men, not boys) became my companions on and off for the rest of that day. After a fast walk along the canal I reached my evening destination, Four Crosses, by lunchtime. I had to decide whether to stay or go on. I knew the site was good, for it was another I had stayed at before. There was a bathroom with thick warm towels provided, meals available if required and enormous packed lunches at a very reasonable price. It was tempting, but lunchtime was far too early to give up on a day's walk. Bill and Pete were going another seven miles and suggested I did the same. I decided to go on. The die was cast and later I would sorely regret it.

The afternoon became hotter and hotter and I hoped that my site that night would have a shower because I certainly needed one. The official path should leave the canal and follow the banks of the Severn for about eight miles but other walkers had already warned us that there was a diversion in operation. The riverside path was closed for the foreseeable future while major embankment works were carried out. The diverted path continued along the canal, which sounded like an easier, more straightforward route. Unfortunately the Inland Waterways Board had failed to clear the towpath along this section which is not walked frequently enough to keep it clear. It was so overgrown, in places you needed a machete to hack your way through. Vegetation of every description was quite literally head height and many walkers had decided that the main road running parallel to the canal was a better alternative to the towpath. Those who stuck to the diversion complained bitterly about the state of the path. Most wore shorts and the evidence of their bramble-scratched arms and nettle-stung legs upheld their complaints. The only consolation was that the overnight rain had dried; pushing a way through wet foliage would have been worse. Providentially I had trousers on, which protected me from the worst effects, but my sleeping mat, strapped to the bottom of the rucksack was never the same again, shredded along its outer edges as I used the rucksack as a shield to push my way through the jungle.

The Montgomery Canal is full of wildlife. Coots, mallard and moorhen abound. Several families of swans with half-grown, fluffy, grey cygnets were either resting on the banks or sozzling heads down in the clear water. Large, unidentified fish, broke the surface from time to time and a kingfisher swept past in a flash of brilliant hues. Despite its over-growth of noxious plants there were also plenty of wild flowers and masses of yellow musk. A man cutting the bit of the towpath adjoining his back garden, stopped to chat. As it was the Inland Waterway's responsibility, I thought it was very noble of him. The waterway's workman who should have been doing the job with a strimmer was sat in his boat further along drinking tea. Bill and Pete, who were at that time some way behind me, told me that when they passed, he was asleep. No wonder the path was in such a state!

Everyone was glad to leave the canal, even if it did involve a sharp climb up to the limestone quarries of Llanymynech. These have been worked since Roman times and were carpeted in a profusion of flowers. On a golfcourse I stopped for a rest, eking out my last dregs of water. Earlier I had bought a milk shake but when I came to drink it, found it had 'gone off' and was lumpy. I had to throw it away. The water situation was so desperate I was on the look out for someone I could beg from. In response to my request, an old lady pottering round her front garden gave me a glass of cider. That was after she had first offered me gin and beer "or would you like something stronger?" Her back was so bent she could barely walk but she was a chirpy soul and delighted to have a visitor. She informed me she was 82 and had squirrel trouble. "They keep eating the nuts." Not wishing to upset her by suggesting that in July bluetits did not really need feeding, we discussed squirrel-proof methods of hanging up nuts while she filled my water bottle.

When I had decided to go on a further seven miles, I had of course checked to see that there was a campsite, but on arriving there that evening, I found it had ceased to exist. The owner had died and the farm was occupied by temporary residents who were quite adamant they did not take campers. I thought they might make an exception for an unaccompanied woman for one night. But with a firm "No" they shut the door. Enquiries at an 'Eight 'til Late' shop, the pub and several houses proved negative. No one offered their garden or field though two people suggested a pub two miles away in the opposite direction. I phoned home for moral support, but there was no-one in. A guest house had no vacancies. A farm which was at least in the right direction had been suggested by several people, so giving up on this unfriendly place I made my way there. The farmer was out but a man washing a lorry in the yard said he guessed it would be OK and if I hung around for a while the farmer would be back, but only briefly. I would have to look out for him and catch him. If I missed him, the lorry driver thought it wouldn't matter if I used a rough bit of paddock behind the sheep dip. He showed me where the water supply to the sheep dip was cunningly disguised as part of the hedge. I was now so desperate I sat by the farm drive looking out for the farmer. He eventually arrived in a cloud of dust, a young man in his twenties, said "Yes" and tore off again. As the lorry driver had predicted, I could use the area behind the sheep dip. The only access was through the foot dip stinking of formaldehyde. All very basic, but after tomato-soup-flavoured-potato-smash, apple pie and custard and two cups of tea, I felt much better. So much for dreams of a good site and a hot shower. I wished I had stayed at Four Crosses after all.

### Farewell to Offa

Trefonen to Chirk was to be my last day on the Dyke. From Chirk I was turning east and making for the Pennines and the start of the Pennine Way. I had spent much time deliberating on which was the best way to link these two major long distance paths. Should I follow the canal all the way from Chirk to Whitchurch, or turn off much earlier for Church Stretton? Would it be better to go further north and use the Cestrian Link, a route designed specifically for this purpose. There was such a wide ranging choice of footpaths, that it really boiled down to personal preference and economic milage. Taking everything into consideration I had decided on a direct line north to Chirk and a direct line east using the Maelor Way and South Cheshire Way to Mow Cop. From there sections of other trails could be used to link up to to Edale.

My wild (and free) site could not have been better placed for the path. The stile and signpost sporting the white acorn of a national trail were right beside the sheep dip, but it took me over half an hour to get any further than the field I was in. Well worn paths and several stiles all marked with yellow arrows, led off in various directions. I followed all of these in turn, each time returning to base convinced they were wrong. I couldn't understand where I was going wrong until it occurred to me that I *should* be following white acorns and not yellow arrows. The correct stile, hitherto unseen, was hiding in the top corner of a field and I concluded it was just too early in the morning for such a taxing exercise on my brain.

The stiles on Offa's Dyke are notorious. There are reputedly around 700 of them whose construction varies according to which county you happen to be in and who is responsible for them. Some are well designed and have an extended post on one side which aids a walker with a heavy pack, but many are not. It's no joke heaving all that extra weight over a high stile when you are hot and weary and your legs are already objecting to too many hills. Feeble efforts consisting of a rickety plank nailed unsecurely on two uneven posts, usually with nettles and barbed wire, are downright hazardous—and those with a narrow two-step iron ladder at the top, in addition to the wooden steps at the bottom, are almost impossible. Some days I just became heartily sick of stiles. They disrupt your walking rhythm, are hard work and in general—a nuisance. Give me a gate any time.

The high land to the west of Oswestry is, like Hergest Ridge, home to a redundant racecourse. A broad circuit of short turf indicates its former use and there are the ruinous remains of the grandstand. There are benches for the weary and a toposcope for the long sighted. If the toposcope is to be believed Cader Idris and Plynlimmon are both visible 35 miles away. Visible when the toposcope was erected perhaps, but now it is impossible to see anything for the surrounding trees. A sculpture beside the grandstand looked as if it had just stepped out of the pages of Dr. Dolittle—a push-me pull-you creature with a horse's head at each end! Bill and his patrol caught up and we shared sweets and biscuits. They knew by now that I was an End to Ender and that I was leaving the path at Chirk so we walked the last few miles together. At least, I walked with Bill, the eldest. The two boys with the fitness and enthusiasm of youth were a long way ahead, with Pete trying to prove he was just as fit, valiantly attempting to keep up with them. We stopped for a second morning break on the top of a hill, while Pete disappeared into the bushes to attend to a grey fly bite on an embarrassing part of his anatomy. And, we took group photographs. In case, they said, I became famous, then they could say they had walked with me.

Shortly after, at a junction of lanes, we wished each other luck with our journeys and, like ships that pass in the night, went our separate ways. We knew little about each other except Christian names and would never meet again, but that is the way of long distance walking. You enjoy each others' company and cherish the memories. It was less than a week since I had left home—yet it seemed longer. The weather was glorious. The trip was for pleasure. When I reached Chirk, I was giving myself a day off before heading for the Pennines.

# 5

# Cows, Canals and Cornfields
## Through Cheshire to Mow Cop

Establishing the link between Wales and the Pennines had given me more headaches than any other section of the walk. The big stumbling block was campsites. North of Stoke on Trent the Peak District had plenty of choice, but between Chirk and Mow Cop, where the South Cheshire Way ended, there was nothing. The flat countryside, criss-crossed with canals, though pleasantly rural is not an area of outstanding beauty. Not, in fact outstanding for anything. It's an area you drive through to get somewhere else. Is isn't high on the list of holiday venues, doesn't rate as a nice weekend break for caravaners and is hardly walking country. In short, if you had a campsite, no-one would use it and the few there are were nowhere near my route.

I had several options. I could abandon camping for a week, although there was every indication that guest and farmhouse accommodation was about as available as a campsite, or I could rely on the goodwill of farmers allowing me to use their fields. This would be fine for the odd night but would mean doing without decent facilities for several days. Neither was really satisfactory. My best bet was to persuade someone to give me car back-up.

But who? I racked my brains for weeks trying to think whom I could cajole, bribe or blackmail into doing this. It had to be someone I liked and could get on with and, given that I could initially give only an approximate date, had to be someone free of commitments and available at a moment's notice. The only person I could think of was an elderly uncle, a widower in his seventies who lives with a daughter in the West Midlands. He's an easy-going chap with a great sense of humour who, apart from a dog and a greenhouse, was pretty much a free agent. I was not sure he would do it and spent two months plucking up the courage to ask him, afraid he wouldn't want to but would feel obliged to say yes. Then I would have felt awful. It was almost time to leave for Land's End before I phoned him and made my proposition. He said he'd think about it and get back to me. Three days later he rang back. He was worried about what it entailed but he would do it on condition he didn't have to sleep in a tent. I assured him there was hardly room for me in the tent let alone sharing it with a bulky uncle and that all he had to do was "be there." A safety net at the end of each day with the all important means of transport to some far flung bed.

Over the last week I had kept him informed of my progress and we had arranged to meet at a pub in a village near Chirk, which I hoped might be able to provide accommodation. It couldn't, but the landlord offered the use of a static caravan. It was being used to store jumble for the village school but his wife would "Tidy it up a bit". The price seemed initially high but weighed against the cost and trouble of finding anything else I calculated it would be cheaper in the long run, and our accommodation problem would be resolved for the next couple of days.

It was terrifically hot and my uncle was not expected for another two hours. I lay in the shade drinking tea until he arrived, when he happily fell in with the caravan arrangement. With two separate bedrooms and a bathroom it was ideal. The boxes of jumble were stacked neatly at one end of the spacious lounge and sheets and duvets were produced for the beds. There was even a glass-covered extension with tomato plants in grow-bags—home from home for uncle who was used to daily potterings in his greenhouse.

After settling in we went to see what Chirk had to offer, which was not much. Mention Chirk and people think of the castle not the town. The few shops were closed and the air was filled with the sickly sweet smell of chocolate emanating from the sprawling Cadbury's factory a stone's throw from the main street. Chirk Bank on the old main highway between London and Holyhead is right beside the Llangollen Canal and was much more interesting. Canal orientated activities offered plenty for the idle onlooker to watch and there was a busy little canal-side shop. There I was able to buy the *Maelor Way Guide* without which I would not have had much idea of the route.

I wanted my uncle to have a holiday and enjoy himself as well as 'doing his bit' for me and told him I proposed having a day off. Where would he like to go? We would both enjoy Chirk Castle or there was the International Eisteddfod currently taking place just along the road at Llangollen. However, the decision was made for us when we found out that it was the final day of the Eisteddfod and all the concerts were booked. So the castle it was to be. We would spend as long as we needed there and then I would walk as far as possible in whatever time was left to shorten the following long day to Whitchurch.

### Tackling the Maelor Way

The nicest thing about having a day off is not having to get up so early. Enjoying a 'lie in' next morning in a real bed was blissful. There was no need to rush. We dallied over breakfast and devised a means of hanging up my damp sleeping bag, washed the previous evening, so that it would dry in the sun trapped heat of the caravan while we were out.

By 11 o'clock cars were already queuing at the castle's magnificent wrought iron gates designed in 1719 by brothers Robert and John Davies who lived near Wrexham. Incorporated at the top of the gate are the Myddleton Arms which includes a gruesome red-painted 'bloody hand'. Legend has it that this arises from a family dispute over an inheritance which was settled by a race. The winner had his hand cut off by a supporter of the loser.

After a long drive from the gates to the carpark we found there was still some distance to walk to the castle and, as my uncle is arthritic, took advantage of the park and ride facility. We found ourselves being transported in a courtesy ambulance. When we telephoned a progress report to my cousin that evening, we were able to inform her that her father had spent his first day being driven off in an ambulance!

For two hours, in gorgeous sunshine, we strolled round the lovely gardens. They were at their best and no words here could possibly describe and pay justice to their impeccable restoration and maintenance, though my lasting impression will be of the glorious displays of roses and the impeccably manicured topiary. To top all of that, there was the opulence and splendour of the 700 year old castle. Walking boots and high heeled shoes are prohibited on the highly polished floors and over-shoes are supplied if considered necessary. My boots were inspected for mud and stones and given a clean bill of health before I was declared fit to enter.

ONE WOMAN'S WALK

The tour followed the usual procedure of stately homes, visitors being gently shepherded from room to room with well primed guides ready to give a brief history lesson and answer questions. It was all too much to take in. The only fact that stuck was that the King's Bedroom—and every castle seems to have one of these—contains a bed which was never slept in by the visiting Charles I in 1645. It didn't arrive at the castle until over a hundred years later.

After boosting my calorie intake with carrot cake from the delightful tea rooms in the castle kitchen, it was time to start walking again. The Maelor Way, which would take me as far as Whitchurch, starts officially at Bronygarth, near where I turned off the Offa's Dyke Path, but could be conveniently joined at Chirk Bank. From there it makes use of the Llangollen Canal towpath for a short distance, then follows field paths to the village of Overton.

To give it full credit, the Maelor Way is well signposted and the guide book is excellent. There is only one major snag. The path is not well walked and was so overgrown it was impassable. At one point, frustrated by brambles, nettles and fields of growing crops, I abandoned the route, fought my way out on to a lane and then had to spend some time working out where I was. The potentially interesting and pretty riverside path along the Dee was also hampered by overgrown undergrowth and under maintained paths. A visiting American pushing her way through a cornfield in the opposite direction observed that she had been there in previous years when the field had been down to pasture and there was no problem. Trust me to choose the wrong year.

Overton has a unique claim to fame. The churchyard yews are one of the seven wonders of Wales and are immortalised in a little verse that goes as follows:-

> Pistyll Rhaedr and Wrexham Steeple,
> Snowdon Mountain without its people
> Overton Yew Trees, St. Winifrede's Wells,
> Llangollen Bridge and Gresford Bells.

I went to investigate and bumped into one of the churchwardens who filled me in on the details. 21 trees form a complete circle round the church, the youngest tree being 21 years old, a replacement for one that died. The others have been carbon dated and are mainly between eight and nine hundred years old. The oldest, chained together in the centre and supported by wooden props, has a hollow core and is estimated to be nearer 2,000 years old, predating the church and suggesting that the ancient yews probably encircled a much earlier sacred site.

Next day saw us back at Overton having said a fond farewell to our caravan. Determined to persevere with the Maelor Way I tried again to stick to the path but eventually gave up. The actual practicality of walking it was not only hard work, but I was getting scratched and stung in the process. The weather was much too hot for such exertions. I was being considerably slowed down over a distance which needed the maximum time available.

I didn't miss anything by walking on lanes instead of fields as most of the interesting places were in the villages and I perambulated from one to another meeting my uncle at each church. These make excellent meeting places as they are a focal point in any village, easy to find and provided something for my uncle to do while he waited for me—and a diversion for me when I arrived. During my entire walk I must have visited 40 churches. For the modern day walker they are as much a sanctuary as for the traveller of the past, providing rest for weary legs, shelter from rain, and shade from the sweltering heat, as well as spiritual guidance. In many a church I have dumped my pack in the porch and sank down thankfully on a welcome pew for a short respite from whatever weather was being thrown at me. Before leaving I always made a few requests concerning my continued safety and well being and a little help with carrying my pack.

We lunched in the shade of trees on a small green at St. Chad's Church at Hanmer. Picturesquely sited beside a mere, this pretty village is peacefully free of traffic. The fine churchyard gates were originally used in the chancel gates and were manufactured by the same Davies brothers who produced the gates of Chirk Castle. The church itself is proud of its association with Owain Glyndwr who was married here in the fourteenth century to Margaret Hanmer, daughter of Sir David Hanmer. The present church was rebuilt in 1892 having suffered no less than two major fires, the first being around 1463 during the Wars of the Roses, the second in 1889. Villagers forming a chain of buckets from a nearby pond bravely fought the flames of the second fire but by the time the fire engines arrived there was little they could do except save the vicarage. Photographs in the church show the full extent of the devastation and the remains of one of the six bells, shattered when they fell from the tower, are displayed.

Hanmer is a border village, geographically in Wales, in the county of Clwyd. But by the end of the day I would be back in England, in

Shropshire. It was now mid-July and the weather was at its hottest yet. This heatwave was forecast to last and, as I was to discover, would continue for the rest of the month. As I was travelling directly east, I was walking into the sun most of the time and when I wasn't, it was beating down on the back of my leg, my right arm and the back of my neck. Shorts, a light cotton blouse and a sun hat were my normal daily attire. Fortunately, working outdoors all the time, my skin is always well tanned and I never burn but I did start to get sunburnt lips and at that time hadn't any sun-block cream. In such flat and open country there was little chance of getting out of the sun and there is nothing worse than road walking in such weather. The heat of the tarmac is thrown back at you and the grey-white of the road surface is not as easy on the eyes as grass or bare earth.

Lunchbreaks sitting in the shade of trees or exploring the cool interior of a church can become a prolonged affair. There was a reluctance to leave Hanmer and a feeling of apathy about setting off again for another dose of uninspiring lanes and unrelenting sun. By the time I reached Grindley Brook on the outskirts of Whitchurch I was glad the day was over.

It had been a long 24 miles. The only campsite was adjacent to two major roads with heavy traffic on both. It was a large and deserted field beside a pub carpark and my uncle was not very happy about me staying there, but the landlord assured me it was one of the safest places to be. It was right on the county boundary and at night the traffic police of both Cheshire and Shropshire forces met in the carpark—a well known local fact—so there is never likely to be any trouble. Uncle had procured Bed and Breakfast not far away and we decided to have our evening meal at the inn. However, we had chosen the wrong day. The landlord was new, had only taken over that week and had not yet bought in fresh catering supplies. We ordered the last two cottage pies in stock and counted ourselves lucky. The canal basin was just across the road and all evening a steady stream of Dutch, Danish and English families came in off the boats for meals, all having the last oddments of whatever the landlord had inherited in the freezer.

### Walking the South Cheshire Way

Several long distance paths converge near Whitchurch but the only other walker I encountered was a man who had just completed the Shropshire Way. His greatest aid to walking was a small monocular which he claimed was a great help for spying ahead for stiles and waymarks. This is something I might consider for the future. It could certainly have saved me a lot of time in some places, especially in areas of large fields, where sometimes you are at a complete loss as to where you are supposed to go if solely reliant on 1 inch maps.

My final destination for the end of the week was Mow Cop, where Helen was to join me for the ensuing ten days. Until then I would be following two other long distance paths starting at Grindley Brook. For part of the time I would be using the canal sections of the Sandstone Trail and for the rest, the 31 mile South Cheshire Way, an entirely lowland walk which ended at Mow Cop. As the South Cheshire Way went across country from Grindley Brook I used the towpath of the Shropshire Union Canal. In hot weather this was far preferable to plodding across fields and climbing stiles and it involved no map reading. It meant I arrived at exactly the same place, by a much easier route. The canal was busy and I wasn't short of company. There were boats passing by every few minutes, their occupants calling out "Good morning" or "What a lovely day." But these heavily used canals become victims of their own success. Unlike the clean waters of the unused Montgomery Canal, the water here was dirty and lifeless. Boats and wildlife don't mix.

Walking on the towpath had the advantage that being beside the water made it seem cooler, even if it wasn't, and I enjoyed the fast walk to a brief mid-morning rendezvous with my uncle at Marbury and a second more prolonged lunchbreak at Wrenbury. My lasting impression of the South Cheshire Way was of canals, cornfields and cows. I seemed to be walking all the time beside a mix and match combination of these. Nowhere have I seen so many black and white cows as Cheshire. If I wasn't pushing my way through a field of corn, I was being followed by curious dairy cows or picking my way through cow-pat splattered pasture. Many of the fields had flooded marl pits, dug out originally to obtain the naturally occurring marl which was spread on the fields to increase fertility. In these, cattle were standing belly deep in their efforts to keep cool.

I had no complaints about the South Cheshire Way and can only commend the Mid-Cheshire Footpath Society on the efficiency of the waymarking. The guide book had easy to follow maps but no less than 44 abbreviations in the text and these not standard map reading abbreviations. Who would ever guess that a POB was a Post Box or that BS, normally indicating Boundary Stone, was in fact a Bus Stop. I found this confusing and irritating and would have liked more information on points of interest.

My uncle met me wherever the field sections came to a suitable road and my time calculations were generally accurate. He rarely waited long before I appeared. After a brief rest, a quick cool drink and a conference on the next meeting point, I would be off again. Nor was it a solitary walk. I met no other walkers, but the locals were friendly and happy to spend a few minutes of their time in conversation. A housewife picking runner beans in her garden was staggered to hear how far I had come — and alone. She had never heard of the South Cheshire Way and was amazed to learn that a long distance path went right past her door. But a smartly dressed young woman with clip board, mobile phone and voice recorder looking strangely out of place in the middle of a field, obviously knew all about such things. She turned out to be the county footpaths officer, checking up on a reported path obstruction. It was nice to know someone does actually take note of complaints and go and look.

### *Farmers — friendly and not so friendly*

Sadly for the people of Cheshire their good character was marred by a farmer who went down in my book as the nastiest between Land's End and John O'Groats. This fellow surely had a problem. He must have got out of bed the wrong side or had a row with his wife to cause such a bad-tempered over-reaction to a harmless woman walking through his farm-yard. I was not lost or trespassing and I was most definitely on the foot-path. The last stile into the farmyard had the SCW of the Way clearly marked on it. The only reason I spoke to him was because he was there, standing in the middle of the yard and there were several gates making it slightly unclear as to which was the correct way out. For something to say and for confirmation that I was where I thought I was, I asked him the name of the farm. This was met with a vicious "You're trespassing." I apologised, said I didn't think I was as I had just come over a stile off the South Cheshire Way. His reply, "Never heard of it. You are on private property and you are trespassing." I decided it was better to comply and pacify him. "OK. I'm sorry. I must have made a mistake. So could you tell me the name of your farm." Another torrent of abuse followed. I was tres-passing. He was a hard-working farmer. He was just going home for his tea and how dare I stand there interrogating him on the name of his farm. It was none of my business. He ended by saying "If you're lost. That's your fault. You've got a map. Find your own way." This left me speechless and wondering if he wasn't slightly unhinged. Without another word, I turned my back on him and walked away, taking the first gate I saw, which turned out to be the right one. Down the track was the road, a sign with the name of the farm and another for the SCW. I was right all the time.

Finding accommodation for the night was my uncle's job. So far we had been lucky, especially in having the caravan for the first two nights. I had known there were few campsites but even Bed and Breakfast accommodation was scarce. For our fourth night, uncle had found a farmhouse where he was warmly welcomed and where the farmer and his wife were kindness itself. They were fully booked and couldn't take me as well but gave me a mug of tea, told me I could camp in the garden, share my uncle's *en suite* bathroom and invited me to have breakfast in the house next morning. In other words, I could have farmhouse Bed and Breakfast, without the bed. We were invited to go and see the calves by the farmer, a stocky, jovial, non-stop talker, who told the most outrageous shaggy dog stories I have ever heard, but whose voice softened as he spoke lovingly to the cattle who were obviously his pride and joy. He was a bit of a comedian as well and breakfast next morning was a jolly affair as he kept everyone amused with his tall stories. The other guests were a couple from Carlisle and some French speaking Canadian honeymooners. I couldn't imagine anyone honeymooning in Cheshire, let alone coming all the way from Canada!

### At the mercy of sun and crops

Under a cloudless sky, the heat was again terrific and with 16 miles to go to Mow Cop I could well have done without the acres of maize and rape that slowed down my progress over endless fields. Shorts weren't the ideal clothes to wear, but it was too hot for anything more and by the end of the day my legs were scratched and sore from the rough stems of the rape. Maize is not too much of a problem as the rows are widely spaced but in July rape is tall, has gone to seed and has collapsed in smelly, abrasive, tangled heaps. The footpaths were no doubt there, but were almost impenetrable. Brute force was needed to push through the fallen plants. When Michael arrived later that evening he commented on the state of my legs. There was a look of consternation on his face when I unthinkingly replied "Oh! That was rape!"

I had met up with uncle several times during the day. We had eaten lunch at a pleasant lockside café on the Trent and Mersey Canal, shunning the parasol-shaded tables outside for the cooler indoor ones. I had no way of knowing what the temperature was, but this must have been one of the hottest days of all. In a cloudless sky the sun beat down mercilessly.

Everyone wore sunglasses and hats and lashings of sun cream. The inland waterway sailors were stripped off to their trendy beach wear and were sunbathing between the bikes and geraniums adorning the cabin roofs. Each time I stopped I was reluctant to set off again in the sweltering heat and was thankful that through at least some of this hot weather I had not had to carry my rucksack.

Mow Cop Castle had been prominent on the eastern skyline for many miles and was drawing ever near. It was the first high ground for 50 miles. There is nothing of any height between the Welsh Mountains at Chirk and this dramatic 1100ft. crag, the Old Man of Mow which heralds the edge of the Pennines. At the end of the day I joined my uncle at Little Moreton Hall, one of Cheshire's famous black and white houses, also known as 'magpie' houses. This is one of the best examples. I was too late to pay a visit but was able to look round the outside and admire the beautiful and intricate timberwork around the doors and windows. The fish in the moat were pretty good too, scores of foot long goldfish lurking just below the surface and waiting expectantly, along with the ducks, to be fed.

I have to confess to falling victim to the temptation of the car for the last two miles. I was exhausted with the heat. It was early evening. We had to find a meal and somewhere to stay the night and all before 8 o'clock when we were meeting Michael and Helen. I couldn't face another two miles, all up hill, at this time of day. So, we drove to Mow Cop.

*A happy ending*

Enquiries from several locals produced no prospect of a campsite. The maps showed none. The Camping Club Handbook listed none. We needed accommodation for my uncle too, but the campsite was the first priority before it got too late. Someone suggested a farm that occasionally took scouts and guides but when we found it we weren't very hopeful. It was beautifully located at the end of a long drive, set amidst deciduous wood-land with stunning views across the Cheshire Plain to Wales. If there were farm buildings they were nowhere to be seen. The house was surrounded by lawns and a swimming pool.

Having driven right up to the house, we could hardly drive off again without looking highly suspicious. So, without hope, we knocked the door, explained our cause and apologised for the intrusion. As expected, the lady of the house told us she didn't think her husband would allow campers and anyway, he was out. "Come in and have a cup of tea," she invited "while I have a think and look in yellow pages." A voluble, bubbly extrovert, she introduced herself as Isobel and told us to make ourselves at home in the lavishly furnished living room while she disappeared to make tea. Fearful of getting a mark on anything, I perched cautiously on the edge of a pale coloured, deep cushioned settee. Seated beside me, uncle nudged persistently, whispering "Tell her where you are going." So far, I hadn't been telling people where I was going, unless it had been absolutely necessary. To me it seemed like showing off and as yet, it seemed a little premature to say "Oh, by the way, I'm just walking to John O'Groats." But when the tea came I waited for a convenient opportunity in the conversation to mention it casually. Isobel's reaction was instantaneous. "Oh! You can stay here." When I pointed out that her husband wasn't around to confirm that it was alright, she said "That's OK. He won't mind." It began to seem as if the mere mention of Land's End to John O'Groats was a passport to anything.

Her husband fortuitously arrived at that moment and leaving him talking to my uncle, Isobel took me down through the woods to show me where I could camp. At this point I felt I should mention that it wasn't just me, but two extra people, a Land Rover and three dogs all expected in about an hour, and that we also had to find Bed and Breakfast for uncle. "That's no problem," she said, "he can stay with us—and if any of you want to use use the swimming pool or shower room, help yourselves." Then came the explanation for this apparent change of heart. She was a born-again Christian and only too happy to help in any way she could. "I went to a prayer meeting to find out the name of my guardian angel" she confided. Everybody else was coming up with names like John, Luke or Gabriel. But mine was Merry Weather!"

After another quick cuppa we left to go and find the church, our appointed meeting place with Michael. The town straddles the end of the ridge. Everywhere you go is either up or down a steep hill. Not having a clue where we were going we drove round in circles trying to find the church, eventually finding it and at 8 o'clock were parked outside waiting. No-one arrived. We drove away again to find a callbox and I phoned Michael on his mobile to see where he was. "Waiting outside the church," he said, "at Mow Cop." It didn't take much working out to conclude that there was more than one church. So we agreed that it would be easier to go to the castle carpark on the top of the hill.

It was an absolutely glorious evening, still very warm, but not the unbearable heat we had experienced all day. The castle is not a genuine castle at all, but an eighteenth century folly. It seemed to be the venue for every teenager in the area and stank of urine, but the view in all directions was stupendous. A local man pointed out what we could see: Arnold Bennett country, Stoke on Trent and the 'Five Towns' of the Potteries to the south, the Pennines and Peak District to the north and east, the Welsh Mountains to the south-west, Liverpool and Merseyside barely discernible in the north-west. The giant dish of the Jodrell Bank radio telescope reflected the evening sun, like a shining star in the smoke-polluted haze of the Cheshire Plain.

We were all feeling the pangs of hunger and drove in convoy to find some fast food, before returning to the farm where we were treated to a magnificent sunset. As the fiery ball of the sun dropped below the horizon and darkness fell, the plain below became transformed by the myriad lights of industrial civilisation.

Uncle was left to the generous administrations of Isobel and later told me that this night had really been "The icing on the cake." They had made him so welcome; he had sat watching the sunset until it faded and afterwards talked late into the night. Meanwhile, we had three tents to erect in the near dark and three dogs, bored from several hours couped up in the Land Rover, to exercise. While they chased round exploring new territory and pursuing rabbits, we exchanged news over hot drinks and revelled in our luck at ending up at such a perfectly delightful spot. Little matters like no loos, and water being obtained from the tap feeding the cattle trough, were insignificant. We were just so grateful to have found such a big hearted lady as Isobel, willing to share her home and help out total strangers.

After four days of uninspiring and often tiring and difficult walking it was great to have finished off the stage on a high note. The unfortunate incident with Mr. Obnoxious Farmer had marred the week and dented my trust in strangers but now I was ready to face the Peaks and the Pennines with a restored faith in human nature, confident that in the face of adversity, there would be another Isobel around to give a helping hand.

# 6
# Hot Days in the Peaks
## Linking up with the Pennine Way

The long distance walker is a hungry animal. On a journey like mine it's a simple life; wake up, walk; go to bed. A dog's life. Nothing to worry about except where your next meal is coming from. Basic animal instincts. Food and its availability becomes the most important thing in your life.

My daily average was 15 miles. To do this continually with a heavy pack requires a high energy intake. You need plenty of food and it needs to be the right type. Any old food isn't good enough. The severity of the terrain, the weight of the pack and the speed of walking can double, even treble the normal daily requirement of calories. On a long walk I switch to a high carbohydrate diet.

To avoid running out of food needs plenty of forethought. After all, you don't set out on a long journey down a motorway without making sure you have enough fuel in your car. I check out food sources beforehand. To cover areas where there aren't any I carry four days emergency rations as well as two weeks basic essentials. Of necessity everything has to be light-weight and suitable for camp cooking. For three months my staple diet was muesli for breakfast, noodles and instant custard for supper.

Whenever I bought food during the day I spent ages reading the labels. I knew the calorie content of many items off by heart—but so much food now is low calorie and sugar free—and I needed food bursting with calories. I considered the weight to see if I could afford to carry it and only bought tins if I was going to use them straight away. Leaving a shop I'd head for a litter bin and de-package all my purchases, discarding everything except bubble packs which protect delicate things like croissants. It's far easier to find space for the contents than the bulky packaging. I had two small, practically weightless plastic bottles filled with instant coffee and instant white tea which lasted for weeks. When refills were required I discarded the heavy jars. Similarly I had a re-usable plastic tube for jam and several empty film canisters for small quantities of dried milk, washing powder and sugar. I used artificial sweetener tablets for drinks and needed only enough sugar for cereals—acquiring extra sachets from cafés to keep my canister topped up. Washing powder if not begged or borrowed could often be purchased in a plastic cup for ten or twenty pence from a campsite laundry—just enough for a washing machine and to fill up my pot. After I ended up washing my smalls in dried milk and putting soap powder on my breakfast a few times, I remembered to taste the contents before using them.

A large plastic margarine container served as my larder. This kept everything in one place and avoided burst packets and leaks. I once punctured the seal on a carton of Pot Noodles and had curry flavoured clothes for a week. One luxury I always carry now is a roll of parcel tape. It's indispensable. Packets can be resealed. Fragile items like yoghurt pots can be taped before they are stowed away and anything, from a mapcase to a camera, can be repaired.

Despite what camping magazines recommend I don't use expensive dehydrated meals. I've tried them and don't like them. They all taste the same whatever it says on the packet, and weigh a ton. Cheap, quickly cooked noodles are just as good and weigh very little. As one packet would provide two meals, several gave me emergency meals for days. To save gas I perfected the art of cooking four-minute noodles in two minutes and made them more interesting by adding a shake of soup powder or an oxo cube. And their big advantage—they are available at any village store. Similarly, instant custard—the sort made with water—is cheap, universally available and can be added to fresh or tinned fruit, any cake you fancy, biscuits or even chocolate bars. A blissful, high calorie fix of Mars Bar and custard is delicious.

The only disadvantage of relying on village stores is that choice can be limited. To overcome this I bought some of my provisions before I left and each time Michael came, he brought up a stock of these supplies and I'd take on all the things normally only available at specialist shops and large supermarkets—individual packs of muesli, Lucozade tablets, pic 'n' mix cheeses, fruit and muesli bars, typically about a dozen of each, and half a dozen packets of peanuts. These were tucked away at the bottom of the rucksack to be used only when I couldn't buy a similar commodity.

### Dogged by heat and heavy packs

So it was with a rucksack full of new long term supplies and the extra maps needed for the next two weeks that Helen and I set off from Mow Cop on a journey into the unknown. There was no definitive path to the start of the Pennine Way. My route had been worked out from maps in the depths of winter, the only criteria being to find a way between Mow Cop and Edale and end up at a campsite each night.

I was sorry to see my uncle leave. After being cajoled into giving me support, I knew he had actually rather enjoyed himself. I suspected that he would have stayed even longer if asked. Helen, on the other hand, having been so keen a year before to complete the whole End to End now wished to be back at home with her friends and had gradually whittled down her walking to ten days.

I was looking forward to her company. I knew her capabilities and we get on pretty well as walking partners. At 16 she was an experienced camper, both with the Girl Guides and on Duke of Edinburgh Award expeditions. She had several long distance paths to her credit: Offa's Dyke at 13; Wainwright's Coast to Coast at 14 and in the exceptional heat of August 1995, the Two Moor's Way. On these she carried a full pack and camped all the way. She is a competent map reader, perfectly at home with a compass, organised in camp and level headed in an emergency. Better than me at everything in fact. When we are together, I let her take over. She leads, I follow — about 200 yards behind.

Our first day together had its problems. We were both having difficulties with our rucksacks. They felt extraordinarily heavy. Helen's because it was her first day, mine because I hadn't carried it for four days and it was crammed with all that extra food. For miles I experienced a sharp pain in my right shoulder which when eventually investigated I found to be the metal adjustment of my bra strap grinding into flesh. Why this had never happened before and never did after I can't understand.

The heat wave showed no sign of abating. So far it had been a fairly dry heat but now it had become humid which is much more debilitating. Helen hates hot weather and had been adamant that she wouldn't walk if it was too hot. I kept my fingers crossed and prayed for unseasonably cold weather.

The countryside was in complete contrast to that of the last few days. From the summit of Mow Cop we remained at a high level along the

Congleton Ridge following the Mow Cop Trail and the Staffordshire Way. It was far too hot to be walking anywhere, let alone on open hilltops. We struggled to the top of the Cloud, the highest hill in the area, and rested at the trig point. Inexplicably, a pile of dog biscuits lay on a flat-topped rock. The view, equal to that from Mow Cop, was hazy. The hills of the Peak District rose invitingly ahead, but to the west everything was enveloped in a thick yellow pall of pollution through which the white dish of Jodrell Bank, glinting in the sun, was still the most conspicuous landmark. Overhead the noise of planes making their approach to Manchester Airport broke the silence with annoying regularity—a sound that accompanied us for the next 100 miles.

We relished every spot of shade. Just to stand beside a scantily branched tree for a few moments was a relief. We wished we could drink more and I realised then how lucky I had been to have had car back-up over the past few days, with ample refreshment on hand all through the day and no need to economise on water. And this was not the only thing we had to economise on. We had almost nothing for lunch. As we had so much other stuff to carry I hadn't bothered to get anything extra for the day's meals, expecting to be able to buy something on the way. But there had been no opportunity.

Finding a picnic table in a most unlikely spot on a disused railway line, we ate a meagre meal of ryvita, cheese and cereal bars. Ryvita was my lightweight standby. It travelled surprisingly well. After several days it has a tendency to end up with rounded corners but generally remains basically intact.

It was fortunate that part of route lay over upland moorland. We were able to supplement our diet with juicy pick-your-own snacks from the abundant crop of bilberries—though our passage was reduced to a dawdle.

### Things get worse

Advance information had reliably indicated a shop at Rushton Spencer but we found it with white-washed windows and empty shelves. It had closed down. Disappointed but not downhearted at that point, we searched for the campsite. It was at a pub called the Crown—but where was it? We established that the village had two pubs, neither of which was the Crown. Two people we enquired of had never heard of it. A third located it a mile and a half away up a long, winding hill. On occasions like this feelings run high; anger and annoyance at the world in general which may rub off in short tempered exchanges with your companion. Frustration causes tempers to fray. Your day has gone wrong.Your plans have been messed up. Body and mind attuned to finishing at a certain time and place seem unable to cope with an unexpected change of programme. You are thoroughly deflated. Energy flags. Legs lose momentum.The thought of more miles is unbearable.

By the time we arrived we were exhausted, dripping with perspiration and dying of thirst. Our carefully conserved water rations had been calculated—to the last drip—to last as far as Rushton Spencer and not beyond. Dumping our rucksacks unceremoniously outside the door we staggered into the bar and collapsed in the cool comfort of the lounge with a line up of reviving drinks. Suddenly the world seemed a better place. We ordered meals. The landlord said he'd have them ready by the time we had put up the tents.

Behind the pub there were two caravans and a grotesque fibre-glass tree in a children's play area. Spoilt for choice in a large field, choosing a pitch was easy. Putting up my tent was not. I had no guy ropes. I knew exactly where they were and why. With three tents to take down that morning, three excited dogs running around and everybody talking and getting in each other's way, my normally well organised packing had gone haywire. On my own I took down the tent methodically, pulling out pegs, counting and bagging them, tying up guy ropes and putting them with the pegs. I distinctly remembered thinking that I was not checking pegs and that if I didn't pick up the guy ropes our youngest, naughtiest dog, would run off with them. I had never picked them up. In fact, as long as the pegs were pushed in firmly enough to hold it taut, the tent stood reasonably well. I prayed we would have no wind and made a mental note to buy string as soon as we reached a shop, to make-do until we reached Buxton and found a camping shop.

Our meal was excellent. Helen managed to put away an additional large helping of sticky treacle pudding. Filling up with reserve fuel. A wise precaution as the pub had nothing suitable for next day's lunch except crisps and confirmed what we already suspected, that there was no shop within walking distance. With our ryvita gone we faced the bleak prospect of walking all day on a diet of Lucozade tablets, crisps and water. The pub could not oblige with milk for our muesli either, though this was nothing unusual. Fruit juice is fine—or at a push, water. We bought orange juice. Later though, the landlord, feeling sorry for us, came down to the tent with a bottle of milk of his own which he insisted we accept without payment. The first of many Isobels!!

Finding the village store closed had been a blow. And it wasn't the first time this had happened. I was frequently finding village stores gone out of business. This one had been logistically crucial. We knew there would be none the following day and the tiny hamlet we were stopping at would be unlikely to have its own store. If we had known in advance that Rushton Spencer's shop had ceased to exist, we could easily have made provision in Mow Cop.

We spent some time pondering the problem and considered catching a bus next day to anywhere with a shop. I went over to one of the caravans to see if anyone had any suggestions and was immediately invited to fetch Helen and have a cup of tea. We stayed all the evening, relaxing in picnic chairs and being plied with slices of melon and dishes of fresh raspberries. This resourceful couple lived in their caravan all the week while restoring a canal barge on the nearby Macclesfield Canal and only popped home at weekends to check their house. They seemed to have found an idyllic way to enjoy their retirement. Their solution to our predicament was to drop us off at a shop next morning on their way to the canal. Our food crisis was over.

"You've pitched your tents on a badger run," they informed us as we said goodnight, "so don't be surprised if you hear grunts and snuffles in the night." We heard nothing. We were both far too tired to be disturbed by badgers. I've never had anything as large as a badger in my tent, but I have had mice—and once a pheasant. Amongst the paraphernalia left in the tent's porch overnight, suspicious rustlings, torn and nibbled packets, the clatter of metal pans, are all the trademarks of mice. The mysterious emptying of a carton of milk at one campsite I put down to a visitation from a cat.

## The Peaks

At 9 o'clock sharp we loaded our rucksacks into Jean and Bill's camper van, squeezing ourselves in alongside two yappy Yorkshire terriers who seemed a little put out at having to share their space. Transported to we knew not where, within a few minutes we were climbing out at a housing estate in the middle of nowhere. Bemused and puzzled we were told that there was no real shop, but that an enterprising housewife sold home-made cakes and sandwiches from her front room along with a few groceries, local garden produce, sweets and drinks. They pointed us in the direction of the right house and five pound's worth of purchases were soon being consumed on the spot or stowed away for future needs.

We were now in the Peak District National Park. Open hill-farming country where careful map reading was essential. It was boiling hot. Helen had bought a long, bright pink ice-lolly sealed in plastic, which she held to her forehead to keep cool. We found our way back onto our original course and rested in the cool sanctuary of Wincle Church, almost hidden by a green shroud of ivy. The strange looking font with an inappropriately small bowl perched on top of a tall narrow column had an inscription round it in which every letter 'S' was back to front. Beside it was a tap. We were both thirsty, and wondered whether we might be stealing 'Holy' water, but thought God would not mind anyway. We drank our fill and replenished our bottles before leaving through a door that bore over it the oddly worded inscription HERE DOE O LORD SURE PLANT THY WORD.

Our last three miles were along a busy main road where heavy traffic kept us jumping on and off the verges. These were uneven with treacherous drainage gullies lurking in long grass just waiting to twist an ankle. Round several hairpin bends there were no verges at all. We nearly burst our lungs jogging up hill round these, when we could catch breaks in the traffic.

Our site at Wildboarclough was of the farm economy variety, which means you get a warm welcome, a quiet site but only limited amenities—in this case a tap, toilet, sink and cold water. Not that we minded. It had again been insufferably hot and though we had walked less than ten miles we were both exhausted. It was a lovely evening. After rinsing a few clothes and making a washing line from our bootlaces—tied between the two tents—we flopped out nearly naked in the long, cool grass, relaxing and recuperating.

My tent was now fully functional again, thanks to the generosity of Jean and Bill who had donated a spare piece of guy rope from their caravan awning. After raiding the emergency rations for supper we recovered enough to stroll down across the fields to the village. Wildboarclough has a fascinating history and owes its existence entirely to its ample supply of soft water. It did not even exist before the nineteenth century. Then it was chosen as a suitable site for the erection of a calico printing factory which was powered by a 30ft. waterwheel. Workers' cottages, a school and chapel were built and a substantial residence for the owner, but there was no church. The present St. Saviours was erected in 1901 by the Earl of Derby in gratitude for the safe return of his five sons from the Boer War and was built using stone from the demolished factory buildings.

We were still in Cheshire but next day, high on the moors, we passed Three Shires Head, where the adjoining counties of Derbyshire and Staffordshire meet. We could tell we were in a National Park by the sheer number of walkers and mountain bikers around—all enjoying the tranquillity of upland wilderness. I could even forgive the two wheeled fraternity for nearly running us down when they approached soundlessly from behind without any warning. They seem to have an aversion to bells, but to make any noise in such glorious surroundings would have been sacrilege.

We stopped for coffee at the Cat and Fiddle—an isolated moorland inn which at 1,690ft. is Britain's second highest public house. Leaving Helen guarding rucksacks while I went in to get coffee I was startled to hear someone say, "Hello, I thought I recognised you." It was the farmer's wife from our campsite, busily polishing tables—obviously a lady with a passion for polishing. She had been brandishing tin and duster in her own sitting room when we arrived the day before. Sitting outside munching chocolate and peanuts we could hear her telling the other staff that we were going to John O'Groats. Furtive faces appeared at the windows curious to see what these crazy women looked like. Somehow she'd got the impression that Helen was going all the way too—but we didn't bother to put her right.

The Cat and Fiddle is situated on a fast road over the moors, a road that climbs steeply through a series of wide bends. On the outside wall of the pub was a gruesome map showing the locations and results of every motorcycle accident for the previous five years. The road is apparently notorious—over 50 accidents in that period—and all the accidents seemed to have occurred on the same bends.

Although we had walked 13 miles, we arrived at Buxton by early afternoon. This eighteenth century spa town was the first town I had encountered on the walk since Truro in Cornwall and at over 1,000ft. is one of Britain's highest towns. We ate the squashed remains of sandwiches and porkpies sitting beside a stream in a wood on the outskirts of the town, then went in search of the campsite.

### Making the most of Buxton

The site was huge and already packed. A canvas city which numbered amongst its occupants at least 30 motorcyclists and some 'travellers' complete with milk churns, dogs and a lorry load of tar. Helen put up her roomier tent and we left our packs inside, taking all our valuables with us. I was always wary of leaving all my stuff, but worked on the basis that as long as I had everything of value with me—that is cashcards, bank books and so on, and my camera, then anything else could be replaced.

Why are campsites always at the top of a hill? Buxton was half an hour's walk away down a long hill. We arrived in the town centre to find the place heaving with people—and we soon found out why. It was Saturday and the first day of the Buxton festival, a two-week long festival of Arts and Music. People were picnicking, eating ice-creams and sunbathing on every spare patch of grass. There were street musicians, people with painted faces and others wearing fantastic fancy dress; above the general atmosphere of bustle and excitement, the air reverberated with the hum of human voices.

Bemused by the sudden wealth of shops in the air-conditioned glamour of a modern shopping precinct we shopped as if we had never seen shops before. My list of essentials were all but forgotten. New and quite un-necessary 'tops' and T-shirts found their way into carrier bags along with so much food we could hardly carry it.

Shopping accomplished we went to see the sights. We looked at the Mineral Water Spa Baths and queued to taste water from the Living Well— a perpetually flowing spring gushing from the mouth of a lion in the town centre. We watched in amazement as local people arrived by car with boots crammed with plastic containers which they proceeded to fill. Some had as many as ten five-gallon containers, taking so long to fill them it was diffi- cult for the likes of us to get so much as a scouped handful. After a long wait we managed to fill a small plastic bottle and couldn't understand what all the fuss was about. It was awful—soft and 'flat'. Nowhere near as nice as our spring water at home.

Outside the elegant Opera House the street was filled with tables thronged with people eating and drinking. The audience was arriving for the evening's performance in full evening dress. As we had both omitted to pack our evening dresses, we had to give this a miss but bought tickets instead for an open-air performance of alternative Shakespeare—*The Fifteen Minute Hamlet* and *Romeo and Juliet Deceased*. We sat near the front with our supermarket bags parked round our feet. I don't think I have ever laughed so much as I did that evening. A fast and furious *Fifteen Minute Hamlet* was followed by an encore that repeated the whole thing in five minutes. The brilliant cast of *Romeo and Juliet, Deceased*, had us all falling off our seats with laughter. It was no surprise to learn they were going on to the Edinburgh Festival in August.

When we left to walk the mile and a half back up that long steep hill, it was almost dark—and I still had to put up my tent. The site was even more crowded than when we left. I dashed off for a shower—only two for the whole site—leaving Helen to put up my tent. We ate a strange supper of yoghurts, Kiwi fruit and rice pudding—all things we had fancied in our manic shopping spree. We had to eat *some* of it as we couldn't possibly have carried it all next day. It was a long and expensive day, but one that still stands out as a highlight of my journey. Once we reached Edale there would be a return to a frugal and much cheaper way of living.

That night there was so much noise that though we were both very tired, we couldn't sleep. Music, talking and laughter and a teenage party in a nearby tent, went on long after midnight. Sleek airliners flew low in their approach to Manchester; heavy lorries rumbled along the main road until the early hours. Another hot and sticky day dawned. Regular breaks were the order of the day as we made a bee-line for Edale on a mainly cross-country and increasingly hilly route. For the first few miles we followed the course of a Roman road but after leaving this, concentrated map reading was essential. I was glad Helen was with me for consultations and for actually reading the map. I am at an age where failing eyesight becomes increasingly frustrating. I need my glasses to read the map but can't see where I'm going if I keep them on and it is so annoying to have to stop every ten minutes to fish them out of the map case—the handiest place to keep them. The only disadvantage of Helen's map reading is that she's too good at it and has an infuriating habit of making comments such as "We've only two more contours to go," as if she can see them painted on the ground.

The heat that morning was diabolical and in such weather water has to be conserved. Unlike many walkers, Helen and I both prefer to carry our water bottles in our hand and not in our packs. This way we can drink small amounts 'on the hoof' without having to take our packs off. We find that this way our water last longer and we don't get so thirsty and dehydrated. Even so, any chance of extra fluids is not to be missed so when we found a small corner shop open in romantically named but far from picturesque Chapel en Le Frith, we grabbed the opportunity to buy milk shakes.

### The Walker's Mecca

Edale is a walkers' Mecca—and not just for those starting the Pennine Way, but for day walkers and all those enjoying the Peaks and Pennines in general. It's outdoor adventure country and as popular with potholers, climbers, cyclists and pony trekkers as with walkers. The village is well endowed with campsites but we were dismayed to find that the first we passed had a sign up saying 'Site Full'. It had taken us nine hours to walk 12 miles and now, this late in the day, we could not afford to be choosy.

When we came to the next site and there were vacancies—we paid up. It was the National Park site and more than I usually paid, but did include shower tokens. The toilets were like Fort Knox. Entry was by a coded locking system, which meant that after dark I needed a torch and specs to get in. Helen was OK. She had good eyes and a brain capable of memorizing the code and the layout of the keypad.

As it was a weekend at the height of the season this site was crowded too. We found a scrappy bit of grass close to the entrance and a waste-paper bin—a busy thoroughfare with people constantly passing. An over-weight man with shoulder length curly hair and long shorts sat cross-legged outside the tent adjacent to ours and stared into space with a melancholy look on his face. He looked as if he wished he was somewhere else.

We walked along to the village to locate the start for the morning. It was obvious. A painted board on the wall of the Nag's Head clearly indicated 'The Official Start of the The Pennine Way.' The footpath was immediately opposite.

If after the previous noisy night we had hoped for a quiet site, we weren't going to get one. Many sites have regulations on groups of teenagers and organised parties and many have a voluntary 'no noise' rule after about 11pm. This one had no regulations for either and in addition, at a nearby hostel, a late night disco was taking place. We were kept awake until some time after 2am by rowdy youngsters further up the field. Then the melancholy man in the next tent finally flipped, swore at them profusely and told them in no uncertain terms to shut up—or else!!! Next morning one of my tent pegs was missing—plucked neatly from the ground and not accidentally kicked. During the night I had been roused by noises near my tent and had been certain someone was outside. I felt sure it had been one of those boys up to no good.

Two exceptionally hot days and two disturbed nights in succession did not auger well for embarking on Britain's toughest trail, but filled with early morning enthusiasm and in anticipation of a great adventure ahead, we left the Nag's Head with about 50 others, all eager to embark on a walk along the Backbone of England.

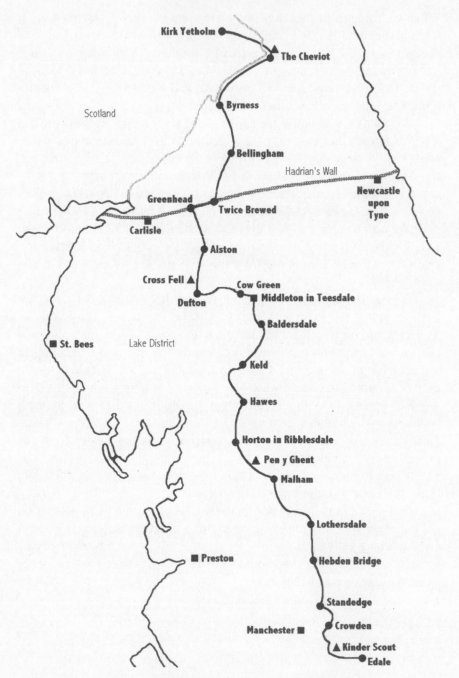

*The Pennine Way; Edale to Kirk Yetholm*

# 7

# The Backbone of England

## The southern Pennines

The Pennine Way is Britain's oldest and best known long distance path. Conceived in 1935 and officially opened 30 years later it provides a continuous upland route for 275 miles from Derbyshire to the border of Scotland. But it is not a path to be treated lightly. Of the 11,000 people estimated to set out from Edale each year only about half actually make it to Kirk Yetholm. Anyone attempting it needs to be well prepared and possess a certain amount of stamina and determination if they are to get to the end.

And just to see what you are made of, the first day is one of the toughest. 18 miles of hard slog over terrain that will test your boots, body and navigation skills, no pub, café or shop to provide succour and not very much in the way of exciting scenery either. With 450 miles behind me I was pretty fit and Helen, now into her fifth day, was getting into her stride. But for those transported by bus, train or obliging members of the family, fresh from the comforts of office or classroom, this is often the first time boots have seen mud for a long time, the first time the rucksack has seen the light of day since the previous year's expedition, and by the colour of the legs, the first time the shorts have been worn this summer!!

The enthusiastic souls leaving the Nags Head and keeping up a fine pace for the first two and a half miles across gentle pastures, soon came to a grinding halt on the rough, rocky steps of Jacob's Ladder. This rugged rock hewn stairway rising 400ft. in about a quarter of a mile comes as a bit of a shock to the system at that time in the morning. Walkers who left after us, soon caught up and overtook us looking tremendously fit and macho only to find that we passed them later as they, like us, flagged and rested. This became the pattern of the day and by that first evening, faces were becoming familiar and brief conversations were being exchanged. The camaraderie of a long distance path was beginning to develop.

After sweating uphill for another mile the barren 2,000ft. plateau of Kinder Scout was reached with relief and life became a little easier. As summits go, this highest point of the Peak District was disappointing—an immense area of peat and gravel strewn with giant gritstone boulders which dwarfed the steady stream of humanity wending its way north. It is the main watershed of England. On this plateau, only a few feet apart, 'cloughs' falling to the west drain ultimately to the Irish Sea, whilst those to the east drain to the North Sea. The path hugged the western escarpment, tracking along sheer, craggy cliffs with far-reaching views across the industrial sprawls of Stockport and Manchester. To the east an unbroken expanse of peat faded into an indistinct horizon. Overhead we still had the almost continuous monotonous drone of planes, which at that altitude, seemed much closer.

Then came the first real encounter with Pennine peat—Featherbed Moss the 1st. The Pennines seem to have a Featherbed Moss every few miles and this is reputedly one of the worst. In wet weather the whole area can be a filthy, oozing, boggy morass though fortunately for us it hadn't rained for weeks and everywhere was dust dry. From now on it was peat, peat and more peat and though in reality this only figured for a few days, there is so much of it ingrained in my memory that, looking back, it seems as if it was peat all the way. In places it is desert-like; almost featureless and a compass is needed even in clear fine weather, to keep on course. And it is no good following in other's footsteps. The whole area is a trampled mass of footprints—probably all going round in circles. If you close your eyes and turn round, you have no idea which way you have come or which way you were going.

In the middle of one of these inhospitable peaty Saharas are the Wainstones, a group of boulders better known as 'The Kiss'; a natural sculpture which if you look at it from the right direction and use your imagination a bit, looks like two romantically inclined heads. I wanted to see these but we almost got lost trying to find them. I spent a long time trying, with little success to get my photograph to look just like the postcards. It was not until later that we discovered I had photographed the wrong stones. We had never found 'The Kiss' after all.

In the blistering heat we drank our water sparingly. With the peat as dry as it was, ground water was virtually non-existent. When we did find a clean supply dripping from a bog in a rocky gully, we drank our fill and refilled our bottles. We carried purifying tablets, but as at home all our water comes from an untreated spring, it seemed faintly ridiculous to use them here, so we didn't bother.

By late afternoon Helen was showing signs of fatigue and her knee, weakened a few years ago when she fell from her horse, began playing up on the long descent to Crowden. She always wears a support bandage, but her knee still has a habit of 'wobbling' and letting her down. The descent seemed to go on forever and at the bottom, work on a reservoir enforced a lengthy diversion along a disused railway track. Helen, her energy depleted, weepy and in obvious pain struggled to complete the last couple of miles. Our conversation was terse and snappy. All she wanted was to go home and I told her she could phone her father as soon reached the camp-site. From experience with homesick girls in Guide Camps, I've learnt that if you agree to their pleas and offer them the choice, they often feel much better. Their spirits are lifted by the thought that they can go home. They don't keep worrying and asking you, because you have already agreed and by the time they actually have the option to go home, they usually decide they don't want to go. I hoped this would work with Helen. But I wouldn't have pressed her to stay if she had really wanted to go.

It was 7 o'clock when we reached the campsite and several of those we had seen during the day were getting concerned at our late arrival. A couple of schoolteachers from Manchester, both men, came over to see how we were, as did two intensive care nurses, also men, who were worried we might have become dehydrated. One of them was unwell owing to the heat and they were considering having the next day off. Two Australians encountered on the final descent reckoned the day had been "A killer!" and they were used to such heat! I suggested to Helen that we too might have a rest day, but told her to ask her Dad to fetch her home if that was what she wanted.

Other walkers were staying up the road at the Youth Hostel, where a range of groceries could be bought by non residents. I went to get milk and some tinned food while Helen phoned. She tried her father, her boyfriend and another friend without success and then went off dispiritedly to shower and wash her hair. Half an hour later she came back looking much happier having talked to some of the others and found out that everyone else had had a terrible day too. There was no longer talk of her going home.

One of the nurses told us he had done the Pennine Way ten years before, when he was 18. He had forgotten how bad it was and couldn't think why he was doing it again. Most of them knew by now that I was walking from Land's End to John O'Groats. Not that I had told anyone but Helen was more forthcoming and in any case it often came out during conversation. Walkers are very nosy. The first question on meeting is either "How far have you come?" or "Where did you start?" and then "Where are you going?" These questions inevitably led to my destination and where I started.

The site warden whose accent I had recognised as belonging to the Monmouthshire-Herefordshire border took particular care of us once he knew we were from his home county. Like most wardens he was in residence for the summer season and ran a well organised site. I had strict instructions to report to him next morning before we left, whereupon I received a good-bye kiss. Not, he told me, something bestowed on all his lady campers.

Walking the Southern Pennines soon fell into a daily pattern; a steep climb first thing, followed by miles of moorland bog and peat and a drop down to a valley in the evening for accommodation. Many of the boggiest and most desolate areas of the moors now have a paved footpath made from flagstones recycled from the floors of redundant mills. To many these are unsightly, hard on the feet and tedious.The only interesting thing about walking on them is fossil spotting. These are many and varied, but mainly the rippled sand effect of fossilised beaches. Flagstone paths sometimes stretched for miles; thankfully never in straight lines, but snaking away into the distance across moorland white with cotton grass. I'm sure that Wainwright would not have approved. They are certainly unsightly. But these previously difficult sections are now undoubtedly safer and cleaner and as long as you stick to them, there's no need to worry about getting lost in a thick mist.

Everywhere was so dry it was unbelievable. Even the notorious Black Hill, more often than not a quagmire of squelching black gunge was not black at all but parched and brown. It was like walking on a trampoline. Walkers here really did walk with a spring in their step. On the summit, if you can call it that, the cairn on a slightly raised island of firmer ground, marks the boundary between Cheshire and Yorkshire and at 1,908ft. is Cheshire's highest point.

As we progressed north, we began to understand Yorkshire's water problem, which had been constantly in the news over recent months. Empty reservoirs became a regular sight. 'No Swimming' signs stood incongruously in acres of parched peat. Somewhere we passed a sign waymarking the Ten Reservoirs Walk but even if it rained for months they wouldn't fill, as it seems much of the water is stored in peat based reservoirs. The peat would just soak it up like a giant brown sponge.

I stopped to cut my toe nails by one of these empty reservoirs, a task I had been meaning to do for days, but kept forgetting. We'd stopped for a breather when I suddenly thought about it and decided to do it there and then. There was no-one about so I removed my boots and socks and began a full pedicure. Neither of us noticed the approaching figure until he called out "You can do mine as well if you like."

### The Pennine grapevine

On Saddleworth Moor we came upon a walker's dream; a refreshment caravan parked beside the busy main road to Manchester. This is 'Brian's', who justifiably boasts the biggest buns on the moor. And, they certainly are. Cut into four, mine lasted until next day. Tea, coffee and chocolate is served in an interesting variety of real mugs. None of your plastic throw away stuff at Brian's. It was ridiculously cheap. We had two each and lay stretched out on the roadside verge along with a dozen other weary wayfarers. Brian is definitely onto a good thing. Not only does he catch all the trans-pennine traffic but he gets about fifty walkers a day crossing the road. He, and various other mobile snack vans are vital links in the Pennine Way grapevine. Information passes up and down the path quickly and efficiently along the network of cafés, pubs, hostels and campsites. They are the unofficial information bureaus and know who has passed through, what the weather is like, where accommodation is available, whether it is good or bad and sometimes even walkers' names. On one occasion Helen and I stopped at a wayside van for a second breakfast of cheeseburgers and later discovered that we were reported to other walkers as being 'the first of the day'. By the time I reached the Northern Pennines, it was not unusual to meet people coming the other way who knew both my name and where I was going!

During these first days, friendships continue to flourish. Christian names could now be put to most faces though even after three weeks a surname might never be known. Most of the men seemed to be named either Dave or Neil and most were getting hairier by the mile. Apart from the tall, dark Australian whose goatee beard was impeccably trimmed for the entire walk, the rest had varying degrees of designer stubble. I had been told that male End to Enders regarded it as a matter of personal pride to arrive with a full beard. Evenings become a time of reunion. Campers were generally heading for the same site—mainly because there was usually only one to head for. Youth Hostellers met up at the hostel, which was often not far from the campsite and, ultimately, most people ended up at the local pub, sometimes for a meal, but mainly because it was more comfortable than their tent. Backpacker campsites, deserted all day, were transformed at night and become home from home for one big happy family of walkers. Sometimes, someone knowing we had not been far behind, would have a kettle boiling for us when we arrived. Then everyone would compare notes and swap events of the day. Most nights we camped with people we knew and this continued after Helen left. 17 days after leaving Edale I was still with people I met on the first day and calculated that roughly half of the 50 who started with us finished about the same time as me.

### Sleep all night—eat all day

Most of the Pennine campsites are backpacker orientated. Facilities may not be of the highest quality but the more important 'extras' are there. Somewhere to dry wet clothes; a shelter for packing up if it's wet; a sink for washing clothes and more important, a washing line. Even if clothes are not wet, sleeping bags and damp socks need airing whenever possible. I had six pegs of my own, but some sites have even thought of this and it's these little things that single out the popular sites from 'the rest'. Many provide packed lunches and a few, a rucksack transfer or pick-up service. One site, as well as providing most of the above, did evening meals, breakfasts, sold simple provisions and hired towels. What a joy to use a big clean cuddly towel instead of my space-saving economy model.

Food was no longer a problem. Breakfast we carried. Lunch was either a prepared packed lunch or obtained *en route*. Evening meals were either tins of something quick and easy purchased on arrival or were bar meals. Walkers never turn up an opportunity to eat, whatever time of day it is and as one person observed, "Pennine Way Walkers don't eat. They browse all day." It was not unusual to have several breakfasts followed by several lunches. A proper breakfast of cereals and possibly yoghurt or cake would be eaten first thing. At about 9.30 there would be a stop for a second 'breakfast', followed by a third about mid-morning. By noon you would be thinking about an early lunch, followed by lunch at about 1.30 and another about an hour later. An afternoon tea break filled the gap until you reached the campsite, where tea kept you going until you got round to the evening meal. Any of these could vary from a pork pie, chocolate bar and apple to a full sit down meal in a café—no matter what the time of day. Helen could keep going on milk shakes alone and I've known her drink as many as five pints in a day, if we had that many opportunities!

The two intensive care nurses, Bob and Phil, were becoming our most regular friends. Both were young enough to be my sons, and not too old to be good company for Helen. Usually we set up our tents next to each other and ended up in the pub for the evening. Occasionally we walked with them for a mile or two, though most people prefer to walk with their partner and soon make some excuse to drop out when they have had enough of another's company. This is something everyone respects and understands, though I'm sure if anyone was actually feeling low and fancied company, someone would oblige. Bob, being an old hand at the Pennine Way knew the best campsites and all the interesting things to look out for on the way. We had our own guide book but first hand knowledge is much better and easier than wading through pages of text.

Surprisingly, many walkers have little interest in what they are passing. For them, the walk is purely a challenge. When not walking, the intervening time is taken up with eating or propping up the bar in the 'local'. That is not my scene at all. I stop and look at anything and everything, whether it be birds, plants, a church, ancient monument or just the view. My walk was not an endurance test. It was for pleasure and interest and a lot of time was taken up with with this. Helen enjoys photography and carried a weighty bit of photographic technology much more sophisticated than my lightweight automatic. Time consuming digressions were spent zooming in on flowers, coaxing green-striped caterpillars to climb photogenically up cotton grass and patiently stalking a family of pheasant chicks, while I grovelled on hands and knees exclaiming excitedly about some plant never seen south of Manchester.

Over the next few days we looked at the Roman road on Blackstone Edge, which is in truth an old packhorse track, photographed the curious double arched bridge over the Leeds and Liverpool Canal at East Marten and climbed Stoodley Pike, a 120ft. tower built to commemorate the abdication of Napoleon in 1814. Later we met two guys camping with a car, who were staggered to find out that we had been up Stoodley Pike and walked 15 miles to do it. They were 'considering' whether it was 'worth the effort' to drive the car as far as they could, and walk the last mile to the Pike. Their most important piece of camping equipment was an enormous coolbox, which they informed us was "full of cold water to keep the beer cold."

## The Cosmopolitan Way

There are few towns along the Pennine Way and the largest is Hebden Bridge, a small mill town that has seen better days. It lies in the Calder Valley and was once known as the Switzerland of the North. Most walkers detour off the route and follow the Calder Canal to the town as it is one of the few places offering any variety of shops and hole-in-the-wall cash facilities. Once again we overshopped in the supermarket. Peaches were cheap, as were Kiwi Fruit and we couldn't resist the temptation of either. I needed a bank not only for cash but to take in a cheque card found earlier in the day. Some poor walker was probably going round like a headless chicken wondering how he was going to pay his way and who was using his card.

Our campsite was, as usual, three miles up a steep hill and we were loaded down with supermarket bags. Helen casually observed it was a pity there wasn't a bus, which rapidly developed into the idea that as we had walked off the route to reach the town in the first place, taking a taxi was perfectly legitimate. It took us nearly as long to locate a taxi as it would have taken us to walk the three miles but once we found one we were whisked away in style, passing Bob and Phil on the way and encouraging the taxi driver to hoot at them as we sailed past gleefully waving from the back window.

It was a quiet farm site in high rolling countryside and the two boys set up their tents next to ours. The last few nights we had been plagued by midges, although as I was to find out later, these were nothing in comparison to the Scottish midges. Towels over the head did little to alleviate their persistent biting. Helen stalked off with a crossword puzzle, and sat behind a wall further up the field where there was more breeze and less midges. In the next field, a herd of Highland cattle grazed providing a foretaste of what was to come when I reached Scotland.

Brontë Country was the theme for the next day, with signposts in Japanese indicating the Brontë Trail. Why Japanese and not any other language we could not understand, until someone explained that the Japanese are apparently fanatical about the English Classics. High on the moor an isolated ruin known as Top Withens is reputedly the Wuthering Heights of the novel and lower down seventeenth century Ponden Hall is believed to be Thrushcross Grange.

Today was a day for meeting people and we seemed to spend much of our time chatting to locals—a woman picking bilberries and another who bred Norwegian Elk Hounds. Her garden overflowed with excited four month old puppies all barking at us as we hung over the wall to admire them. "They're Pennine Way Hounds," she told us. "They bark at all the walkers."

We stopped for a break in an area where roughly built huts dotted the moorland. Some of timber, some stone, some of corrugated iron, but all sporting a substantial chimney indicating some form of heating. Many had a water butt and seat outside. We were sitting on one of these when an elderly couple came by. They were from Keighley and owned a neighbouring hut. They explained that they were originally shelters used by game hunters but were now used by local people as weekend retreats. Without at that time knowing where I was going, they said they had met two girls a few weeks before, walking from Land's End to John O'Groats. Helen immediately piped up and said "That's where Mum is going."

This part of the Pennines was much prettier and more interesting than anywhere we had seen so far. We were not far from the industrial sprawl of Leeds and Bradford but far enough to be unaffected by it. The villages we passed through were small and sleepy though most were originally small mill towns. Many had a huge mill dominating a few houses. We stopped at a public house called the Black Bull for an early evening meal. It was only 3 o'clock but we were both starving. "Where are you staying tonight?" asked the landlord. I named out destination. "There's no camp-site there." he said. I assured him that my accommodation guide listed one. "Ah Yes!" he said "But that's my sister-in-law and she's gone to Canada for three months. I'll see if I can fix you up somewhere else." A few phone calls later, he came back to say he had arranged for us to stay at the pub in Lothersdale who didn't normally take campers but would let us stay in the beer garden. "I can see all the walkers from here," he told us as we left. "I'll wave when you get to the top of that hill," indicating the far side of the valley. Feeling rather foolish, half an hour later we waved furiously from the top of the hill, just in case he really meant it.

Lothersdale was another mill town with a rayon and silk mill claiming to have the largest waterwheel in Europe. We duly reported to the Horse and Hounds for our tiniest site yet in the small but totally private beer garden. The only customers who used the beer garden that night were Bob and Phil, who having made the discovery that there was no campsite, had taken Bed and Breakfast down the road. The four of us spent the evening wandering round the village and ended up chatting over drinks in the pub. The landlord would accept no money for our overnight stay, though he added that he would have done if we hadn't gone in for drinks.

## A cyclist with 'ormones'

Many people had been looking forward to the area we were now in saying it was easier, more pleasant country for walking, but Helen and I prefer mountains and moorland and wide open spaces. We could think of nothing worse than toiling uphill and down dale over a rural landscape of stone walls and pasture. It is far easier to get lost in areas like this, than on open hills with a compass or with a well worn path to follow. And get lost we did. Having crossed four or five identical fields all with numerous gates and no signs of stiles, we came out onto a lane at a gate that had evidently not been opened for months. We knew we were in the wrong place, but three farms in the distance could be used to orientate our map. A flat capped, elderly man appeared, pushing an ancient bike along the lane, two Tesco bags hanging from the handlebars. Local knowledge was better than the map we reasoned so we asked him the name of the nearest farm. This was met with the enquiry, "You from the city?"

"No," we replied, "we're from Wales." A long pause ensued while this was digested.

"Ahhh! Oi've 'erd of Wales. It's got a mountain. Snowdon! Do you live anywhere near Snowdon?"

"No! That's North Wales. We live in South Wales. Can you tell us the name of that farm?"

"Cardiff then!" he persisted, "that's a town in Wales. Do you live anywhere near Cardiff?"

The conversation was not getting us anywhere so I changed the subject, thinking if we found out where he was going, it might help us. "Are you going to work?" I asked.

"Ohh no-oo! I don't work. I'm on medicaments." And with sudden enthusiasm "Do you know anything about medicaments?" We shook our heads and edged a bit further down the road and his face fell.

"Oh! Well, I don't know why I 'ave 'em. But I've got 'ormones. You've got 'ormones in yer body—and genes and things. I don't know what for." And suddenly brightening, "Are you going north?" We nodded eagerly. "Oh, well," pointing, "that's South. And if you're looking for the path, it's down there on the right. I've seen lots of people like you with big bags going up there." We thanked him and made a further move down the road before the conversation took another turn.

This was a day when we should have been well endowed with shops, but it was not to be. The first at Lothersdale we had not bothered with as we wanted to be up and gone before it opened. We were not particularly worried as we knew we would go though several other villages and could buy lunch on the way, but at the next, Thornton in Craven, we discovered there was no shop and to add to our despondency, it started to rain. We made the brief acquaintance of a party of about eight walkers who arrived in the village in a minibus. A Ramblers Club we thought at the time, but later found out they were on a Pennine Way Guided Walk. The minibus collected them each evening and took them to their pre-booked accommodation, returning them to the start again next day.

We were still having no luck with a shop. The next at the canalside village of East Marton had a sign on the door announcing that it was 'Closed All Day' and we had to wait until Gargrave, a much larger village, before we could get something to eat. But it was worth waiting for. Gargrave has a most wonderful café which specialises in catering for the cyclists. The walls are covered from floor to ceiling with posters and photographs of cyclists, cycle races and cycling memorabilia. It is well patronised by walkers too and outside, propped against a wall, were two large rucksacks. Inside we found Bob and Phil tucking into bacon sandwiches and joined them over a pot of tea, toasted sandwiches, and two milk shakes for Helen. It's a small friendly café where everyone talks to everyone else, though conversation has a tendency to revolve round village gossip and cycling. Walkers are requested to sign the Pennine Way Book before they leave.

### Magnificent limestone country

Later that afternoon, in superb weather, we arrived at Malham. We were now in the Yorkshire Dales National Park in an area of rugged limestone scenery, tumbling waterfalls, flower rich countryside, and a rural landscape dominated by stone walls, neat stone barns and sheep. Malham's famous cove, one of Britain's best known glacial formations, dominates the landscape with its 240ft. high cliffs as the village is approached. This was a place I had heard much about but never visited, so it was great that we arrived early enough to spend some time in the National Park Visitor Centre before setting up camp. Bob had recommended a farm garden campsite where he had stayed before as being a much nicer option than one of the larger sites, so we camped there with them, and discovered the Guided Walk people from the minibus Bed and Breakfasting at the same place.

After taking advantage of a café for our evening meal we went off to explore with the aid of a Village Trail leaflet and found that despite being crowded with tourists, Malham still manages to maintain its old world charm. A small river crossed by an ancient stone bridge and several foot-bridges wends its way past buildings steeped in history. The resident ducks dabbled happily along its banks and a herd of dairy cows straggled unac-companied and placidly along the main street, returning to their pastures after milking. Malham was at one time a centre for the Calamine Industry, the only visible remains today being the Calamine House where, after being brought down off the moor, Calamine was stored before being trans-ported from Gargrave on the Leeds and Liverpool Canal. A fascinating area. It would have been nice to have a day off, see Janet's Fosse, a pretty waterfall just up the road and walk to the dramatic gorge and towering cliffs of Gordale Scar, but Helen wanted to go as far as possible in her allotted time. The next day was her last. She was returning home for a more appealing camping holiday with friends, though I think, secretly, now that we had made so many friends and she was enjoying herself, she would have liked to have completed the whole Pennine Way.

She would have made it too. Most walkers who get as far as Malham will probably get to the end. Those first two or three days from Edale are the worst. If any one is going to give up, they will give up then. If you survive that, you can manage the rest. We had heard of a few that have given up. One man with a lad about nine had started well, but they soon gave up and another with a ten year old daughter had done four days, though in their case, that was all they intended to do. He was a walker but a first time camper and was introducing the girl to the pleasures of both. She carried her own rucksack with sleeping bag and clothes, but by half way through the day he would be carrying hers in addition to his own and her conversation was restricted to "How far have we come?" "How far have we got to go?" and "Are we nearly there?" This is really not a walk for children. Apart from being physically demanding, there are too many long and tedious sections with not enough to interest the young mind.

The climb to the top of Malham Cove's great limestone cliffs is up a short, steep series of rocky steps. Approaching the cliffs you are very much aware of the intricate pattern of drystone walls carving up the countryside, many of them centuries old and a reminder that this area has long been settled by man. At the top, you find yourself standing on the deeply fissured limestone pavement formed firstly by the scouring action of the ice and later by the dissolving properties of rainwater on the limestone. There is no fence to safeguard the unwary and as you get your breath back, you stand in awe peering nervously down the sheer rock face to the green fields below.

The pavement is criss-crossed with crevasses 2ft. or more deep and wide enough to take a walker's boot with ease. Full attention to walking is needed if a broken leg or sprained ankle is to be avoided, not to mention the accidental dropping of a camera or some other bit of equipment. The deep cracks are more correctly called grikes and provide a safe habitat for many plants. You might even see, as we did, a rabbit hiding in the shady depths. The whole landscape is dominated by limestone. Bare, white, rocky crags, water sinks, shakeholes, scars and gills and, quite clearly visible, the dry valley of the Watlowes sweeping towards the edge of the cliff. To me, all reminiscent of earlier days at Cheddar. Not far away, and soon reached, is Malham Tarn, the highest lime-rich lake in the country and home to a variety of wild life in a unique and scientifically important habitat.

The whole day was one of mountain and moorland rising to over 2,000ft. on Fountains Fell, with a fair amount of map reading required through an area riddled with water sinks and ground disturbed by mining. And, although it was a fine, sunny day, there was a keen wind and we lunched huddled in the shelter of rocks somewhere near the summit, wearing every bit of warm clothing we possessed.

The final obstacle of the day was Pen-y-ghent, one of Yorkshire's highest and best known summits. We had already agreed not to go to the top. Purist Pennine Way walkers would not dream of missing it, but Helen was not that bothered and my argument was that I was not walking the Pennine Way, only making use of it. The distinctive outline of Pen-y-ghent loomed ahead scarred by a line of white bags, full of stone and dumped by helicopter to continue the National Park's ongoing battle against erosion. Walkers swarmed up the side like ants, but we turned off before the final ascent, taking a short direct path into Horton in Ribblesdale.

### Three peaks—or Pennine Way?

Horton in Ribblesdale, we now belatedly realised, was the home of the Yorkshire Three Peaks Challenge Walk. There was only one camp site and it was packed. Tents numbering about 80 were pitched on every square yard of grass with only feet between them. Cars, which were not allowed on the site, were packed equally closely in the parking area. There was no way one could be choosy on this site. It was a matter of finding a vacant patch of grass large enough for your tent and staking your claim before someone else did. In our case, with Michael's arrival imminent, we had to find a patch large enough for an additional tent and 'bagged' an extra pitch by putting up my flysheet and inner separately.

Bob and Phil having conscientiously conquered Pen-y-ghent, arrived soon after us and squeezed in beside us. Then we adjourned to the Three Peaks Café, which is the start and finish of the Three Peaks Walk, a gruelling 25 miles which takes in Pen-y-ghent, Ingleborough and Whernside each well over 2,000ft. It was a Saturday. The café was packed. Walkers and hill runners arrived by the minute. Clocking in. Checking their times. They come from all over Britain. Some camping for the weekend, others arriving at dawn, doing their walk and leaving again in the evening. A nearby carpark was full of support vehicles heavily laden with crates of water and cold drinks.

You could barely move in the café for sweating, scantily clad bodies and booted walkers. Tea and coffee is served in pint mugs and as you placed your order you were asked "Are you Pennine Way or Three Peaks?" Here they are proud to possess the oldest Pennine Way Walker's book, with records going back over 30 years and, depending on your reply, produce the appropriate book for you to sign. Tucking into toasted sandwiches and sipping our 'pints', Helen and I listened to the exploits of some of the competitors, my efforts paling into insignificance to those of one athletic, sunbronzed, middle-aged woman. She claimed she had beaten her previous week's time for the Three Peaks and was telling anyone who would listen how she had run the Coast to Coast in five days, (190 miles from St. Bee's in Cumbria to Robin Hood's Bay in Yorkshire). Many people do the Three Peaks as an annual challenge but there are some, like this super fit lady, who do it more frequently, continually trying to improve their time.

The café also sold outdoor gear so I was able to replace my map case, which was falling to pieces and was already held together with parcel tape. I had a tendency to use it as a handbag. Usually it contained three maps, one recently redundant, the current one and the next one. As a map was used for only two days or sometimes less, this saved having to stop and unpack the rucksack every time a map ran out. All sorts of other items were crammed in the map case for convenience. My glasses. Essential. I couldn't read the map without them. My notebook and pen, for jotting down anything interesting and to write my diary during the day, if I had chance, while things were fresh in my mind. Plants collected were pressed temporarily in the notebook and transferred to the folds of redundant maps to be sent home. All my personal papers, chequebook, post office book and credit cards were discreetly hidden between the maps, the advantage of this being that I always had everything of importance with me. Never did the map case leave me. Whenever I left the tent on a site, or the rucksack propped outside a shop, the map case was always round my neck. Postcards and guide books also ended up there to keep them dry and flat until they were posted home. I wore out three map cases before reaching John O'Groats.

### Helen's last night

One of the problems with a walk of this length, is keeping up with normal family affairs. There is mail to be attended to, bills to pay, birthdays to remember and in my case the welcome, but ill-timed sale of a house taking place. The sale of a property we owned had been going ahead at the usual frustratingly slow rate before I left. I had signed some papers while I was home in July. Now there were further papers to sign and financial matters to discuss, all of which was to be done that evening.

Knowing that Helen would not want to be bored with our business, as it was her last night, I asked Bob and Phil if they would mind if she went along with them for the evening. They had worked out that from now on there was a pub every night and they wouldn't have to cook any more meals! They had no objection, so when Michael arrived at around 7 o'clock, they went off to the village, leaving us to work our way through a mountain of correspondence and paperwork. This took several hours and it was late by our camping standards when we went to bed. With so many people, most of them in high spirits, it was a noisy site. At about two minutes past midnight one group, having presumably just noted the time, burst into a rowdy rendering of Happy Birthday. It was all good natured revelling. After all, most of these campers were either already worn out or needing to be fit for the long arduous challenge next day. Everyone wanted a good night and the site soon lapsed into silence, broken only by the rustle of plastic groundsheets and the nasal renderings of the snorers.

Michael had again brought my box of supplies. I stuffed in two weeks supply of cheese and muesli and the rest of the maps up to Fort William. Not as many as you might think as an excellent map published by Harvey's covers the whole of the West Highland Way and eliminates several standard OS maps. Even so I would be carrying nine maps, the most I had needed at any one time. Not bad going when you consider that to walk from End to End I would have used 40 maps. Michael was expecting to come up again to the Scottish Lowlands, but when and where was all a bit vague and might never happen, so I took all the maps to be on the safe side. From Fort William I was going to purchase maps as required.

The whole site was on the move early next day. By 8.30 Helen and Michael were on their way home and I was on my way north. Bob and Phil had left even earlier having last night woken up to the fact that they were half way through their time but only a third of the way up the Pennines. They had rapidly revised their schedule and from now on were stepping up their daily distance. I would not see them again. I was as sorry to see them go as I was Helen. They had been great company and it would have been nice to have still had them around after Helen left, so it was with not without a tinge of regret that we exchanged addresses and said our good-byes and I gave them some packets of Lucozade tablets as a parting gift.

Once more I was walking alone. The first time for ten days, longer if I counted the four days with my uncle. There was still almost 180 miles to go to the end of the Pennines and then the whole of Scotland. But the good news was that by the end of the day, on arrival at Hawes, I would be half way there. A mere 600 miles to go and another six weeks of walking.

# 8

# Friends, Romans & Cheviots
## The Northern Pennines

The first day without Helen was not as bad as I feared. It was such a delightful day's walk along old packhorse trails and a Roman military road through wonderful limestone countryside, that I barely noticed that I was alone. For several miles all three of Yorkshire's challenging peaks were clearly visible as was the magnificent 24 arch Ribblehead Viaduct prominently stretching across the broad expanse of Batty Moss, the source of the Ribble. For a few miles the Dales Way ran concurrently with the Pennine Way increasing the chances of meeting other walkers and all too often the Sunday influx of mountain bikes whizzed past, arriving silently out of the blue. Like jet planes, you don't hear them 'til they've passed.

The area is noted for its caves and potholes. I passed one right beside the track where a tiny stream plunged dramatically 50ft. down a gaping 'pot' to pass through a tortuous subterranean passage before re-emerging in a cave. As I peered with some trepidation over the edge, a group of potholers arrived and under the watchful eye of their leader began putting on harnesses and uncoiling ropes. They looked very proficient but when I asked them if they objected to being photographed they looked rather dubious and replied, "Well. OK. But don't expect a look of confidence.This is our first time!"

Further on, Ling Gill Gorge nature reserve, a rare example of upland woodland, was fenced off to protect it from grazing sheep. I could barely see the 200ft. gorge, but the contrast in the quantity and variety of flowers and vegetation within the boundaries of the fence, compared with the sparsely covered open moors was quite extraordinary.

It was over 15 miles to Hawes and it was exceptionally hot. I walked all day with barely a stop and didn't realise how exhausted I was until I arrived at my farm campsite. I was directed to a corner of the field where a young man lay motionless on the grass, rucksack abandoned beside him. I flopped down a few yards away and closed my eyes. Neither of us spoke, recovering our energy before setting to work on the tents. Mine was up in minutes. I was drinking tea in no time. His went up eventually, after a bit of a struggle, then he came over and asked if he could look at my tent. A first-time backpacker, he had recently purchased a hundred pounds worth of tent and rucksack and this was only the second time he had put a tent up. He was impressed with how quickly I was organised and we sat companionably discussing walking, camping and related matters.

Although it was Sunday, I learnt there was a supermarket open until 5pm in Hawes. I could get there in time if I hurried. "Ask them to stay open until 7," said the farmer's wife, "I'm expecting a lot more campers tonight." It was a mile away by road, but less across the fields and I found Hawes to be a delightful little market town with cobbled streets, every other shop selling antiques and a hotel called Herriots to remind you that this was TV veterinary country. But Sunday was not the best day of the week to be there, as half of the North of England were also there, the young on motorbikes, the elderly on coaches. Gift shops, cafés and the chip shop were doing a roaring trade. An outdoor pursuits shop was busy as a pre-Christmas Saturday. I treated myself to a mosquito coil. I had seen how effective Bob and Phil's had been, burning slowly in front of their tent on midgey evenings and had a suspicion one would be a valuable asset further north.

I wanted to go to church and checked the time of the service before returning to the tent to change into something reasonably tidy. Remarkably, this was the first time since leaving Land's End that I had actually been near a church on a Sunday which was holding a service. However, my faith was put to the test. By the time I reached the site, the first drops of rain were falling. Within minutes it was pelting down and was unquestionably set in for the night. Clutching my bags of shopping I dived into the tent and feeling very guilty, spent the evening reading, writing, eating and drinking endless cups of tea.

*The wettest day*

Hawes was roughly my half way point. It was time for a break. An old college friend was going to accompany me next day to Keld. Then I was going to stay with him for a day or two. His wife, also a friend from student days, was several hundred miles away looking after an elderly parent, but had no objection to me borrowing her husband for a few days.

Rain hammered down all night and showed little sign of abating as I crossed waterlogged fields to meet Ben at 9am. 50 miles away Preston had been dry and sunny with no hint of rain so Ben was appropriately dressed in trainers and shorts and was not expecting the deluge that awaited him in Hawes. But rain had not been forecast so undaunted by the grey, unfavourable conditions, which we were quite sure would soon improve, we left the car in a puddle-filled carpark and set off for Great Shunner Fell. We passed Hardrow Force, England's highest waterfall, but didn't stop. We had enough water falling on us to want to see more. I was fully clad in waterproofs, but my small day sack was not waterproof and was soon soaked. Ben had only a light cagoule which covered most of his top and shorts, but did nothing for his legs. Water trickled from his thinning hair and dripped from his beard. Ankle-deep in liquid peat, our feet squelching in sodden socks, we made a sorry looking pair.

The summit of Great Shunner, one of the Pennine's highest points is attained by five miles of ascent which, if Wainwright is to be believed, can be 'delectable' in fine weather and 'not a step too long'. I wouldn't know. We never saw it. The whole peaty surface was a sea of water. If it were not for the firm, grey trail of flagstones which replaced the old peaty path, it would have been impassable and it is doubtful whether we should have even found the summit as the cloud layer was so low and dense. Shivering, drenched and dripping, we munched soggy sandwiches huddled on the leeward side of the summit cairn at 2,340ft. The only half-wits abroad we thought—until a group of lads materialised like ghosts out of the impene-trable mist just yards away. We had been completely unaware they were approaching.

Relying on the old saying 'Rain before seven, fine before eleven' we were still confident it would clear up. From time to time the cloud layer lifted slightly giving rise to dramatic atmospheric scenes with enticing glimpses of sunlight. All just enough to raise our hopes but never coming to anything. The rain never ceased in intensity and the sun never managed to break through. In the charming hamlet of Thwaite some cyclists poked their heads out of a café to enquire if it had stopped raining. Then shaking their heads and muttering that only lunatics walked in such weather, disappeared back inside. If they had witnessed us round the corner photographing the reflection of one of Ben's passions, a Victorian letter box, in a traffic mirror on a concealed entrance, they would have thought their comments well founded.

It was the sort of day a walker hopes to avoid and was certainly not the sort of weather to be fell-walking alone. If it were not for Ben's company, I would not have gone. I would have sat the day out in the tent or visited one of Hawes' several attractions. If I had felt impelled to walk, I would have taken a low level road route. As it was, in spite of the appalling conditions we both actually enjoyed the walk. Yes! It was cold. We were both soaked. Even wearing waterproofs rain of that nature gets into every nook and cranny. But we had some laughs along the way and enjoyed each other's company. In a way, the weather made the day all the more memorable though Ben constantly reminded me that he "would not normally have dreamt of walking in such weather" and that I was "highly honoured to have his company."

As walking days go, 12 miles was fairly short for both of us and by the middle of the afternoon we were sat on a damp bench in Keld waiting for a taxi. Not surprisingly, apart from the lads on Great Shunner Fell, we had met no other walkers and back in Hawes, judging by the number of people crowding the various tourist attractions, most sensible humans had plumped for a much more comfortable activity. The taxi driver, an enterprising young man who managed to fit in a one-man taxi service while at the same time working on his father's farm, dropped us in the still puddle-bound carpark, just yards from a working ropewalk. Here, visitors may freely enter and watch ropemaking in progress, in the expectation that they will then part with their money in the extensive gift shop. It was the ideal place to drip dry and warm up. All types of rope are made there from conventional stuff thick as a man's arm made by traditional methods, to modern hi-tech climbing ropes manufactured automatically on intricate machines whirring away behind glass safety screens. We parted with just a little of our money before driving back to Preston.

At Hawes it had rained for 21 hours. All day Ben had been gleefully rubbing his hands congratulating himself on the fact that he would not have to water their large garden and two greenhouses. On our return we found that Preston had not seen a single drop of rain. It had remained as fine and sunny as when he left that morning!

## *Spares and repairs and expensive noodles*

I really needed a break. Apart from the fact that practically everything was now wet and needed drying out, I had not had a day off for 15 days and there were several things I needed to do, the most urgent being to get my rucksack repaired. Over the last week the stitching of one of the shoulder straps had begun to pull apart. I worried constantly that it might suddenly give way completely and in addition I was obliged to keep re-adjusting the tension as it pulled further apart. Only an industrial machine was capable of effecting a good repair. I also had to replace a pair of leggings. I had washed my only pair at Horton in Ribblesdale, put them in the Land Rover overnight to dry and promptly forgotten them. They were now back in Wales and I had no spare warm trousers. They were essential as my leg wear was carefully planned to meet every eventuality. Shorts for hot weather; windproof fast drying walking trousers with endless pockets for normal and general wear; shell-suit pants for cold weather; leggings to wear under anything if it was really cold, to double as night-wear if required and as spares if everything else was wet.

The local town came up trumps. Replacement leggings were a bargain at the first shop I tried and after a few enquiries, we found a tailoress who repaired the rucksack on the spot for free. During the after-noon I washed my sleeping bag, dried my tent and boots and earned my keep picking black and white currants for Ben's home-made wine. Then, unsuitably attired, we rounded off the day with a meal at a swanky Chinese restaurant. The most expensive noodles in three months.

Returning to Keld, it was difficult to believe we'd sat shivering on a bench in such miserably wet conditions two days before. The weather now was bright and dry, though not as hot as when Helen and I had camped there two years previously during our Coast to Coast walk. Keld is the half way stage and we camped beside the River Swale in weather so boiling that Helen, her friend Lydia and two other young walkers had gone swim-ming in the river below Wainwath Falls. They had no swimsuits but swam in T-shirts and shorts and softened their feet so much they all got blisters the next day.

My feet were still in good shape. My West Country blister had long since healed and I'd had no further trouble. Years ago I'd asked a chiropodist friend what was the best way to deal with blisters. "Don't get them" was his reply. "Don't wash your feet. The worst thing walkers can do is find a stream, take off their socks and give their feet a good soak. If you must wash them—have a quick shower. Don't soak in a bath." It was good advice. Perhaps not to be taken too literally but I heeded his word. The soles of my feet were like leather. I showered quickly, always changed into clean socks and light trainers as soon as I reached my destination and tried to avoid getting my feet wet at all other times. At the slightest hint of rubbing, I slapped a length of adhesive fabric strapping tape right across the affected area and left it there until it fell off of its own accord. And I swear by sheep's wool—a tip I picked up from an octogenarian walker. It's free—available in fields nationwide, full of lanolin and perfect for stuffing down the socks if a boot begins to chafe.

## A cosy evening

Keld is no more than a cluster of houses at the head of Swaledale. The many tiny stone barns and the surrounding patchwork of fields, enclosed by drystone walls, are typical of this particular dale. You can stand on a hill and count 30 or more barns without turning round, most of them in good repair and still in use. No-one had ever heard of Keld until long distance walking was invented. Now the Coast to Coast and the Pennine Way cross here and have really put it on the map.

Waving goodbye to Ben, I set off for Tan Hill using the road instead of the official Pennine Way as everywhere was now so wet underfoot. Coal used to be mined at Tan Hill but the only remaining habitation is the Tan Hill Inn. At 1,732ft. it's the highest inn in Britain and is licensed for marriages. Walkers have been known to swap their cagoules and boots for wedding finery, get married and then continue along the Pennine Way for their honeymoon. It's a desolate spot by any standards. People who have never been to any part of the Pennines can have no idea of their scale. Mention Britain's mountains and most people think of Wales or Scotland, but the massive chunk of high country running up the centre of England is longer than the whole length of Wales and is as wild as many a Scottish Glen. Standing at Tan Hill on a clear day, with nothing but bare desolate hills stretching in each direction as far as you can see, you get some idea of their size.

I was apprehensive about the next five miles as it involved crossing Sleightholm Moor, a flat featureless peat bog, which after rain Wainwright likens unto 'walking in Oxtail soup'. Some walkers had already warned me to take care, as one man that morning had already gone in up to his hips. Passing walkers had come to the rescue and heaved him out but he was, apparently, "in one hell of a mess." Just out for the day and clad in shorts, he had no change of clothing and was returning home by train, which must have been an embarrassing experience. For some reason through this trickiest bit of bog there are no safe, boring flagstone paths. You are left to find your own way though the mire. And, as everyone chooses their own route, there is no distinct path. I would have been happier with a companion and was glad to get over safely.

After this the countryside became more attractive. Hilly, with rushing becks and heather moors. We were now in County Durham and back into limestone country and one of the most fascinating features that day was God's Bridge, in the valley of the River Greta. Here the relatively small river has eroded a passage through the limestone forming a natural bridge which has been used for centuries. Nearby a busy trunk road is crossed in safety by the more modern aid of a pedestrian underpass.

That night I borrowed another husband! My intention had been to stay at a campsite in Baldersdale, but the onset of rain coinciding with my arrival at Clove Hill Camping Barn caused me to make a snap decision to stay there instead—if they had room. A practical decision. I didn't want to get my dry tent wet again. As I signed in at the back door of the farm a voice from behind said "I know you. You're the lady going to John O'Groats." It was a man Helen and I had seen several times and dubbed 'The Big Blacks man," from the logo on his T-shirt. We were the only occupants of the barn and while the farmer lit the woodburner, we made ourselves at home and got to know each other better. "What is this Big Blacks T-Shirt anyway?" I asked and was embarrassed to learn that the 'Big Blacks' were my own Black Mountains. Keith, a teacher from Northampton was a keen challenge walker and had stayed in a neighbouring village several times while taking part in the Big Blacks Challenge. He knew my area well and we spent a cosy evening in the unaccustomed comfort of armchairs, chatting and feeding logs into the fiery depths of the stove, while his underpants and my socks kept company as they dried by the heat of the fire.

As Keith had ordered a meal, it would have been churlish to sit in a corner eating noodles, so I ordered too. It was enormous. Steak for Keith. Mushroom flan for me. "I don't have another steak" the farmer's wife apologised. Both were served with prodigious quantities of carrots, cauliflower cheese and potatoes. Far more than we could eat and brought out to the barn, beautifully served as if we were at a high class restaurant. When the generous helping of apple pie and custard was brought out we eyed it with misgivings. We were both so full, neither of is could eat it. I couldn't bear to see it go to waste and transferred mine to my own dish to eat later for supper. I could see Keith thought this mercenary, but he was staying in accommodation every night and didn't have to rely on what food he carried. I might not have the chance of a pudding like that for a long time.

All the facilities were in redundant farm buildings and taking a shower was an experience in itself. Each 'mod con' was in a converted but still recognisable cattle stall. Undeniably rustic but clean and warm. The sleeping arrangements too could only be described as 'simple'. Wall-to-wall mattresses, camp-beds and settee cushions on the loft floor. Access was up an open staircase from the dining area. Warmth amply provided from the woodburner below. Keith diplomatically gave me first choice of bed and then slept at the opposite end himself. That is my story anyway and the version I stick to!

I have to admit, the idea of Youth Hostels has never appealed to me, mainly because I could never contemplate sharing dormitories and kitchens with so many other people. The original idea of cheap and basic overnight accommodation for the young and adventurous seems to have been lost. These days many are fully booked by people who arrive by car and expect meals provided and as one walker remarked, the word 'Youth', ought to be removed from the name. He reckoned at 30 he was usually the youngest. Most hostellers were more like 50 plus. The camping barn system is much more down to earth. A sturdy trestle table serves for meals. An area is set aside for cooking on your own campstove, with a few basics like teabags and electric kettle sometimes being provided. Furnishings are minimal. Cost is low. Popular walking areas are providing more and more of this type of accommodation. The Coast to Coast Walk has a network of barns along its whole length and another network is being set up on Exmoor and Dartmoor. This was the first time I had used one and I was impressed. I would certainly consider making more use of them in future.

*Only one million two hundred thousand more steps to take!*
Baldersdale is the home of Hannah Hauxwell, that remarkable elderly lady who found fame when the BBC 'discovered' her living alone in spartan conditions on her isolated hill farm. They omitted to say that the Pennine Way goes right through the fields of her farm, Low Birk Hatt, passing the house and never mentioned the fact that her 'isolation' was interrupted by about 50 walkers a day. Nor did they mention that there are several other farms within half a mile or so and that her farm is only just off a good metalled lane. Several people observed that it was nowhere near as isolated as they expected and to me, compared with home, it wasn't isolated at all.

Hannah no longer lives there and the farmhouse has been sold and modernised, but the fields, flowery meads unadulterated by inorganic fertilizers and chemical sprays, are now a nature reserve known as Hannah's Meadows.

Keith, being a challenge walker and carrying only a small light pack, was a fast walker. He left shortly before me and was soon miles ahead. Occasionally I would catch a glimpse of him, almost out of sight, but it was reassuring. There was a difficult stretch of fieldwork over which almost everybody seemed to have trouble. If I could see him I knew I was right, or else we were both on the wrong track. With a choice of paths, stiles and gates, everyone seemed to have a different idea as to which was the correct route and it was not unusual to find someone you had already seen marching off confidently ahead, returning and admitting that they didn't think they were right.

Middleton in Teesdale, an attractive village with lime trees growing along the road flanking the green, was reached by lunchtime and seemed to be the meeting place of every Pennine Way walker so far encountered. I could hardly believe this. Having lost a day at Hawes I never thought to see any of them again, but it seemed many had taken a day off, mainly because of the rain. As I crossed over the Tees, I bumped into the Australians, who stopped to say "G'day". Over lunch in a café I chatted to the two Manchester school teachers and later encountered other familiar faces in the Post Office and supermarket. As I left, the eight Guided Tour walkers emerged from the same café I had patronised earlier and struck up a conversation.

I remained in their company for the rest of the day. A gentle pleasing walk for some eight miles along the River Tees where time and distance passed quickly with congenial companions. I walked mainly with Ron and Maureen, a couple from Essex, but also in turn with most of the others. The tour, I learnt, was fairly flexible and could be joined on a weekly basis. Only four were doing the whole length over three weeks, the others doing just a week. The eldest, a 77 year old gentleman from Edinburgh had done one week the previous year and was finishing off the final lap the next year. David, a balding Oxford professor in white baseball cap and trendy all terrain sports sandals, worked out that I had only one million, two hundred thousand more paces to take to John O'Groats. Put like that, it sounded an awful lot of walking.

Along the banks of the Tees, the flowers were breathtaking—by far the most varied and colourful since the clifftops and hedgerows of

Cornwall. A natural herbaceous border. The yellows of ladies bedstraw, bog asphodel and various compositae made sunny splashes amongst purple vetches, betony and hardheads. Fragrant orchids perfumed the air; dainty pansies peeped from sunny banks beside waterfalls. Everywhere juniper bushes tall as a man flanked the path and hung over rocks. There are few places in Britain where juniper grows in its natural state and the unobservant may well mistake them for gorse bushes. Much of the area is a Nature Reserve. A botanist's paradise. Plants grow in Teesdale that grow nowhere else and I would dearly have loved a day crawling round with a flora and hand lens. This was one place I would definitely come back to in the future, and of all the areas I had seen on the walk this was somewhere I regarded, on a scale of points out of ten, as a most definite ten.

If you are neither geologist, botanist nor walking addict and simply like to drive out in the car for a picnic, then Teesdale is equally well known for its waterfalls. At Low Force and High Force the walking party guide allowed official photo-stops where we joined the snap-happy day-outers who had paid an extortionate carpark fee on the other side other the river, to stand and gaze at what we were seeing for free.

The River Tees must be counted one of England's most beautiful rivers. The waterfalls though not of great height, cascade over the rocks providing scenes fit to grace any calendar, birthday card or jigsaw puzzle. Low Force, a series of white frothy waterslides is the prettier but as its name suggests has little height, whilst further upstream the water at High Force plunges 70ft. into a deep dark pool with a roar that can be heard long before it is seen. We duly waited our turn to get to the fore of a small promontory, the only point to get a really good photograph, hopefully excluding the heads and sun hats of other spectators.

Later I joined the group in their afternoon break, my provisions being supplemented by generous donations of an apple and crisps. We took group photographs for the holiday album and one of the party, hearing that I was already booked for a fundraising talk when I returned home, donated five pounds for our Church Restoration Fund. At Longden Beck, a sign on the bridge read 'EDALE 149 - KIRK YETHOLM 121'—still a long way to go, even for those doing the Pennine Way, and for me, a long way to the most important milestone of my journey—the Scottish Border.

My companions turned off for the Youth Hostel and I continued up the Tees alone to a more or less wild campsite at a small hill farm. It didn't look a very prosperous farm, but the farmer's wife was welcoming and provided simple meals and snacks in a tiny, shabby living room. She made me a cup of tea and poured one for herself, then as the place was quite isolated with no public phone, let me use hers. Throughout the walk I used a BT Chargecard. In places like this it was indispensable. I never had to worry about having the correct change, and enough of it and didn't feel guilty about having to use someone's private phone, if the need arose. From the itemised bills when it was all over, I was able to see exactly what it had cost—£104. Not bad for making a call practically every night, from one end of Britain to the other.

### Pennine gems

Camping was permitted anywhere in the pastures bordering the river where three other tents, occupied by a Dutch couple and two pairs of German boys, were already tucked into sheltered nooks behind a wall and below the banks of a river terrace. There was nowhere to wash and the toilet, in a shed in the farmyard, could have been better. Paper, a light and a lock on the door would have been appreciated, but at 75p I was not complaining. On some sites I had paid two or three pounds for just as little. With the weather deteriorating and a heavy mist creeping down from the hills the temperature fell rapidly. I put my tent up close to a wall, had my supper and went to bed.

The next 12 miles were through wild country and as was my practise in isolated and potentially hazardous areas, I set off early the next morning, to be ahead of the crowd. A safety precaution I considered essential for a lone walker. These were the upper reaches of the Tees. The river flows fast and wide in a narrow valley through high craggy fell country and the Way, which was by no means indicated by a path, followed the north bank. The opposite bank was a military 'no go' area. Strategically placed notices warned that it was a Danger Zone. On the steep rocky slopes, wild, shrubby potentillas grew alongside more juniper bushes. Upper Teesdale is a Nature Reserve of international importance with plants so rare they are collectively known as the Teesdale Assemblage. Many I had never seen before—tiny Alchemillas and Euphrasias, yellow mountain saxifrage and minute white milkworts—and I lamented the lack of a flora and hand lens, the latter being so small that I could easily have carried it in my pocket. If only I had thought to take it. I was so frustrated at not being able to make the best use of a great opportunity.

After about half an hour the gentle drizzle of dawn became a cloudburst. But it was not particularly cold and the exertion of walking kept me warm. I didn't bother with waterproofs, just draped the jacket over my shoulders and rucksack and allowed the rest to get wet. The path, or lack of it, involved hazardous scrambling along the bottom of steep craggy screes where huge boulders blocked the way along the river. No mean feat while carrying a cumbersome weight on your back. In the rain the rocks were treacherously slippery and as much work was done with the hands and knees as feet. By the time I reached the largest and most dramatic of the Tees waterfalls the rain was torrential, sheeting down like the very waterfall itself and blotting out the tops of the fells ahead.

Cauldron Snout is certainly the most impressive waterfall I have ever seen and was on this occasion not lacking in water. Not a waterfall of the type that tips over a cliff and plunges unhindered into the depths below, but an impressive torrent of creamy foam as the infant Tees crashes 200ft. down a steep rocky gully in a boiling, peat-stained fury, creating its own mist-hung atmosphere. There is no fixed path to the top. The walker is left to clamber up the rocks best he can, soaked in spray and conscious of the fact that one false move could result in a disaster. The reward at the top is a view back down the 450ft. long cataract as awesome as the one from the bottom—and a not so rewarding view of the monstrous dam of Cow Green Reservoir.

When the Pennine Way was first planned no reservoir existed and much controversy surrounded its construction as the site was of such great scientific importance. But against all opposition the march of progress overruled. Some of the unique plantlife was saved by removing whole pastures to a new site, but the famous loop of the Tees at Cow Green known as the Wheel has gone forever, submerged in the waters of the reservoir. A sight never to be enjoyed again by walkers.

The downpour at Cauldron Snout seemed to have emptied the clouds of their load. From then on the weather steadily improved. My wet clothes dried quickly and I enjoyed an idyllic walk along an old miners' track which meandered across lonely silent moors for about six miles. Scenery very much like Dartmoor I thought. Wild yet not unblemished by man. More Military Zone warning signs and spoil heaps, and near a cairn an untidy clutter of spoil heaps and derelict buildings—the desolate remains of the mines.

A man with a dog caught up and overtook. Doing a circular walk, he said, but the dog had lost his collar, so he had to return by the same route and see if he could find it. The dog, a black labrador happily unaware he was the cause of a thwarted walk, bounded along finding interesting sniffs and sloshed carelessly through all the muddiest puddles. I caught up with them again at High Cup Nick where we both stopped for drinks and gazed at the stunning view. He offered to take my photograph with my camera before retracing his steps to Cow Green and his car, hopefully reuniting dog with collar on the way.

High Cup Nick is yet another spectacular geological feature. An outcrop of the Whinsill, formed of a hard grey volcanic rock which would be seen again on Hadrian's Wall. The 'Nick' itself is a deep cleft in the high rocky cliff face of the horseshoe shaped 'Cup' and below lies a perfect U-shaped glacial valley. To the west lay the Lake District—a panoramic view of the Cumbrian Hills with the air so clear after the rain that the best known summits could easily be identified. The path round the rim passes an isolated column of rock which is said to have been climbed by a local cobbler who proceeded to repair a pair of boots on the top.

By early afternoon I was in the fellside village of Dufton. Although I had seen no sign of anyone behind me all day, except the man with the dog, the others soon began to arrive. With my tent already erected I was in the process of pegging out my washing on a barbed wire fence when I was hailed by teachers Dave and Neil coming across the field. I thought this rather odd as I knew they had given up camping. Their gear was too heavy and they had sent it all back home and were now staying at pubs and youth hostels. However, they had just come to check up on me; to see if I had arrived OK, which I though was very thoughtful of them. This was typical of the camaraderie that builds up on a long walk, between people from all walks of life. Age, sex and status are irrelevant. A common aim makes everyone equal and there is certain security in knowing that everyone is looking out for everyone else.

Later everyone congregated at the Post Office which doubled as the village store and was doing a fast trade in cold drinks, ice creams, yoghurts and chocolate. One way and another with a range of accommodation, several campsites and a Youth Hostel there were Pennine Wayfarers liberally distributed all round the village. The guided tour walkers were staying overnight, but the next day was Saturday, their change over day. They were being taken to Penrith to meet their new guide and anyone joining them for the coming week. I thought it was unlikely I would see them again. In fact, Ron and Maureen who I promised to send a postcard to from John O'Groats, phoned when I eventually returned home and have kept in touch ever since. They and the other couple who were on the guided tour, have since embarked on the End to End themselves, filling in all the bits they had not already done before.

I was completely captivated by the lovely North Pennine villages. Picturebook villages. Stone cottages clustered round tree-lined greens, nestling against a backcloth of outstandingly beautiful hill country. In Dufton, whose name means that it was the farm where the doves were kept to provide meat for local nobility, the houses were of local red sandstone, which gave the place a warm, rosy glow. Many houses had dates and initials and sometimes names carved over the doorway—a tradition in these parts; the initials or names being those of the original owners. An elaborate nineteenth century sandstone drinking fountain which dominates the village green was originally erected as a horse trough by the London Lead Mining Company. They were also responsible for the extra houses that were built for the miners and for the development of Dufton's present layout.

Mature lime trees, heavy with flowers, bordered the green, their fragrance attracting many thousands of insects most of them bees. In the warmth of the late afternoon the sound of so many bees busily gathering nectar was incredible. I wandered round, took photographs, talked to other walkers and then joined the queue at the phone box to call home. Ever since the rain had departed the weather had been gorgeous and the day ended with a superb sunset. By then I was back at the tent cooking supper and just happened to turn round to find the sky every shade of pink and the western flanks of the Pennines bathed in an an almost unreal orange glow. I grabbed the camera. It was one of those satisfying moments when you are glad you are camping and not glued to a television in a comfortable guest house.

### High hills and strong winds

Delightful as the Pennine villages are, you are obliged to come down off the tops every night to get to them. And this means a long climb up again every morning. Alston, where most of us were going next day, was 21 miles away and meant an early start. I left at seven and walked for nine hours with hardly a break over very hilly terrain. To start with there was the four mile ascent back up onto ridge to the summit of Knock Fell. Not satisfied with one summit cairn, Knock Fell at 2,604ft. has several though only one has the distinction of a name, Knock Old Man. These are the highest hills of the Pennines and this was the first of the day, closely followed by Great Dun Fell at 2,780ft., Little Dun Fell, slightly lower and ultimately Cross Fell at nearly 3,000ft.

These hills are subject to a notorious local wind, the Helm Wind and it was blowing furiously up on the tops. A strong Easterly is caused by a combination of warm air rising on the lower ground to the west, a cold cloud cap sitting on the top of Cross Fell and the resultant turbulent air currents. From first thing Cross Fell had been shrouded in low cloud and once up on Knock Fell it was nearly impossible to stand in the fierce, bitterly cold wind. Looking back towards Dufton a steady stream of walkers were plodding doggedly upwards as the village divested itself of its overnight population. On the tops, weekend walkers were also about and on the summit of Great Dun Fell there were so many people I wondered where they could have come from so early in the day.

The fenced off summit is home to an extraordinary assortment of modern technology, including a massive white sphere which can be seen for miles around and is, I was given to understand, 'something to do with Global Warming.' It was certainly not very warm at that point on the globe and battling against the wind I was finding it difficult to keep my balance. The summit of Cross Fell was still obscured by cloud so I decided not to go up and contoured round the side instead, almost losing my way while making a sweeping detour round treacherous waterlogged moss beds. When at last I rejoined the track at an old lead mine I stopped for a cheese and biscuit break, the first stop in 10 miles. This old miners' track was popular with mountain bikers sweating and toiling over the rough uphill bits. I may be mistaken, but it always seems to me that mountain bikers carry their bikes as much as they ride them! I met several walkers heading south. One couple, prompted by my Offa's Dyke T-shirt, wanted to know if I had walked it and what I thought of it. They were preparing to walk Offa's Dyke the following week. Another couple toiling up a long hill as I was on the way down, stopped to ask the usual questions, discovered I was going further than the end of the Pennines and asked what make by boots were. One of them had a new pair of boots which he had 'broken in' before leaving Kirk Yetholm and which had fallen apart after four days. The soles were now held on with bright yellow insulating tape which he hoped would last until Edale. My Scarpa boots were ten years old and had done over 1,000 miles before having them resoled before the start of this walk. The boot equivalent of going round the clock and putting a new engine in your car. They were as comfortable as an old pair of slippers and I was confident they would see me to the end.

Before continuing on their way these walkers passed on the useful tip that an enquiry at the Post Office in Garrigil would produce an excellent pot of tea. On arrival I found that the Post Office, though not a café, provided this service for walkers and I was soon in possession of a tray with a large brown tea pot, mug, milk and sugar which I took out on the Green. There, under under a lime tree humming with bees, I ate a rhubarb crumble and drank three mugs of tea—enough to recharge the batteries for the last 4 miles along the flowery banks of the South Tyne until I reached Alston.

Alston claims to be the highest market town in Britain and the old town, reached by steep cobbled streets, is built on the side of a hill. My first impressions were not favourable. The unusual assortment of shops, one selling nothing but old bottles, seemed dowdy and run down. There place seemed unkempt—as if its residents had given up bothering, and the only campsite was not camper friendly. It was essentially a caravan park with no special area for tents which were subsequently squeezed between or behind the caravans. As more and more people arrived for the weekend, more and more tents were packed into these small spaces. The static vans were owner occupied and regularly visited judging by the tidy little gardens around them. Youngsters hurtled round on bikes and played football dangerously near the tents. The Dutch couple who camped at Longden Beck were already there but the Australians came and looked and left. These two were lovely guys, both businessmen, extending a working visit by three weeks to do the walk. Most of the time they camped, but they were very fussy about where they stayed and always checked out everything meticulously before booking in. In this case they turned up their noses and went off to try and find a Bed and Breakfast. I couldn't say that I blamed them. Apart from everything else it would have been no good getting caught short in the middle of the night. The toilets were a five minute hike away, beneath a garage on the main road. The entrance was through what appeared to be two huge tanks, which looked as if they might at one time have been undergound fuel storage tanks. A corridor led into what should have been well appointed toilets, shower rooms and laundry, except that none of it was very clean and half of it didn't work.

I spent the evening in town, making up for lack of food during the day with a huge fish supper in a café. Afterwards I browsed round St. Augustine's Church, fascinated by its restored and working seventeenth century clock whose mechanism is operated by stone weights slung from the ceiling. The size of the church reflects the fact that 100 years ago, Alston was the centre of an important lead mining area with a population of 10,000. Today it has dwindled to 1,400 and even the once busy railway line from Haltwhistle is now only a tourist attraction. The South Tynedale

Narrow Gauge Railway, now a preserved steam railway, runs just a mile or two hauling its freight of holidaymakers on a short journey alongside the river.

Returning to Alston on the way home in September, it seemed more attractive. The tourists had vanished. Everywhere looked cleaner and fresher and with time to explore the town's hidden corners, I saw it in a different light and appreciated its many old buildings.

My impression on the way up were perhaps clouded by fatigue — and compounded by a bad night. Firstly I discovered I'd lost my torch! And I was annoyed because I always packed and unpacked in the same order and with the utmost care. Everything had its place in the rucksack and in my tent, the layout was always the same. Sleeping bag in centre, all my food on one side, torch, maps, first aid, books and camera on the other side. Boots, rucksack and cooking utensils went in the porch. The torch, a small and expensive one was a birthday present from Michael before I left. I could not think how I could possibly have lost it. The only time I opened the rucksack was when I stopped at the old lead mines. It must have fallen from a side pocket while searching for a knife to cut the cheese. What was more annoying, if I had discovered my loss earlier I could have replaced it as there was a shop in Alston with the same torch in the window on offer at a sale price. Tomorrow, Sunday, the shop would be closed. The second reason was I just could not sleep. It was an incredibly noisy site. Weekenders continued to arrive until dark. Practically every caravan was having a late evening barbecue. The children never seemed to go to bed and grown ups sat around laughing and drinking. Music and TV commercials blasted from the open windows of caravans and a well amplified Country and Western Night taking place at the local Football Club went on into the small hours. The Australians were wise to choose B and B!

The following morning I overslept. By the time I left the youth-hostellers were on the move and for a time a group off us walked together. One of these was Tony who I hadn't met before even though he'd started on the same day. He had the worst sunburn I have ever seen. On his first day he wore shorts for the first time that summer and never noticed how burnt he was getting. The calves of his legs were purple and black where blisters the size of the palm of your hand had begun to dry and heal. Apart from shorts, he had only heavy denim jeans which were far too hot for the weather we were having and although he was in agony from their chafing, he dared not bare his legs again to more sun. For all that, he was amazingly cheerful and regaled us with details of a close encounter with a bull the

113

previous day. "He was a big fellow," he said. "I would describe him, but there's a lady present." One of the others piped up, "It's OK. She isn't a lady. She's a farmer's wife. She won't mind."

I also met for the first time Alicia, a music teacher from Essex. She too had left Edale on the same day and was staying at youth hostels. She said she had heard I was an End to Ender and had been hoping to meet me so we walked together for a while before parting to go at our own pace.

It was not an easy day. The path followed the valley of the South Tyne all the way to Greenhead and our first acquaintance with Hadrian's Wall. It was seemingly straight forward, but in practical terms involved precise map reading, and a lot of concentration. It was hilly and much too warm. The flowers along the Tyne were glorious; masses of great burnet, hare-bells and ladies bedstraw. Curlew, snipe and oystercatchers were every-where—and other creatures if you kept your eyes open. A grass snake slithered off the path where it had been soaking up the sun. A magnificent hare grazed alone in a field and a small herd of deer, disturbed by my approach, vanished into the undergrowth. I came across Keith stretched out in the heather, sun hat over his face, snoozing and warned him I had just seen a snake. He said he was too hot to care. For a while we walked together, but he always walked faster than me and after a companionable interlude he left me behind. The heat was exceptional. When I rested Alicia caught up again and we finished the remaining miles together.

Another walker tipped me off about a short cut to a campsite which he highly recommended. And he was right. The appropriately named Roam 'n' Rest was a lovely site; small, friendly, beautifully maintained and despite being full, was not noisy. There were children in the play area but they were well behaved and under control. I was given a super pitch between two unoccupied caravans, reasonably private and sheltered from anything that might arrive in the way of severe weather. Several people spoke to me including three French students. I had only noodles for supper, but eaten in the warm evening sun in such pleasant surroundings I could not have wished for anything more.

Less than a quarter of a mile away was the Youth Hostel. Just about everyone who wasn't camping was staying there and most of them were queuing outside the phone box. This was always a general meeting place. Most people were in the habit of ringing wives, husbands, girlfriends and children nightly and it was not unusual for me to have to make two trips to the phone, or cut short a call to let someone else have a turn and phone back later. Several times that day we had heard the distant, tantalising sound of an icecream van's chimes. Now, rather belatedly, it put in an appearance and those of us waiting to phone sat on a wall eating icecreams, watching in astonishment a flock of harlequin ducks waddling up the main road, heedless of traffic.

### Exploring Hadrian's Wall

Each time I phoned, Michael gave me the current weather forecast. That night he advised "Find a camping barn and stay put!" The forecast for the next few days was terrible. Heavy rain and thunderstorms were expected. Almost everyone was planning to have day off on the Wall to explore its associated milecastles and forts and visit the various museums. Carlisle was only 30 miles away and the Hadrian's Wall Bus provides a service both east and west. The purchase of a day ticket enabled you to travel backwards and forwards along the wall as much as you like. I decided that if it did turn wet, I would go into Carlisle for the day.

The rain didn't materialise and I left at 9am with the intention of going to Vindolanda which everyone said this was a 'must'. Outside the Youth Hostel Alicia was boarding the bus for Once Brewed Youth Hostel, doing what a lot of walkers were doing—taking a bus to their next destination and dropping off their rucksacks leaving them free to walk the wall unburdened. I made a quick change of plan and decided to do the same—leave my pack and tent at the next site, visit Vindolanda and then walk back along the wall later.

Twice Brewed and Once Brewed are next door to each other on the main road which runs parallel to the Wall roughly on the line of the vallum. There is a logical reason for the two names. Twice Brewed is the name of an inn where in the eighteenth century General Wade, on his way to construct military roads in Scotland, found the beer too weak for his taste and ordered it to be twice brewed. Once Brewed is the Youth Hostel a few hundred yards away, where, so they story goes, they make only tea, which is brewed once.

Alighting from the bus at the Youth Hostel, I popped into the Tourist Information Centre next door to find out the time of the next bus to Vindolanda. I calculated I had time to walk the half a mile to the campsite at Twice Brewed, put the tent up and get back before the bus left—if I was quick. I did a route march down the road, booked in, threw the tent up, whilst other bleary-eyed campers were just considering taking theirs down—it was still only 10 o'clock—and was back at the bus stop by 10.30. The girl in the Information Centre had taken great pains to point out that I must be sure to get on the right bus as two left at 10.30 from the same place, one for Vindolanda, the other for Carlisle. About 30 people were waiting at the bus stop, all strangers but all talking to each other and all except me, going to Carlisle. The Vindolanda bus arrived first, barely stopped, cruised slowly by and disappeared down the road before I had collected my wits. It didn't matter that much. It wasn't far and I started to walk. Ten minutes later the bus came back up the road. It was the same driver that had brought us from Greenhead earlier. He stopped and called out of the window "Were you waiting with that crowd at the bus stop?" I said I was. He apologised most profusely, insisted on turning the bus round, and took me to Vindolanda for nothing.

Anyone visiting Hadrian's Wall should certainly put Vindolanda at the top of their list of places to see. Not only is it a superb open air museum, with a lot of visible remains of the third century fort but there are also reconstructions of other Roman buildings. You can stand in a Roman shop or kitchen and listen to a young housewife describing her daily life and what she is going to cook for her husband's supper, or admire the temple of the Water Nymphs, with its lavishly painted internal walls. Excavations have established seven successive forts constructed one on top of another, each sealed with soil and turf before the next was built and thus preserving in each oxygen free layer an extraordinary wealth of information. Over 2,000 written documents have been found, revealing a great deal about the lives of the people who lived and worked there.

Three hours passed quickly. I could have stayed longer but there was still the Wall to walk. It was again hot and humid and though the promised thunderstorms had not arrived there was a thundery feel to the air. On the way back to Once Brewed I was offered a lift which I gladly accepted. It saved me time and gave me more time on the Wall.

From Once Brewed it's only a short walk to the Wall which is probably patrolled today by more feet than it was in Roman times. Walking on the Wall itself is now prohibited owing to the amount of damage and erosion taking place. The most badly affected sections are being restored. There were walkers everywhere and not just the Pennine Way brigade. There were also those doing the Wall Walk, the 80 odd miles from the Solway Firth to the North Sea near Newcastle upon Tyne, and a considerable number of tourists. Hadrian's Wall seemed particularly popular with Italians and French.

Once on the Wall it wasn't long before I began meeting those walkers who were just arriving from Greenhead. Most of them were going to visit

*About to set off from Land's End with my dog Fern
who walked almost 50 miles in two days*

*Walking with Robin and Helen along Offa's Dyke Path in 1993
(Photo courtesy of the late John Beardsmore)*

*Unusual signs spotted* en route, *in Cornwall,
the Yorkshire Dales and Scotland*

*My tent, one of the lightest on the market is too small for me
to sit up inside*

*On the summit of The Cloud on the boundary between
Cheshire and Staffordshire*

*Taking a break in Teesdale with Maureen and David, two of the walkers
on a Pennine Way Guided Walking Holiday
(Photo courtesy of Ron Parkes)*

*Pen y Ghent, near Horton in Ribblesdale with Helen striding out along a typical section of Pennine paving*

*The Three Brethren. A popular viewpoint on the Southern Upland Way where each cairn stands in a different parish*

*People encountered* en route
*Top: The French students who invited me to share their supper of noodles*
*Bottom left: A cyclist on the Great Glen Cycle Way with her dog*
*Bottom right: Eric the Viking guards the entrance to the craft village at*
*John O'Groats*

*A sighting of 'Nessie'*

*Top: The view of Ben Nevis from my campsite near Fort William*
*Bottom: Seals on the beaches of the Moray Firth near Brora*

*Top: Michael and Land Rover ready to accompany me*
*through the final miles of Caithness*
*Bottom left: My arrival at John O'Groats*
*Bottom right: With Janet Street-Porter by the Stone of Revenge*
*on the hill above my home*

Vindolanda, except Keith who came along much later as I was sitting propped up against a rock eating a second lunch. He had been to visit the Military Museum at Greenhead. It was hot, sultry and thundery and we sat chatting for some time, neither of us in a hurry to move. Anyone who thinks walking Hadrian's Wall is a nice easy stroll is sadly mistaken. The Romans chose every inch of high and difficult ground and built their wall on top. Walking it is a strenuous occupation; steep scrambles onto craggy ridges and descents down eroded slippery slopes. Steps have been constructed on badly eroded areas to save further wear, but these are still hard work in hot weather. Milecastles survive in various states from scant walls, looted in the past for their stone, to complete floor plans, but all bring to your attention how far you have walked.

There is a misconception by many people that Hadrian's Wall marks the boundary of Scotland, but at this point Scotland was still some three days walk away. Looking north over the Wall, which is only head height in most places, there is as far as you can see—nothing much. A vast, empty country of boggy moorland and rolling green pastures with barely a farm to be seen. On the distant horizon, darker shades of green mark the beginning of Wark and Keilder Forests. This is Northumberland. There were hardly any signs of life. No roads. No animals. The only ones I saw were horses; manes blowing in the breeze, heads stretched over the wall hopefully waiting for Wall trekkers to offer a word or titbit.

The sun was setting by the time I arrived back at Twice Brewed. I had walked as far as time permitted and then made my way back across the fields. My neighbours were a family with two children and a black poodle and not far away were the Australians, this site presumably having met with their approval. I now knew that they were from Canberra and that the one had run out of time. His flight back to Australia was already booked and he had to catch a bus to Newcastle next morning and return to London. John, the other, was carrying on alone.

In addition to my human neighbours there were peacocks and ducks. The ducks waddled from tent to tent looking for scraps and I had two very persistent muscovies practically inside the tent. I have a theory why so many campsites have peacocks. They are such noisy birds they wake everybody up really early, a sort of green alarm clock. I'm sure this is tactics on behalf of the site owners to get people up and on their way as soon as possible!

*Friends old and new*

Overnight there was a strong, blustery wind, but still no rain. Carlisle was still on the cards if it rained, but if it was dry at dawn, I would carry on to Bellingham. It was dry, but not for long. At 7.30 I was on the Wall walking along a high craggy outcrop of the Whin Sill at an altitude of 1,200ft. and shrouded in mist, when it started to drizzle. On rocky crags like this there is no Wall. There is no need. Sheer cliffs dropped down to a lough (lake) where a family of swans huddled on a small island. It was now far too dull to be worth bothering with photographs and I was glad I managed to get most of them taken the day before.

I was still meeting people who told me they had started on the same day and yet our paths hadn't crossed before. It seemed impossible after all this time. A family camping wild in the boggy wastes beyond the Wall were just breaking camp. But they hadn't come far. They had started the previous day from the Wall and were going to Kirk Yetholm accompanied by an indeterminate and bedraggled mongrel. The drizzle continued, occasionally becoming heavier, with visibility permanently poor and flies being a continual nuisance. A rough looking chap in shabby jeans with a deplorable rucksack and worn out boots asked in a strong Birmingham accent where I'd spent the night. He told me he'd slept in Wark Forest and said the deep carpet of pine needles was the most comfortable bed he'd ever slept on. I felt sorry for him—he was young, in his early 20s and looked as if he had little to his name and was making do with what equipment he had.

For miles every gate had crudely written notices pinned up advertising 'Tea and Snacks'. This service was being offered at a remote farm and seemed to be the holiday occupation of a boy and a girl of about 12 and 14. Orders were taken at the back door where, in a none too tidy kitchen, the boy was up to his elbows in a bowl of soapy water washing mugs and plates and the girl was making sandwiches on the draining board beside. It was a miserable morning and walkers are always hungry and thirsty. Everyone was turning in at the farm gate. Some were sheltering from the rain, sitting on upturned crates in the recently vacated cowshed. I chose to sit in the rain at a picnic table on the tiny grassy patch that served as a garden. I ordered jam and scones and a pot of tea. After some delay, the girl came out to say she couldn't find the scones, would I like fruit cake instead. When my order did arrive, it was all nicely laid out on a tray, with sugar in a stainless steel bowl—and she had managed to find the scones. Even the jam and butter were served in separate dishes. I was impressed.

The three French students arrived and shared my table. The ham sandwiches they ordered were made with the crusts of the loaf. These children wasted nothing. By the time I left there were at least ten other walkers keeping the enterprising pair busy and mother was probably somewhere in the background scratching round for extra cups and thawing out more bread.

This was the most exciting thing that happened in a day of dreary weather and dreary walking. There were forests from time to time and once a glimpse of deer, but little of interest and no outstanding scenery. We were all glad to reach Bellingham at the end of the day, but within minutes of my arrival it began to rain. I sought refuge in the Post Office, bought a padded envelope and packed up a parcel of maps, books and gifts to send home. The aromas drifting from a bakery tempted me to a delicious meat pie and a hardware store was able to furnish me with gas and a replacement torch.

Bellingham (pronounced Bellinjum) is a quaint old village and the farm with the campsite was in the village centre—just off the street and behind the shops. In torrential rain the tent went up in record time. The French students arrived and put their tents beside mine. We settled down to sit out the downpour. In a brief respite I made a dash for the supermarket where Alicia was also stocking up. The rest of my acquaintances were distributed round the village in various pubs, guest houses and the Youth Hostel.

The French students who had introduced themselves as Lauren, Agnes and Bertrande, were from Lyon and were all studying chemistry. They were such a charming group, always laughing, and so polite and friendly, both amongst themselves and to others. After completing the Pennine Way they were catching a bus to Glasgow to do the West Highland Way and then, from Fort William, were travelling to Mallaig for a week on Skye.

By 5pm, the rain had returned with a vengeance. As it is impossible to sit up in my tent, all I could do was lie on stomach and elbows and pass the time reading and writing, on this occasion consoling myself with cakes and hot chocolate. Two hours later, supper was a banquet. No noodles this time. Instead, a baker's meat pie, tinned potatoes, peas, mince and onion pie filling with gravy poured over it all, followed by tinned apricots and cream. The supermarket had gone to my head, or more correctly my belly. During another nearly dry interlude I nipped out to phone and met Keith with similar intentions.

The only other occupants of the site were two families in adjacent caravans who were either related or close friends. They were Geordies, with six children between them, all under the age of about nine—and I could not understand a word they said. They were constantly yelling at one or other of the children, none of whom took any notice. This would result in a good walloping followed by prolonged crying. All six were boys and despite the rain all, even the smallest, were kicking a football around, much encouraged by the two fathers. A football landed on the side of my tent several times, but no one told the children to keep away.

During the night the sound of rain lashing against the tent woke me several times. At 6 o'clock it was still raining and not worth getting up. When I did leave, the youth hostellers, always later than the campers, were turning out. Alicia walked out of the door as I passed and we spent most of the day together. She was the same age as me. We got on well, walked at the same pace and talked about everything under the sun. I learnt a lot about her and she about me. Quite a different experience to the conversations held with the men, which was usually based on walking, camping or the events of the day and was rarely what one might describe as 'deep and meaningful'. She was an interesting woman who walked for the most part in a flowery skirt and always wore a pretty headscarf. We talked about religion and our beliefs and she divulged without saying too much that she lived in a religious community. This, coupled with the fact that officially she had only two weeks holiday and had obtained special permission to extend her holiday by a few days to complete the walk (which I thought strange as teachers have about six weeks holiday), gave me the impression she might be a nun. Oddly enough we never learnt each others surnames or swapped addresses, which was a pity. I would have liked to have kept in touch with her.

This was the day of the Keilder Forest; 17 miles of upland moorland and monotonous conifers, the highlight of the day being a difficult calving at a farm passed first thing in the morning. When I'd passed, the vet, farmer, his wife and another man had been attaching ropes to the protruding feet in an effort to deliver the calf, which was upside down and wrong way round. As the day wore on, reports filtered through, from other walkers seeing different stages of the proceedings, that the calf was alive and well, was soon standing and suckling and suffered no ill effects from his traumatic arrival.

It was a day for passing the time in the company of others. Alicia introduced me to Frank, a lean, fit looking fellow from Middlesborough—

yet another man not met before. We met up with others from time to time—all at the end of the day aiming for Bryness. Australian John joined us for a while but was so tall and had such long legs we could not keep up with him. I enjoyed my conversations with him, enthralled by tales of backpacking in Australia and his experiences with the local Bushwalking Club. So far that year he had flown round the world five times and was, he said, fed up with everybody saying he should be used to hot weather. When he arrived back in Canberra it would be mid-winter and his wife had been reporting temperatures of minus six degrees.

Several miles of featureless, heatherclad moorland at the start of the day was uninspiring and not improved by the dull, hazy weather. Views if any were invisible. The path was ill defined and, worst of all, the flies were intolerable. Everyone was accompanied by their own personal swarm, buzzing annoyingly around the head. Most of us donned waterproofs, put up hoods and pulled the drawstring tightly round our necks, using maps as swatters to flap the persistent pests from our faces.

I was unimpressed with Keilder Forest even if it is the largest man made forest in Northern Europe. You don't even get to see the only interesting bit, the vast reservoir of Keilder Water. If you like cycling or pony trekking along forest trails it is probably fine, but to walk through for several hours it is unbelievably dull. And the forest tracks were the worst I have ever come across, constructed of large, sharp-edged, flinty hardcore; awkward and uncomfortable to walk on and chopping the soles of your boots to pieces.

The main topic of conversation now was of getting to the end. For many, the next day was the last. The distance between Byrness and Kirk Yetholm is, depending on which guide book you refer to, around 28 miles. We were all fighting fit by now, but it was still a long way over challenging terrain and there was a tiny problem. The route is entirely through the wild, remote hills of the Cheviots, and is the longest section of the Pennine Way with absolutely nothing *en route*. No farms or villages to offer sustenance, no accommodation, in fact no habitation at all. Just endless hills, mostly over 1,400ft. and many well over 2,000ft. You need to have plenty of confidence in your navigational skills and in your ability to make the distance and should have some contingency plans for bad weather or any other mishaps. Youth hostellers and Bed and Breakfast people have little option but to walk the entire distance in a day. Campers have the freedom of stopping where they like and making two days of it.

There are advantages and disadvantages for both. Most of us had taken about 17 days for the whole path, but many walkers have only a bare fortnight's holiday, so a day gained here, albeit a long one, is for them a necessity. Alicia was one who officially had only two weeks holiday but had been allowed the extra two or three days if she needed them. Other people already had coach or train tickets booked and sometimes needed another whole day to travel back to the other end of the country. Several had relations driving up to collect them and these were being pressed into providing pack carrying services to enable their hard pressed loved ones to do their long day without rucksacks. These unsuspecting souls were ending up with a car full of the packs belonging to all their loved one's mates as well.

For those camping wild, the absence of food and even water means all has to be carried. Not too great a problem if it is cool, but more of an issue if it happens to be hot. But at least campers don't have to get up early. Those doing the whole distance, especially if they were hoping to catch the last bus at 6 o'clock, planned on leaving at 4am. Everyone was well aware of what they were up against. We all knew it was going to be an arduous and challenging walk and people were anxiously comparing notes, checking what time others were starting, trying to find out where the best wild camping was likely to be, deciding how much extra water to carry and wondering what the weather would be like. One or two were worried about their compass reading abilities if it should be foggy. Others had been told, and were quite confident, that you couldn't get lost as long as you stuck religiously to the border fence.

The coniferous monotony of Keilder Forest finally comes to an end on the banks of the River Rede. And after hours of sweat and toil Byrness is no big deal; a tiny hamlet on the Edinburgh to Newcastle road, consisting of a church, hotel, filling station and not much else. The bulk of Byrness's population lives half a mile along the road in the community of forestry houses, but even some of the these are now surplus to requirements. Several have been taken over by the Y.H.A. and most of my acquaintances were spending the night there. The few of us who camped were on a large campsite a good mile short of the village at a place with the unlikely name of Cottonshopeburnfoot, which holds the record for the longest name in England. There is no shop at Byrness, but the campsite sold tins of beans, canned drinks and milk, which helped eke out the food being carried for the next day.

When the French students arrived they put up their tent close by and Lauren, the most fluent English speaker of the three came over and invited me to supper. I accepted and told her I would be expecting the best French cuisine, but all I got was a communal pan of noodles, exactly the same as I would have cooked for myself. I enjoyed their company. They were happy-go-lucky and full of fun. I never heard a cross word or the hint of any disagreement. The midges were biting well that night and I lit my mosquito coil outside their tent while we sat round talking and dipping into the noodles. It seemed they were supposed to be walking in Norway, but last minute travelling problems had caused them to change to Britain. Norway was now planned for next year. It was a pity they were taking a bus to the start of the West Highland Way; I would have enjoyed their company through the Lowlands. By the time I reached the start they would be finishing at Fort William. They were not even walking the last day across the Cheviots either, as Lauren had twisted her ankle. Rather than risk such a long trek, they were catching a bus to Jedburgh.

It was late by the time I walked the mile to the only call box outside the Youth Hostel, and it was a spooky walking back through the woods in the dark. For some reason I slept badly and didn't wake until after 7. Lauren, Agnes and Bertrande were eating breakfast at a picnic table when I went to say goodbye, and with charming powers of persuasion, insisted I had another breakfast with them—to help them eat their spare muesli so they didn't have to carry it. It was difficult to refuse, though I had already eaten a whole large can of beans. We swapped addresses and they invited me, should I ever go to France, to look them up and they would give me accommodation. The sort of thing often promised during short term holiday friendships. I never expected to hear from them again so it was a lovely surprise to receive a card from them at Christmas.

### The Scottish Border

It was fortunate I was not hoping to complete the 28 miles in one day as I would never have done it. I was fraught with delays.When I eventually left, it was to get no further than the filling station on the main road whose café I had learnt sold canned and bottled drinks, cakes and biscuits. As the only source of water between Byrness and Kirk Yetholm was going to be oozing out of a bog, I wanted some bottles of spring water to supplement my normal daily litre. As it was now nearly 10am, I was astonished to find Alicia sitting there drinking coffee. She was supposed to be making an early start to ensure she caught the bus to Edinburgh which connected with her train back down south. Unfortunately, she had fallen on the steep climb up Byrness Hill and had

123

injured her leg so badly that she knew she would not be able to complete such an arduous day. She had managed to get herself back down and was now waiting for the bus to Jedburgh, from where she could make the shorter walk by road to Kirk Yetholm. She had no option but to go there because someone had already taken her rucksack by car and she had no means of letting them know she had injured herself.

This sort of disaster can upset all your plans. I resolved never to be parted from my rucksack again when a similar thing had happened in the Lake District during our Coast to Coast Walk. Helen and I had sent our packs ahead one day on the packhorse service, only to get lost in poor weather in a thunderstorm. By the time we had discovered we were not where we should have been, pinpointed where we actually were and retraced our steps back to square one, we had lost four hours and there was no way we were ever going to get to the same place as the rucksacks before midnight. With visions of search parties being called out it was only by the extreme kindness of someone whose door we knocked on in desperation when we came down off the hills that all ended well. This generous lady drove some way to fetch our rucksacks and let us camp on her lawn. As long as you have your rucksack, you have all your necessities should illness, bad weather, injury or exhaustion overtake you and though conditions may not be ideal, you can set up camp anywhere.

The Jedburgh bus was going to be pretty full as apart from Alicia and the French students, the family with the hiking mongrel had also decided not to do the last day. As far as I could make out, everyone else had successfully made an early start and I was the last to leave. I bought two bottles of water, said goodbye to Alicia and began the steep climb to the top of the hill.

The ascent was straight up; almost vertical and with no proper path. A hands and knees scramble up rocky crags. Hard going and in places I was unable to get up the rocks with the rucksack on my back and had to take it off and haul it up behind me. It was more of a rock climb than a walk and I was not at all surprised that Alicia had fallen. I prayed it wouldn't happen to me and was relieved to reach the top in one piece. Looking back, Keilder Forest was a dark sea of conifers as far as the southern horizon. Ahead stretched the lonely miles of the Cheviots. After about four miles the Scottish Border was reached, an ordinary post and wire stock fence wending a tortuous course almost all the way to Kirk Yetholm. The rumours were right. Follow the fence and you can't go wrong.

I don't think I have ever seen such hilly hills. The terrain is good underfoot, but the hills are desolate and open to the elements. In bad weather there would be no chance of finding shelter. In every direction dozens of peaks all much the same height, look to the uninitiated almost identical, despite the fact that according to the map each is a named Hill, Law or Knowe. I wondered what distinguished a Law from a Knowe and why some were just plain hills? In between, deep valleys and hundreds of tumbling burns gave the landscape the appearance of a crumpled quilt — and the Pennine Way progresses upward and onward always with the border fence to the left.

The Romans seemed to like the Cheviots, though heaven knows why. In the middle of nowhere, in the valley of the River Coquet, a Roman camp, one of several, is clearly discernible and Dere Street, a Roman road is followed for a little way. I dread to think what the poor soldiers who were stationed here thought of these hills. A posting here was probably used as some sort of a threat against young troublemakers. The ultimate deterrent. Behave or we'll send you up the Cheviots!

### A wild and lonely night

Except for occasional glimpses of the two Dutch boys, recognisable by their broad rimmed hats, on the summit of some distant hill, I saw no-one else until at around 4pm when I met a runner. Wearing only shorts and a running vest, but carrying a rucksack he was running from Coast to Coast and had left Holy Island (about 25 miles away) that morning. He was intending spending the night at Bellingham, a further 20 miles, and was finishing somewhere in the Lake District. As he pounded up to me, barely stopping, he said "Are you Shirley? There's an Australian with a beard been asking after you." John was apparently two miles ahead and had been trying to find out if I was in front of him or behind. I found this reassuring as he was camping wild too and there was a possibility that I might catch him up. An hour later I found the Dutch boys setting up camp on a patch of short springy turf on an exposed hilltop. I was tempted to join them but it looked a bit too windswept for my liking. Finding a wild camp site is not as easy as you might imagine. In all these hundreds of acres of hills there were actually few places suitable for camping. Most areas were too exposed. The ground is either too wet and boggy, thick with heather and totally unsuitable or covered with tall, coarse, tussocky grass, equally unsuitable. Patches of short grass are almost non-existent and likely spots have usually some other detrimental

125

feature, like being too much of a slope, uneven and bumpy or full of stones.

A mile further on John had found a level dry patch just large enough for his tent—which was like mine, a very tiny one. I stopped to talk to him and told him I was going to try and push on a few more miles to the mountain refuge hut, which I had been told was warm and cosy. It most likely was, but I never found out. Within a matter of half a mile from John it suddenly began to spot with rain and there were ominous rumbles of thunder. With the ground still rising, getting increasingly boggy and the Cheviot summit ahead, it was time to call it a day, get the tent up and myself in the dry before the heavens opened. Luckily there was a tent-sized patch of none too dry ground right beside the path. More peat than turf, but it looked suitable and I quickly put up the tent.

There's a wonderfully smug feeling about beating the rain; of being warm and dry in your tent before the onset of a storm. Warm and content, I enjoyed a huge meal of meat pie, noodles and beans followed by chocolate cake and custard while it thundered and blew outside. Then did the washing up—a simple matter of pushing everything out of the tent and leaving the rain to do the rest. Despite the soggy sponge-like ground, there was no useable water. What I had with me had to last not only overnight, but the whole of the next day, so economies were essential.

This was my highest campsite. Not only of the Pennines, but of the whole of Britain. I can be absolutely certain of the altitude and the precise spot as King Seat trig point at 1,743ft. was the other side of the border fence in Scotland. Me, my tent and the Pennine Way were just yards away in England. The rain, in the manner of thunderstorms, was heavy and shortlived, though thunder continued to rumble around the hills all evening. The sun came out again giving views better than there had been all day. At 2,676ft. the Cheviot summit was silhouetted clearly against the still angry looking, orange-tinted sky. I swished the rainwater round the dishes and pans in rain water and left them to dry, then wandered on along the path where fruiting cloudberries grew in large numbers. These grow only at high altitude in the north and are related to blackberries. The fruit is red, similar to an unripe blackberry, but the plant, unlike the rampant, prickly bramble, is less than six inches tall, thornless and consists of one single stem topped by a berry. It's a plant already suffering the effects of global warming. In recent years the seed, dependant on very low winter temperatures, has not been receiving enough cold weather, resulting in poor germination and poor regeneration. Warmer winters may well cause the cloudberry to decline and disappear.

Rain and thunder returned overnight, waking me several times. By dawn it had passed over and the hills were blanketed in thick mist. Low cloud sat on the summit of the Cheviot so it was as well I had seen and photographed it the previous evening. In true survival fashion I had left every suitable container out overnight and accumulated enough water to rinse my cereal dish, have an extra cup of tea and top up my water supply for the day. John appeared on the scene just as I finished packing and we walked together. He told me he had strolled along last night to see where I was and was relieved to find I was only just over the brow of the hill from him. He had been concerned that I might still have tried to get to the mountain refuge hut and got caught in the storm. He too had collected enough water for an extra breakfast cuppa.

After so much rain the ground was a morass of brown peaty slush. If it were not for the wooden walkways laid in the worst areas it would have been impassable. Pools of peat-stained water fringed with cottongrass might have looked attractive on a nice sunny day, but in thick mist with only a wooden duckboard between you and it, looked murky and uncomfortably close.

At the foot of the final ascent to the Cheviot Summit, the Pennine Way turns away to continue its alliance with the border. Those determined or with enough spare energy to go to the top, must make a detour of over a mile. John was going up and left his pack hidden amongst the peat hags so that he could make a quick dash for the top. It was still so misty I could see no point at all in this exercise. For all the effort it was doubtful whether you would even see the summit let alone any view. I had done Great Shunner in the mist and rain and not seen it, missed Cross Fell because of strong winds and was quite happy to give the Cheviot a miss as well!

I bid him farewell and turned off to follow the border fence through a wild and desolate area of yet more swampy peat. This gave way eventually to craggy cairn topped hills followed by steep rocky descents, with the ground becoming firmer and drier and the weather steadily improving. The mist, when it went, lifted suddenly, revealing blue skies, fair weather clouds and sunshine. The Mountain Refuge, a substantially built hut on a high prominence came into view and I popped in to see what I had missed last night. Inside a family of four were sitting drinking coffee. I was greeted with "You must be Shirley!" Somewhat taken aback at this I said I was and expressed surprise that they knew my name. "Oh they're all talking about you. We heard about you in the Youth Hostel in Kirk Yetholm" they said. We sat talking and they told me they were going to Edale. Not many people do it this way round. They were only the third lot I had met going south. The two children were barely teenagers so it would be quite an achievement if they made it all the way.

Although the distance to Kirk Yetholm from my wild camp was not great, it was still very much mountain walking and tough going. I laboured up to the top of the Schil and ground to a halt, relieved that at nearly 2,000ft. this was the last hill of the Pennine Way and the last in England. The view was stupendous. The difference between north and south dramatic. Behind, lay the Cheviot and the empty hills of yesterday; ahead an unobstructed unsurpassable panorama of Scotland. I sat on the craggy boulder strewn summit, not unlike a Dartmoor Tor, eating cheese rolls whilst fending off a persistent ewe and her twin lambs and savouring the scene. It was an exquisite moment—standing between two nations, having walked the length of one and about to walk the length of the other. I was jubilant and felt like jumping up and down and shouting wildly with joy. On reflection I was more exhilarated then than on reaching John O'Groats—perhaps because there was still more to look forward to while at John O'Groats there was only anti-climax.

The path descended steeply from the Schil and at last, 700 miles from Land's End, a stile in the border fence gave access to Scotland. For the last few miles there was a choice of paths but I could see no point in further hard work and had already decided on the easy, low level route. For the Pennine Way walker this was the end of the road. For me, the end of England. It was August 9th. I had a month of Scotland ahead and over 400 miles still to go and I was feeling on top of the world.

# 9

# Scotland the Lonely

## The Southern Uplands

The elation of not only completing the Pennine Way, an achievement in itself, but of crossing the border into Scotland and knowing I had walked the full length of England was short lived.

As I made my way those last few miles, pausing briefly for a rest on the banks of the Halter Burn, there was a deep sense of regret that the camaraderie of my fellow Pennine Way walkers was about to cease. For them, it was a time of celebration, in fact Dave and Neil, who had been picked up by Land Rover somewhere in the middle of the Cheviots and off-roaded to a farmhouse Bed and Breakfast, had already asked me if I would join them in the pub that evening for a final get-together and celebratory drink. But for me it was just the end of Stage Three. It would take me another four weeks to walk the length of Scotland and for much of the time I would be completely alone.

My spirits took a further plunge as I realised that having started early and John having gone off to make his bid to conquer the Cheviot, I was the first of the day to arrive. There was no-one to even share a coffee and mull over the morning's walk. I hovered outside a café peering through the window at the pristine white-clothed tables and smartly dressed middle-aged couples genteelly sipping coffee. It didn't look particularly walker friendly and I decided that this middle-aged lady was too scruffy and unwashed to venture inside. Had I been with a fellow walker I would have dumped my pack, removed my boots, and made short work of a large pot of tea, ignoring the looks of distaste.

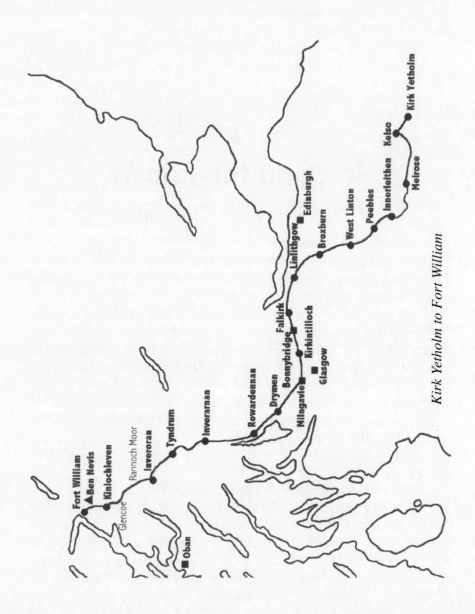

*Kirk Yetholm to Fort William*

The Border Hotel appeared to be closed and lifeless. Having sent my copy of Wainwright home to save weight I couldn't claim my free drink anyway, so I didn't even bother to try the door and pressed on down the road to find the campsite. There I could make as much tea as I wanted in the comfort of my tent. A bus passed by, made a circuit of the village and departed again, something I passingly noted but without realising its significance.

My morale dropped even lower when I reached the campsite and discovered that this, the only site in Kirk Yetholm, would in fact not take tents. I was astounded! In a village which must be known to every serious walker in Britain at the end of the toughest and probably the best known long distance path, there is nowhere to camp. The handbook says there is; the Ordnance Survey map indicates that there is; the sign at the campsite clearly says not. I was told that caravanners complained about walkers getting up early and making a noise—and that some walkers left without paying. Scarcely an insurmountable problem—allocate a separate area for the early rising campers, request quiet between certain hours and take payment on arrival. Other sites do this without any problem.

Two local ladies confirmed that there was nowhere else and suggested camping wild by the river. A grey haired village elder, who couldn't understand why people wanted to walk hundreds of miles for pleasure anyway, told me that there was a campsite about a mile and a half out of the village on the road to Kelso. I thanked him and decided that would be my last option. I would try and find accommodation in the village, then I could still meet up with the 'gang' in the evening. Meanwhile, I needed cash and lunch in that order and went off in search of the Post Office and shop.

It was obviously my unlucky day and the last straw was about to be dropped on the backpacker's back. It was lunchtime. Both Post Office and shop were closed for an hour. I had no better luck trying to find Bed and Breakfast. In such a small place choice was limited and everywhere I tried was fully booked. "It's Friday." I was told. "If you'd been here last night we could have fitted you in, but Friday is the day new walkers arrive for the weekend—sorry!" Looking for consolation, I thought I'd phone home. There might just be someone available to listen to my tale of woe and cheer me up. But the phone box was out of order.

I was rapidly coming to the conclusion I hated Kirk Yetholm and reluctantly accepted that I would have to miss the evening's get-together and catch the bus into Kelso, but when I checked the timetable; the bus had gone. It was the one I had seen earlier and there was not another until late afternoon. Despondently I sat on a bench on the village green, parched and hungry, counting the minutes until the shop opened. As soon as the Post Office opened I withdrew enough cash to last a few days then, with money burning a hole in my pocket, I hotfooted it down the road to the shop where my expectations of lunch were severely dashed by the limited stocks available. There was not even any bread. I bought a few items to keep me going and a milkshake which I drank outside the shop—and left by the road to Kelso feeling thoroughly deflated.

### A night of luxury

Thankfully, the campsite I had been told about did exist, but was a Caravan Club 'members only' site. I had camped at these before, one warden telling me that he would never turn a backpacker away, so I approached with high hopes. Repeated knocking at the door of the owner's bungalow bought no reply and I concluded they were out at work. Near one of the caravans a youngish man was playing cricket with his two children. I asked him if he thought a camper would be accepted. He thought not and said the owners would probably be away all day but I was welcome to wait there with them if I wanted. Meanwhile, his wife offered me a plastic chair and a mug of tea, both of which I gratefully accepted. They were a lovely family with a tiny new baby daughter just a few weeks old, experiencing her first caravan holiday and apparently being as good as gold. She certainly looked a picture of health and contentment suckling her mother as we drank tea in the blazing afternoon sun.

The couple told me there was a Bed and Breakfast sign further along the road and that the house looked "very nice". This instantly appealed to me. It wasn't far to go and take a look and I could return to the campsite if I had no joy. I thanked them for their hospitality and took to the road once again, but when I saw the house my heart dropped. It was indeed "very nice"—a large, well appointed country house in its own substantial grounds, loch included, and the thought flashed through my mind, "I'm never going to be able to afford this." But time was getting on. It was late afternoon. I was getting desperate. Two children playing croquet on a neglected lawn asked what I wanted and ran off to ring the elaborate doorbell. This summoned a smiling lady who I liked immediately. She didn't seem at all perturbed at the sight of a none too clean backpacker on her doorstep and "Yes" she did have a room. From the expression on some people's faces I'm sure they say no, even when they do have a vacancy.

The price to my surprise (and relief) was no more than a small guest house I had tried in Kirk Yetholm and I was invited in and shown upstairs. I queried my boots and offered to take them off, but the suggestion was waved aside with a cursory "They look clean enough to me." I was led through a spacious hall and up a magnificent polished staircase, the walls hung with splendid oil paintings. Faces of ancestors and sea-going gentlemen stared down at me probably wondering what vagrant was tramping through their ancestral home.

My room was palatial—or seemed so after the confines of a tent. High ceiling, two enormous sash windows overlooking the gardens and Loch Yetholm and a bed of such dimensions it almost needed a ladder. It reminded me of the bed I had as a child which had two layers of deep straw mattresses and a feather mattress on top. If you fell out it was a long way to fall. I wouldn't have wanted to fall out of this one either. It was so high I could almost have pitched my tent underneath! The *en suite* bathroom was almost as big as the bedroom where every comfort was provided: easy chairs, a TV—I'd almost forgotten what a TV was, writing table and magazines and, best of all, tea and coffee making equipment with biscuits and a little tin of sweets.

Left to 'sort myself out' I could have wept with relief. I unpacked everything. The first time my rucksack had been completely emptied since I had it repaired. I laid everything out on the bedroom floor and found a few long lost items. It's surprisingly easy to lose things in the depths of a rucksack. Helen lost a packet of toffees for almost a week and I once lost my hairbrush for four days! Having done this long overdue chore I bathed and went downstairs to cook tea. I had already established that an evening meal was not provided. Most people drive into nearby Kelso. I asked if I could take my stove out into the garden to cook something, but Mrs. Hurst wouldn't hear of it and invited me into her kitchen to use the Aga. She supplemented my noodles with soup and delicious homemade bread, and sat and talked, pleased I think to have company. She said I was welcome to do any washing—an offer I couldn't refuse. Having done that, I wandered down to the loch before returning to the house where I discovered a piano in the drawing room. I missed music, especially the piano. I don't play well but I do love to sit down for a couple of hours in an evening and play for my own pleasure. I had piano withdrawal symptoms. I hadn't heard any decent music for weeks, my middle-aged tastes not being catered for by loud modern blasts from pubs or passing cars. After rifling through the limited range of music available I retired to my room to see what was on Television—something I did not miss. All I could find was a programme in Gaelic with rather a poor picture. I gave up and lay on the floor reading. The two armchairs didn't seem appropriate after weeks without such comforts!

It seemed strange sleeping in a bed too, especially such a high one. I had no alarm clock and was afraid I wouldn't wake up in time for breakfast. Most mornings I was awakened by the birds at first light. I hoped the habit would continue. The large sash windows of my room were open at the bottom with a net curtain pinned across the open gap to keep out the flies and midges. They overlooked the garden and a group of tall trees. Perhaps a passing rook would wake me.

There was no need to have worried. I was awake in plenty of time and the superb cooked breakfast was a treat after weeks of Alpen. Mrs. Hurst had hinted that she preferred staggered sittings as it made life easier for her, so I ate at a highly polished round table, in isolated splendour in the lovely dining room. I had almost finished when the only other guests put in an appearance. They were a Sheffield couple breaking their journey north for a birdwatching holiday. Conversation inevitably came round to where I was going and they urged me to go to the Orkneys when I reached John O'Groats. "They are not a bit what people expect and you will be sure to love it there" I was told. It was an appealing idea and would certainly be the 'icing on the cake'—a splendid way to end the walk.

### Border Country

After the disappointments of the previous day I decided, as I was already nearly there, to take the bus to Kelso and shorten the journey to Melrose where I knew there was a campsite. When I stopped to think about it I could hardly believe that many of the things I was now doing without a second thought were all things that in the past would have scared me silly. Bed and Breakfast—at a posh place too—and by myself. I could never have done that five years before. Now here I was calmly deciding to take a bus and not only considering but looking forward to taking a ferry to the Orkneys. Never in my life had I felt so self-confident. A whole new world was opening up—one which I could enjoy to the full instead of forcing myself to go somewhere and pretend to enjoy it.

The bus stop was at the end of the lane. By the time it arrived it was raining and I was glad to be sitting comfortably in the dry. I had been warned by Mrs. Hurst that the bus would actually be travelling from Kelso and not to it. It would go to Kirk Yetholm and return to Kelso by a circular route. In order to go about three miles, I would travel seven. The only

134

person to board the bus at Kirk Yetholm was Frank—the man introduced by Alicia during the latter part of the walk. I think he was as pleased to see me as I was to see him—a last tenuous hold on three weeks of fellowship and pleasure. The journey passed quickly as we exchanged news. Apparently I didn't miss out on the celebratory evening after all. It turned out to be a non-event. The atmosphere in the pub was far from jolly so the few walkers of our group that remained had adjourned to the café and celebrated over coffee instead of beer.

I was pleased to have Frank's company and as it was still raining on our arrival at Kelso and he had some time to wait for the Edinburgh bus, we too adjourned to a café. Being a gentleman he insisted on paying for the coffee and donated his unwanted sachets of sugar to top up my supplies. Frank said he would love to tackle Land's End to John O'Groats, but could never get enough time off work. It would have to be when he retired. This is the problem most people have. Many walkers I talked to said they would dearly love to do it and one of the first things they ask is "How have you managed to get the time off work?" I felt so guilty that I had selfishly taken the time to be able to do it while I was still fit. The 'time factor' was probably the reason why most Pennine Way walkers fell into the categories of either students, teachers or the retired—all people with long holidays or unlimited time.

Frank was amazed that I was doing it so cheaply. My estimate for the trip was £1 per mile, based on fairly accurate costings of previous long distance walks. I expected that it would cost me something over £1,000. He had spent £700 for the three weeks of the Pennine Way, though this included staying full board each night and taking pub meals during the day.

We parted at the bus station. His destination Edinburgh, mine Melrose. It was a dank and miserable morning. The countryside was now much gentler, the Cheviots getting more distant with every mile and the three peaks of the Eildon Hills coming ever closer. As the day wore on the weather steadily improved and by mid-afternoon was gloriously sunny. Melrose, famous for its abbey and ever popular with tourists, was overflowing with visitors, mostly from overseas and many of them American. The abbey is the main attraction but there are others: the Motor Museum, a Teddy Bear museum, Roman Exhibition, and Priorwood Gardens. Far too much for me to see in my limited time. There was time to visit the abbey and its museum and I was able to spend the long, warm, sunny evening exploring the rest of the town. Now that I no longer had the companionship of other walkers I was glad to be somewhere with plenty to see and do. There is a limit to how you can amuse yourself in a tiny tent for several long hours, especially if the weather is inclement.

The campsite was located in the town itself, on the edge of a football pitch beside a school. It was filled to capacity and was well camped with the grass in the tent area almost non-existent. I had to remind myself I was in Scotland. It could well have been the continent as apart from the warden, I think I was the only British person there. There were many nationalities: French, Dutch, German, Belgian and Italian, all with cars or motorbikes. Two cyclists arrived with heavily laden panniers, but I was the only backpacker.

Normally at warden controlled sites like this a deposit of £2-3 is made for the keys to the toilet and washing facilities. This is refundable on leaving and as most wardens aren't generally available until around 8 o'clock this can be a bit of a nuisance if you want to make an early start. As the distance to Innerleithen was over 20 miles I needed a long day and was up by 5am. Fortunately the procedure here was unusual in that no deposit was required and I was able to creep out of the site just after 6.30, leaving everyone else still in dreamland.

My route for the entire day was to be via the Southern Upland Way which I rejoined on the edge of the town on the banks of the Tweed at Chain Bridge. Here, the monks of the abbey used to cross the river on stilts to reach their fruit-growing plots on the other side—an area still known as Gattonside, a corruption of Gardenside. The footbridge in use today is the toll bridge erected much later for the passage of vehicles.

Although my route to the start of the West Highland Way was already worked out, I had spotted a book in the Tourist Information Office entitled 'From the Pennines to the Highlands' by Hamish Brown. This appeared to be an almost identical route and as well as being a guide book, included many points of interest. Although it was not exactly pocket-size and was extra weight to carry, I bought it anyway as I thought it would make the route easier to follow and more enjoyable.

For the moment, the Southern Upland Way was far from upland, and followed the banks of the Tweed to Galashiels. Once of lesser importance, Galashiels is Melrose's larger, industrial neighbour and a thriving manufacturing town best known, perhaps, as the home of the Barbour jacket. My fears of getting lost in the maze of industrial estates and sprawling suburbia were groundless—the path was a smooth black ribbon of tarmac, a cycleway along a disused railway line. It was still early. The only other signs of life were the odd jogger and dogs out for early morning 'walkies'. I stopped to have a word with a Sheltie before leaving the town—again along the banks of the Tweed. My dogs were something else I missed and I missed them desperately. All my life I've had dogs around and never walk at home without canine company. Whenever I met a dog I had to stop and speak to it and if, as now, it happened to be the same breed as mine it made my day. The brief exchange helped to fill a gaping hole in my life.

Just outside Galashiels is Sir Walter Scott's imposing residence, Abbotsford, built on the site of the former Cartleyhole Farm whose name was presumably not imposing enough for the new house. I would have liked to visit it, but if I had stopped to look at everything on my route progress would have been very slow indeed. As I left the river behind it began to rain, rapidly becoming heavy. Fortuitously, I was near woods and able to shelter through the worst of the downpour before setting off across more open country. I had thought that perhaps I would be lonely walking by myself after the company of the past four weeks, but so much concentration was needed following the map and guide book that there really wasn't time to be lonely. The Southern Upland Way is adequately signposted, but there is not an arrow at every turn as there is on some long distance trails. Even a brief lapse in attention can result in a long hike in the wrong direction at the cost of much time and energy, so I took no risks and if in doubt double checked and closely scrutinised the map.

The departure from the River Tweed at Abbotsford was not to be final. I crossed it again before climbing steeply through monotonous forest for over two miles. It seemed never-ending but eventually gave way to open moorland at the summit cairns of the Three Brethren. It had been an arduous morning's walk. I was exhausted and relieved not only to arrive at the top, but to leave the forest behind and find myself in the type of country I really enjoy. One thing I had discovered about myself over the past weeks was that my strength was in my stamina. I think this is often where a woman has an advantage over a man. What we lack in muscle power we make up for in other ways. This may be sheer determination or a will to succeed or, as in my case, a bit of both coupled with the fact that I can keep going for hours whatever the difficulties, allowing my body to set its own pace and mentally programmed to not give in.

The Three Brethern are stone cairns marking the boundaries of three counties, each cairn being a different shape. From there the rolling hills of Ettrick Forest stretched as far as the eye could see and lived up to my expectations of the Southern Uplands. It was all very reminiscent of the

Pennines—but where were the walkers? The Southern Upland Way is the oldest of the Scottish long distance paths but is nowhere near as popular as the much shorter West Highland Way. It was Sunday and the only people encountered had been a party of ramblers easily identified by their sheer numbers, small brightly coloured day packs and thermos flasks. Later I passed two, obviously serious, long distance walkers, equally recognisable by the size of their rucksacks. One of these, a woman my own age, was eager to talk. The hoops of her dome tent had broken and she had been sleeping for days without it, until last night when the midges had got the better of her. The only Bed and Breakfast she could find had cost £25 and was not even *en suite*. Now she was considering giving up, even though she was nearing the end. The midges were intolerable and owing to the proximity to Edinburgh, accommodation was proving difficult to find and was too expensive—the Edinburgh Festival was in full swing. In the Melrose Information Office I had overheard people being booked 40 miles out from Edinburgh. I commiserated and went on my way thankful that I had taken the advice of my local outdoor centre to stick to a ridge tent. I only had two short poles and if either broke any suitable stick would have held the tent up.

The path across the hills was a clearly defined old Drove Road. I passed an engraved stone beside a tiny, muddy spring. This was the Cheese Well where in the past travellers placed small pieces of cheese, not in the spring, but nearby, to appease, the water spirits. The water looked undrinkable and I didn't have any cheese. I left nothing and hoped the water spirits were in a benign mood. Then I was back into yet more forest on the descent to Innerleithen. Traquair House, just outside Innerleithen, is Scotland's oldest inhabited house and reputedly visited by 26 monarchs. It was another place I would have liked to have visited—and another I had to miss. I found myself making mental notes of places I would visit next time I did the walk!

### St. Ronan's Wells and Smail's Printing Works

In sharp contrast to Melrose, Innerleithen seemed dowdy and run down, the town consisting of a main street flanked by small lock-up shops. By-passed by the tourists, it lacked the bright floral displays and trendy gift shops of its more popular neighbours, though behind the door of one ordinary looking shop was a surprise. From the outside Smail's Printing Works had the appearance of any other shop but inside was another world. To step through this door is to step back in time into the world of a small family run printworks, unchanged since the turn of the century. When I visited it the following morning I had a fascinating tour. All the guides had worked there in the past and were fully conversant with the various operations. I was the only visitor and had their undivided attention until a Dutch family arrived and I was asked to wait while they caught up with my tour. I sat outside by the waterwheel which once powered the entire works. The stream flowing under the wheel was apparently home to numerous eels. "We feed them on mints." I was told by one of the workers. When I observed that this must give the fish a funny flavour he laughed and said he meant mince not mints.

I found the most interesting department was the compositing room demonstrated by an amazingly dextrous and talented lady who told us she had trained for seven years to do this highly skilled work. It was astonishing to watch her deftly picking up miniscule letters without even looking at them. "It's all done by weight and feel" she said. She described in detail how a page was set up and with great patience let us all set up the type for a personal bookmark—mine read Land's End to John O'Groats.

The tour was worth every penny. The National Trust Shop offered a tempting range of items which I had to disregard as I could not afford to carry unnecessary weight. This was always a great incentive to save money. I had to think twice before buying anything.

Meanwhile, that evening, a chip shop was equally alluring and armed with a greasy parcel of sausage and chips I went in search of the campsite and found it eventually after trailing along endless streets of identical looking 40s style houses. It was a much bigger site than I would have expected of such a town, largely made up of static vans and with an excellent shop. Several acres along the banks of the river, (the Tweed again needless to say) were set-aside for camping. There was one solitary tent. Feeling lonely I plumped for company and pitched nearby in the hope there would be someone friendly to talk to. But the occupant, a cyclist with his hair tied in a pony tail, didn't seem the chatty type and spent the entire evening reading outside his tent without ever seeming to notice me.

To waste such a lovely evening would have been a crime. I washed my socks and trousers and pegged them on my guy ropes to dry, then strolled along the river bank. A disused railway line ran beside the river crossing it on a high stone bridge—a popular venue for small boys on bicycles and teenage lovers. An elderly couple walking dogs stopped to chat as I leaned over the bridge parapet looking for fish. During the previous January, they said, the river had flooded right up to the caravans. There had been fish swimming over the fields. The man was a retired farmhand and pointed to a cow alone in the next field. "See that cow," he said, "she belongs on the other side of the river. Everyday she comes over here and every night she goes back. None of the other cows ever bother to come over. She likes being on her own." I asked if it was possible to walk to Peebles along the river, but he assured me it wasn't. Although there was a path in places there was no public right of way all the way so it seemed I would be 'stuck with' the road. There was a good route recommended in Hamish Brown's book but I wanted to visit the museum first, and was looking for a shorter, faster way that would get me to Peebles in time to look round.

It was a long way back to town to make my nightly phone call. I was too tired to be bothered and went at 7 o'clock next morning instead— before taking down the tent. Then, making the most of having no pack, went to see St. Ronan's Wells. Surprisingly Innerleithen was at one time a Spa town, its waters being made famous by Sir Walter Scott who wrote a novel *St. Ronan's Wells*. The Wells and Victorian bottling plant, which is now a museum, were closed that early in the day, but the gardens ablaze with colourful bedding were open. I was able to partake of a glass of water from the tumblers provided at the original Victorian drinking fountain. As we discovered at Buxton, the water was not very nice. But there is a choice: either unpleasantly chlorinated or absolutely foul, sulphur flavoured, which smells and tastes of bad eggs. St. Ronan was a seventh century monk who is said to have taken the devil by his hind leg and slung him into the well, which is why the water tastes of sulphur.

### Peebles—a home town look-alike
The next morning dawned bright and clear with a cloudless blue sky, and by the end of the afternoon I was in Peebles. It was my first visit and I loved it. A busy, thriving town bustling with vitality. Broad streets with a mixture of essential and touristy shops and a large supermarket discreetly tucked away up a back street. I was struck by its similarity to home. A tall clock tower and ancient river bridge. Meadows along the river and the shapes of the surrounding hills. From a distance it was nostalgically an Abergavenny look-alike.

My main concern was to get my rucksack repaired again. The opposite shoulder strap to the one repaired earlier was now beginning to pull apart. An enquiry at a while-u-wait shoe menders established that they could repair it if I could bring it back empty before they closed at 5.30. As the campsite was on the outskirts of the town this involved a hike against the clock to reach it, book in, put the tent up, tip the contents of the rucksack out, then dash back self-consciously carrying the now floppily empty pack. The job of stitching was speedily accomplished and cost less than two pounds. A small price to pay for peace of mind. I had worried constantly that one day in the middle of nowhere I might find myself with a useless pack.

It was now August 12th, the height of the tourist season. All day it had been, indeed still was, extremely hot. The River Tweed was still with me only yards from the town centre, just behind the shops. At 97 miles it is one of Britain's longest rivers and is an SSSI from source to mouth with 16 different species of fish. At Peebles it is wide and shallow and on the broad stretch of grass along its banks every available bench was being put to good use by sunbathers and picnickers. The shingle beaches were thronged with children messing about in the water. Watchful parents lazed on the banks while their offspring threw stones, paddled and swam. People were practically treading on each other's heels along the riverside path leading upstream to Neidpath Castle.

The Tweed here is particularly scenic with scots pines and views of the castle which anyone with a camera cannot ignore. The castle was the location for the making of the film Robert the Bruce and although unoccupied and partially derelict, it is more intact than many castles and parts have been carefully restored. My visit was brief but worth the walk and I learnt a fact I never knew before—what a mural is, and it is not a picture; it is a room constructed within the depth of a wall. Neidpath has several fine examples.

The campsite was the largest I had used so far. Pitches were marked out with brown lines, sports field fashion and by evening they were filling up fast. As Michael was coming next day, I booked in for two nights.

The amenities included a TV room, Pool Room and Bar and while not wishing to partake of such amenities myself, it does keep the children occupied and saves quite so many footballs being kicked around the tents. The disadvantage of such a big site is a complete lack of privacy. Fine if you have a massive frame tent which you can get lost inside, but I felt quite out of place amongst the canvas palace community. All my activities had to be conducted outside the tent in full view of all.

### Respite from a heavy pack

Taking only the bare essentials and armed with Hamish Brown's book I set off next morning to enjoy a day's walking without a heavy rucksack. I was soon into an upland landscape of forests and hills. The route quite off the beaten track and unwaymarked. In fact most of the time there was not even the remotest trace of a path. But the book was so clear in its directions that I had no trouble at all finding my way and made no mistakes. Through wild, unpopulated hills, I saw no-one. It was incredibly peaceful—the silence only broken at times by the distant buzz of chainsaws as gangs of forestry workers cleared some of the extensive conifer plantations. Passing between a group of dilapidated farm buildings my attention was drawn by faint noises and a strong odour to several cages in an old shed. These I found to be occupied by creamy-coated ferrets with litters of young. The sight of a human presumably signified food as each cage became a tumultuous writhing mass of squeaking fur, swarming up and down the bars. Ferret farming? This had to be Scottish farm diversification.

Everywhere was carpeted with lush green ferns and luxuriant cushions of moss. Keeping my eyes open for interesting flora and fauna occupied much of my time and to my delight I was able to add clubmosses to my plant records. Prehistoric settlements and hill forts were a frequent feature. There seemed to be one on nearly every hill! I ate my lunch at 1,300ft. in the ramparts of an immense circular fortification from where the surrounding hills stretched endlessly in each direction. Scenery not unlike the Cheviots—extremely 'hilly' hills, some reaching 2,000ft. and providing challenging walking. Once the final summit of the day was reached a track lead down to the village of Romannobridge. The next obstacle, the Pentland Hills, lay prominently ahead.

Four miles of fast, un-rewarding road walking was unavoidable to reach West Linton, the only diversion a Dutch backpacker who I heard long before he came into view, striding along playing a harmonica. He asked if I had come from Peebles and which way I had come. But his understanding of English was limited and he had only a small scale road map. My advice could not have been very helpful. I hoped I made him understand that it was not a good idea to go the way I had come. With his map he would never have got there.

I was not expecting Michael until about 3 o'clock and as I entered West Linton it was just turned 2.30. Once again it was hot and sunny. I was dying for a drink. A tea room on the edge of the village green looked inviting with tables outside. Despite a fair scattering of residents exercising dogs and watching over children in the nearby play area, the café was empty save for the proprietor, a man about my own age. I ordered coffee and asked for a sandwich. He only sold cakes, but said he'd see what he could find in the fridge. He produced cheese and salad, chatted while he prepared it and established where I was going. Having been alone all day I was glad of someone to talk to. He had no other customers so I invited him sit outside with me while I looked out for Michael. He commented that a number of End to End walkers seemed to go through West Linton and wondered why? I showed him Hamish Brown's Book, which was new to him, and he produced another cup of coffee—on the house. When a local woman came in he immediately introduced me. "This lady's walked all the way from Land's End" which prompted an impassioned conversation about Cornwall—where she took her holidays every year.

Refreshed, I made an unhurried circuit of the village and phoned Michael to find he was still 60 miles away at Lockerbie. I wasn't bothered. There was plenty to occupy me. West Linton is a very attractive village, once an important stopping place for drovers on their way from northern Scotland to England. It lies at the foot of the Pentland Hills on the banks of the Lyne Water amidst beautiful countryside. I first made for the church-yard which had the most wonderful gravestones I have ever seen, grue-somely carved with skulls and crossbones, hourglasses and grim reapers. This was at one time Scotland's most notable centre for stone carving. The remains of an earlier church and the incumbent's house lie within the graveyard with Bee Boles built into one of the walls. It was while photographing these that my camera failed. While rewinding a film, the rewind motor went berserk and broke the film. By a stroke of luck I had noticed that the village had a chemist's. They produced a light-proof bag, removed the film and told me the camera was now useless. The rewind mechanism was slipping on the sprocket and the motor was continuously trying to keep it moving. This was a disaster as the camera, a fairly good automatic one, was compact, light and produced excellent results. I relied on it for my 35mm transparency films. I now had to consider buying another. An unexpected and unbargained for expense.

With this little problem to chew over I browsed round the odd assort-ment of antique and second-hand book shops, galleries and gift shops and called in at the Post Office to send a birthday card to my eldest son (such things have to be remembered even when walking!). I was wearing my Offa's Dyke T-shirt, chosen for the walk because it was grey, always looked clean and dried rapidly. I never expected anyone this far north to have even heard of Offa's Dyke and was surprised when the girl on the counter asked if I had walked it. Her cousin lived right on the path near Hay on Wye. Another case of the 'small world' syndrome.

Hungry again, even though only an hour had passed, I bought crisps, peaches and a milk shake, and picnicked in the shade of a tree until Michael arrived. His journey had been long and tedious, running in a new Land Rover and he was in need of a break. We dallied in the village and it was evening before we returned to Peebles. I was relieved to find my tent still standing. Whenever I left it, I always had a sneaking suspicion that it might not be there when I returned.

That evening we located a photographic shop in Peebles but a sign on the door told us it closed all day on Wednesdays. The next day was a Wednesday. I would have to buy a camera somewhere else. I caught up on news from home. Michael said he could stay until I reached Milngavie (pronounced Mul-guy), the start of the West Highland Way and would help me through the difficult area between here and Glasgow. Difficult because, as in Cheshire, there were virtually no campsites. Without car back up I would have to rely on Bed and Breakfast—which would not be easy owing to the Edinburgh Festival. There was also the more worrying aspect that for the next few days my route involved walking through areas which were likely to be highly undesirable for a lone woman. I was much happier knowing that help was at hand if needed and that someone was fully aware of my whereabouts. Without a pack to carry I reckoned I could cover the 60 miles to Milngavie in three days.

### In the steps of the drovers

My route from West Linton followed the old drove road across the Pentland Hills via an ancient pass called Cauldstane Slap. It is a straight forward and delightful walk. Rising gently from the village a rough track took me to Baddingsgill Reservoir and the higher reaches of the Lyne Water. Here, on a grass-covered tump in the middle of the river I found some tall, overpoweringly fragrant, cowslip-like flowers. I knew these were not wild and were much too late in the season for native cowslips, yet there was no habitation nearby. I thought they were *Primula florindae*, a garden plant, and pressed a small specimen of flowers. When identified six weeks later that is what they proved to be and I found that they are occasionally found naturalised in this part of Scotland. I was extremely fortunate to find it.

It was a beautiful day. Perfect for walking. I had the hills to myself and thoroughly enjoyed the solitude and beauty of the hills. From the summit of the pass the wide views over the lowlands were partially obscured by heat haze. Below lay another reservoir—a natural lake until the Edinburgh Water Company had other ideas for it in 1859. One of their iron boundary markers still stands nearby. There are the ruins of a castle and a farmstead. Drovers halted here overnight to water their cattle in the level, rough pastures and the farmers had to ensure all their hay was gathered in before the tens of thousands of cattle arrived to trample their fields.

What a tremendous sight it must have been; difficult to imagine the noise of all those cattle, men and horses in what is now a peaceful spot. Today only a handful of cattle graze where once were thousands.

Michael was to meet me at Little Vantage, a place named from its position on slightly higher ground where there is an excellent view along the length of the Pentland Hills. At the end of the range the famous 'crouching lion' shape of Arthur's Seat pinpoints the city centre. I'd been there several times, and so had not included it on my route; this was the nearest I would be.

It was 1 o'clock and Michael had not arrived. Coming directly across the hills I had done eight miles, but he had to make a 40 mile round trip to get to the same point. In addition I had suggested he went back to visit Smail's Printing Works. I ate my lunch until he arrived and we made a new rendezvous for 3.30pm in the carpark of the Almondell Country Park. Meanwhile, he went off to Livingston to try and find a replacement camera.

### Country parks and highland flings

The Pentland Range was the last hilly country I would see until I reached Loch Lomond. Now that I had reached the lowlands the countryside was intensively farmed with larger fields, many of them full of cereals ready for harvesting. Combines were busy and straw was being baled. The route now was not particularly pleasant; minor roads and the urbanised outskirts of Livingston—an extensive industrial sprawl. A woman walking her dog near some houses couldn't believe I was alone. "I wouldn't walk on my own round here" she said. The Almondell Country Park embraces the River Almond in an area known as the Calder Valley. Unlike other country parks I've ever come across it was a busy place. Cyclists, families with small children, older youngsters just messing around, people exercising dogs—and a few walkers, though these appeared to be people taking a short cut home from work. Much of the park is wooded with thick under-growth and a labyrinth of paths. Notable features include the aqueduct carrying the main feeder for the Forth and Clyde Canal from the River Almond and a bridge built in 1800 and designed by the artist Alexander Naismith. Until recently this was a picturesque ruin, but when I passed it was an ugly building site. Amidst the noise of heavy machinery and shrouded in dust it was being restored by a small army of civil engineers.

The information board at the park entrance had shown the location of the visitor centre and carpark, but thereafter there were no signs to indicate anything. It was more by luck than judgement that I arrived at the carpark at the appointed time—only to find that Michael was again not there. The visitor centre is housed in an old country house which still retains its gardens and I was attracted by the sound of Scottish music. Collecting a take-away coffee from a vending machine, I found a Scottish folk group in the walled garden entertaining a party of elderly people, most of them in wheelchairs. I sat on a bench sipping scalding coffee from a polystyrene cup enjoying the lively foot-tapping music and hoping that Michael would come so that he could hear it too. But he didn't. The musicians packed up their instruments. I went and looked at the canal wildlife display; large tanks, stocked with all the species of fish to be found in the Forth and Clyde Canal. Then I decided to carry on towards Broxburn along the road which Michael would surely use, and hope to meet him on the way.

Broxburn. And still no sign of him. I phoned from the first call box I could find and found he was still in the carpark at the country park where he had been waiting since 3.30pm. The wrong carpark. We didn't know there were two. He arrived ten minutes later while I replaced some of my energy with a Mars milk drink. Packed with calories, I had become addicted to these over the weeks.

We camped at another country park at Beescraig near Linlithgow. This one was in a scenic, afforested area with herds of deers and splendid views of Edinburgh and the Firth of Forth. It was quiet with small secluded camping areas separated by screens of trees. The excellent facilities even extended to the luxury of bathrooms. Once the tents were up we drove the short distance to Linlithgow to try out the replacement camera. A good opportunity soon presented itself in the carpark adjacent to Linlithgow Palace. Kilted pipers were busily getting bagpipes out of the boots of their cars. They fiddled about tuning up, had an impromptu practise, then marched off towards the palace. We followed and found Scottish dancing taking place in the great courtyard. It was a colourful scene attended by several hundred people, many of them tourists. We watched from one of the upper rooms where we had a bird's eye view of the whole courtyard, vibrant with the sound of music, laughter and dancing. A real highland fling with people wearing anything from full highland dress to jeans and T-shirts. It was by now almost dark, and framed in the narrow unglazed stone windows of the palace the sun was setting in a breathtaking blaze of gold. A memorable evening and a grand finale to my first week in Scotland.

# 10
# Through Silicon Glen
## Canals and the Antonine Wall to Milngavie

Vast brick red shale 'bings' dominate the countryside around Broxburn. Great ridges of waste that are all that remains of the flourishing Victorian enterprise which extracted paraffin from oil bearing shales. At its peak 13,000 people were employed locally, but the industry collapsed once oil was discovered in America. After years of decline the last works closed in 1962. Now, the bings have a beauty all of their own and provided a dramatic backdrop to Niddry Castle where I joined the Union Canal next morning.

The next two days were spent almost entirely pounding canal towpaths and for the first few hours this was rather a novelty. Without a rucksack I felt weightless and with such easy walking rapidly clocked up the miles. The Edinburgh and Glasgow Union Canal, to give it its full name, was opened in 1822 to link Edinburgh with the Forth and Clyde Canal at Falkirk. When new it was nicknamed the mathematical river, because it followed faithfully the 240ft. contour and had no locks for it's entire 31½ miles. Now, the old canalside stables have been converted into a museum and a replica of a Victorian steam packet makes regular trips from the canal basin in Linlithgow. But long sections of the canal are still overgrown and full of rubbish. The many bridges make easy disposal points for supermarket trollies, road cones and drinks cans. Green lanes of duckweed stretch for miles. Old mattresses and car tyres are recycled by coots and moorhens as prime nesting sites and wildlife abounds. Families of swans became a familiar sight; father on guard and alert while mother and the almost fully grown youngsters sozzled head down in the weed.

Mallard approached, quacking hopefully for tit bits and the occasional kingfisher swept past—a streak of blue low over the water. On the towpath my boots were in danger of crushing hundreds of newly transformed baby toads and under one road bridge I watched enthralled as a mink played on the opposite bank ignoring my presence.

After seven fast miles I reached Linlithgow Basin, my pre-arranged meeting point with Michael. Beside the canal a sixteenth century doocot— dovecote to sassenachs—stood midst carefully tended beds of red roses. A giant bell of stone restored in a vandalproof manner, its doorway walled up so that we couldn't see inside. The romantic ruin of linlithgow Palace surrounded by trees, blue skies, sparkling loch and majestic swans was defaced by scaffolding and shrouded in tarpaulins: a malady that currently seems to affect ancient monuments throughout the land. We ate lunch at a picnic area beside the Loch in the company of many tourists and twice as many swans. The loch is a bird sanctuary and any amount of tourists was no deterrent to the hundreds of geese, assorted waterfowl and numerous seagulls competing noisily for food. The swans were a particular nuisance practically grabbing sandwiches from your hand if you weren't vigilant.

We lingered awhile in the cobbled market place admiring the elaborate Cross Well, carved by a one handed mason. Then I made tracks back to the canal for my next session of towpath bashing. Almost immediately I came to the great aqueduct over the River Avon; twelve stone arches 85ft high stretching impressively for 900ft. across a wooded glen, the sun casting their shadows on the meadow below. Narrow, cobbled footways and iron railings on each side of the barge-width trough make safe passage for horse and walker. I walked level with the tops of the trees.

Like other little used canals, the Union Canal is full of wildlife and in places has jungle-like qualities. Banks are a tangle of rampant vegetation and there is so much duckweed the water has the appearance of a swamp. But the presence of stone staging posts and well preserved examples of kick-stones, angled stones set into the towpath for horses to kick against when negotiating bends, remind you that this was once a thriving working canal.

The only other users of the towpath were two small girls and their father, cycling. They stopped so frequently looking at flowers and butterflies that I overtook them several times. Each time they caught up again they stopped to talk. I was glad of the company.

Under most circumstances, I was perfectly content with my solo state. Indeed, part of the enjoyment of the entire walk was the self-imposed solitude. I loved the remote wildness of the hills and undisturbed hours rambling through deserted countryside. Time passed quickly where attention was constantly focused on following the route, watching where you put your feet, admiring views and stopping for any amount of interesting diversions. Indeed, there were times when I actually regretted the fact that I had company. Walking along busily chatting I would later find I could recall little of the route. I would have missed things I had intended to see, not stopped to savour a scene, been unaware of the terrain and at the end of the day feel that a chunk of the walk was a 'blank page'. To get the most out of the walk I needed to be alone. But there were occasions when human company became desirable—even longed for. On wet days for instance. Being alone when you are cold, wet, weary and thoroughly fed up is depressing. Two cold wet and weary people can joke about it and cheer each other up. And there are bad days when nothing goes right. No food. Losing your way. You just feel the need for a shoulder to cry on and someone with whom to commiserate.

And here, towpath walking was becoming a tedious affair. In places it had been surfaced with hardcore and was more or less a road. I needed no map. The view was unchanging. I enjoyed the wildlife—but even this was the same for miles. It was a day when a walking companion would have been welcome and I was looking forward to the day's end. Passing under each of the canal's 62 numbered bridges became something to look forward to—all bringing Falkirk significantly closer. The most notable, No.61, had a face carved in the stonework on each side; a grumpy face on one side, a smiling one on the other. No-one seems to know why. Perhaps the stonemason was as bored with building bridges as I was walking under them. Finally, just before reaching Falkirk basin there was a 633 yard tunnel to negotiate. This was apparently quite unnecessary except to accommodate the whim of the local landowner who would not allow the canal to pass through his estate. In order to maintain its contour the canal had to be tunnelled through a hill, no doubt at much extra expense.

A dank wooded cutting led towards the tunnel and the towpath suddenly plunged into the hillside—and within seconds, became invisible. A wooden handrail on the canalside was the only guide in the fast diminishing light. With eyes straining and one hand groping along the handrail, I walked cautiously along the cobbled walkway prepared for unexpected potholes and puddles. By the time I reached the half way point, the two ends were mere pinpricks of light. It was totally black and very eerie. Water dripped from the roof into the canal and odd noises, sounding strangely like ghostly voices, echoed through the darkness. My greatest

149

fear was that someone walking or cycling the opposite way would collide with me. I wished I had my torch. Nearer the end, as more light filtered through, the reflection of the walls in the canal made the water look frighteningly deep. It was an experience I would not wish to repeat and I was mightily relieved to step out into sunlight and see the Land Rover waiting to take me back to Beescraig.

It had been another day of perfect weather and making the most of a lovely evening after supper we drove to Blackness, the ancient port serving Linlithgow. Blackness Castle stands on the shores of the Forth Estuary with its walls in the water. An austere and formidable guardian of the seaward approaches to Linlithgow. Down river, the Forth road and railway bridges could be seen spanning the Firth side by side. It was quiet and almost deserted and the tide was out. As darkness fell the sun setting behind the distant hills cast a golden shaft of light across the mudflats. After a 19 mile long day, it was moments like this that made all the effort worthwhile.

### A botanist's dream

One more long day was needed to reach Milngavie, and this was mainly more fast towpath work, interspersed with short sections of the Antonine Wall. The Union Canal had now become the Firth and Clyde Canal although it no longer actually makes a a 'union'. Originally the two were linked by a flight of eleven locks soon after emerging from the tunnel at Falkirk. All this and much more I learned from information boards along the towpath which graphically displayed the canal's history and made interesting reading. It was constructed as a 35 mile long ship canal with 39 locks (or 40 depending on where you get your information) and is a broad, deep canal which would easily pass for a river. In its heyday romantically named steamers like the *Fairy Queen*, *Gipsy Queen* and *May Queen*, carried hundreds of passengers on pleasure trips from Glasgow.

My day was filled with interest. The canal is a botanist's dream. The water, like a giant freshwater rockpool, was crystal clear with a green forest of submerged plants and a diverse range of surface floating species. I wished desperately I had thought to ask Michael to bring my flora for the week. Waxy white frogbit flowers bloomed over large areas of water. In places arrowhead, a plant not common in the north, was the dominant species. Water lilies grew in massive circular 'islands' merging in places to form a continuous river of plate-sized leaves. The rampant growth on the banks ranged from tall, brown, spiked bulrushes growing with their 'feet' in the water, to the many flowers preferring the drier parts of the towpath.

Vast banks of rosebay willow herb were mirrored in pink perfection in the still water, paler valerian and greater willow herb blended with the purples and blues of hardheads, woundwort and water mint while toadflax and ragwort flowers added bright splashes of yellow. The air was thick with the unforgettable scent of creamy, frothy flowered meadowsweet.

Thanks to the aquarium at the Almondell Country Park and the clarity of the water, I was able to identify all the fish I saw, the most common being pike. I have never seen so many pike in all my life. Everything from babies a few inches long to full size grandads, basking in the sunny patches between the water lilies. They fascinated me as they didn't dart away and hide but remained, almost motionless, in the water, not moving even when I leaned over to look more closely and attempt to take photographs.

The views from the towpath were not inspiring, but at least there were views. The towpath ran along the north bank. On the southern side acres of golden corn and gentle pastures bordered the water. Cows grazed. Swans sat with their heads tucked under wings. Dead trees, victims of disease, stood gaunt white and skeletal, but graceful still, their reflections beautifying death. Two miles away lay the broad silvery sweep of the Firth of Forth, the low lying ground between it and the canal almost entirely industrialised. A huge oil refinery at Grangemouth; a vast chemical plant, cooling towers and tall chimneys; the M9 and the roar of traffic. Beyond the Firth a blur of blue mountains were discernible in the urban haze.

As an alternative route to the canal, the Antonine Wall provided a fairly direct path in the same direction and made a welcome change. But it was hillier and I found it tricky to follow. As it was unbearably hot and the canal was so simple, it seemed sensible most of the time to stick with the towpath. In truth, the Wall isn't a wall at at all, but a massive earth embankment very much like Offa's Dyke. Constructed by the Romans much later than Hadrian's Wall, it was relatively short lived and is less well known. It was built of turf and runs for 37 miles between the rivers Forth and Clyde, but very little has stood the test of time. What is visible today are surviving sections of the vallum (or ditch). The canal follows the same route and runs almost parallel with the Wall—in many places only a few hundred yards away in the fields. Some of the canal locks were actually constructed within the ditch itself—something that would never have been allowed had they been building the canal today. Or would it?

Although the canal was an easier option, I wanted to walk some of the Wall and chose sections featuring high, clearly visible embankments. At times this proved to be a scramble through overgrown woodland past spoil heaps of old open cast mining. There was no clear path, and only by sticking closely to the line of the vallum could I ensure I was going in the right direction. At one point the so-called footpath was obstructed by a fence and obliterated by a broad unsurfaced track where heavy plant were busy excavating the spoil heaps. Lorries trundled by in clouds of dust. Taking Hamish Brown's advice, I aimed for a line of prominent pylons, trusting I would come out in the correct place at Rough Castle, one of the many Roman forts along the Wall. With its closely mown sward, gentle contours and scattered groups of trees, I thought at first the fort was a golf-course. Here a well preserved and unobstructed length of wall can be walked and on the defensive banks of the fort, an excavated area of lilia can be seen. These booby trap pits have sharpened stakes driven into the bottom, a cruel method of stopping the charge of a mounted enemy.

### Airguns: abuse and rubbish

I met Michael at Kilsyth in a seedy looking area where everything showed advanced signs of dereliction and neglect. The only way from the canal seemed to be through a dubious looking old industrial tunnel which had a cobbled roadway and a stream running through it, the water flowing over cobbles. We lunched beside a waterfilled quarry at an attractive picnic site in the Kelvin Valley and were appalled to find that, in the modern way of the world, the whole valley, which is a Site of Special Scientific Interest, was under threat of destruction, earmarked to provide a bypass for Kilsyth.

I was now going through the area I had been dreading the most. This strip between Glasgow and Edinburgh is known colloquially as Silicon Glen and is either industrialised, urbanised or both. It is not the most pleasant area to be walking alone whatever your sex. Towns merge one into another; Falkirk into Bonnybridge, then Cumbernauld, Kilsyth and Kirkintilloch. If I had known in advance how bad it was I would not have chosen to come this way. Friends of mine planning to use the same route after I returned were advised to "walk through it very quickly." I did this instinctively. There were occasions when it was not wise to hang around. I was uneasy and at all times wary. Near one bridge a man and two boys were shooting with airguns ahead of me on the towpath. I was certain they were shooting at the ducks, though they behaved suspiciously innocently when I passed. I had the distinct feeling that if I looked in any way disapproving I might have met violent verbal abuse—or worse. On this canal, as on others, there were many swans with young, but this was the only canal where I saw dead swans; grey sodden masses of feathers floating head down in the water. After I passed the high steel perimeter fence of a young offender's prison, bridges were daubed with the lurid colours of spray painted graffiti. And there was the all too common sight of house-hold rubbish, road cones and traffic signs deposited beneath the bridges, and in one town the bridges were used by cardboard box dwellers for shelter. Wooden benches were occupied by shabbily attired, ill-kempt characters bedding down for the night.

I was surprised that the towpath was not used more. Perhaps even the locals were wary of potentially unsafe areas. A few people walked short distances with dogs or children. The occasional cyclist rode past. Most of them spoke as they passed, making comment on the weather, the view, the swans and in one instance, the multitude of butterflies. At Kirkintilloch the evening rush hour was under way. Roads were conjested with traffic and in the town centre where the canal had a towpath on each side, people were going home from work. A group of youths jeered and called to me from the other side. I could not understand the unfamiliar accent and ignored them, but from the tone it sounded derogatory. I felt very uncomfortable. I was relieved when a couple walking a dog joined the path in front of me. They walked at a snail's pace but I slowed to the same speed in order to walk behind them until I was well clear of the town.

Michael was of course never far away and I needed his reassuring presence. He was driving ahead and walking back to meet me, but conve-nient meeting places were not always at convenient distances. And places I would have liked company were sometimes difficult for him to reach by road. I was usually on my own for four or five miles at a time.

### Wigwams and a wedding

On its way to the mouth of the Clyde the canal continues through the outer regions of Glasgow but I had no reason to go that far. I turned off at Cadder to go across country to Milngavie, north of the city where I met Michael in a layby at Balmore. It was 6.30. I had done 20 miles and I'd had enough for one day even though I was still four miles from Milngavie.

Our intention was to stay at my first campsite on the West Highland Way; a small farm site near Drymen catering specifically for walkers. A mere quarter of an acre of rough grass behind a barn, and that partly taken up with two wigwams. The barn was made over for walkers' use and contained toilets, showers, sturdy benches and a long, equally sturdy table for cooking under cover. The wigwams are a feature of several of the West Highland Way campsites and similar structures can be found in other parts of Scotland. Constructed of wood they are, as their name implies, a solidly built wigwam-shaped structure raised above the ground with a single door at the front. Inside there is a basic sleeping shelf on three sides with room to sleep six persons. No doubt you can cram a few more in; I'm not aware of any restrictions. They are very popular, though of more use to a group than a single person and at the time of my walk cost £6 per person. They always looked very cosy and I believe on some sites were heated.

In the scrappy area of grass between the wigwams, choice of pitch was determined solely on where you could fit your tent. Terrain was not worth considering. We erected our tents a few inches apart and went off to spend the remainder of the evening in Drymen, a tourist orientated town on the southern end of Loch Lomond where many of the boat owners congregate. A forest of masts met the eye as a multitude of small craft bobbed up and down at their moorings to the sound of chinking rigging and fluttering flaglets. Close to the shore was a large white marquee where wedding guests were arriving for an evening reception, the men resplendent in highland dress as colourful as their elegant behatted partners, and all clutching odd shaped gift wrapped parcels.

When we returned to our quarter acre more tents had materialised. Four German boys were so close their tent was practically in Michael's. We hoped they didn't snore—and for that matter that we didn't! On the Pennine Way there was one terrible snorer amongst the hostelling fraternity. Those staying at youth hostels prayed every night that he would be far enough away that they couldn't hear him. One chap told me he actually got up one night and moved to an armchair in the common room in order to get some sleep. But no-one liked to say anything to the snorer—and possibly he didn't even know he snored.

I fell asleep contemplating the next stage of the walk. I had clocked up another 100 miles since leaving Kirk Yetholm and still had over 300 to do. These would be my longest totally unsupported miles. It was a daunting thought, but I didn't dwell on it. My target was Fort William. My main concerns were weather, food and whether I had enough warm clothes if it should turn colder further north. I was still not thinking in terms of the ultimate end. I wasn't particularly looking forward to being on my own, but I was looking forward to getting to Scotland's more mountainous regions. The next 97 miles would be in the company of a new band of walkers and unless it slipped out in conversation, no-one would know where I was going. For a week I would become just another walker on the West Highland Way.

# 11
# The Ultimate Insect Experience
## The West Highland Way

Somewhere in Teesdale, in conversation with the elderly Edinburgh man who was on the Pennine Way walking tour, I asked if he had done the West Highland Way and what he thought of it. He told me that he had and added that he thought I would be disappointed—it had not come up to *his* expectations. Now, having done the walk myself, I have to agree. Quite possibly at the right time of the year and in better weather I might have enjoyed it more than I did. But when people ask me which part of the trip did I like least, I have to say that The West Highland Way came a close second to the Cheshire Plain.

I had no complaints about the rugged and spectacular scenery, apart from the fact that for most of the time visibility was too poor to see very much, but I was disappointed with the route itself. Much of it is on forest tracks and old military roads and is so well marked by the tramping of thousands of feet a map is scarcely necessary. Like many walkers I do enjoy the challenge of reading the map and finding my own way. And I had not anticipated the sheer number of people and the fact that for much of the time it was impossible to enjoy peace and solitude when road or railway was never far away.

The West Highland Way is probably the most popular of all the long distance paths, part of its appeal being that it can be accomplished in a week. For most people this means starting on a Saturday. My arrival at the official start, marked by a plinth in the bustling, pedestrianised shopping precinct of Milngavie was, by pure chance and a stroke of bad luck, on a

155

busy Saturday morning. August 17th—the middle of the busiest walking season. According to *The West Highland Wayfarer*, a free guide I'd picked up in an information office, an estimated 50,000 walkers used the path in 1994, increasing to 66,000 in the hot summer of 1995, so it was no surprise to find walkers were leaving the town centre in constant procession, almost as if they were being set off at timed intervals with a starting pistol.

Unlike the serious, dedicated walkers encountered on the Pennine Way, many of these seemed to me grossly overloaded yet not adequately equipped for whatever might be ahead. Some were students and young people who perhaps out of necessity had to make do with what kit they could acquire. Others looked as if they were using new gear for the first time and in later conversations I discovered that this was often the case, this being their first attempt at a long distance walk. Others were inexperienced walkers, backpacking for the first time.

If I had given my arrival date enough forethought, I could easily have taken a day off at any of the historic border towns or spent time exploring more of the Southern Uplands and timed my arrival at Milngavie for mid-week. But now I was here I had little option but to join the eager throngs setting off full of enthusiasm on their big adventure. I found it more than a little disconcerting to walk on the heels of someone else. I had either to slow my pace or put on a spurt to pass and get ahead. And I knew that not far behind another walker was having exactly the same frustrations with my progress.

Four German lads talking volubly in their native tongue set off before me in great spirits and at a great pace. They soon slowed and I passed them after the first couple of miles, quickly leaving them far behind. A few miles later I 'fell in' with a single man who was walking at the same pace as me. We had passed and repassed each other so many times that on reaching one stile at the same time, decided to walk together. The stiles, if that is the right word for them, were like nothing I have ever encountered before, consisting of two upright metal poles fairly close together and held by chains. With both hands you pushed the two poles apart, squeezed through the gap and hoped that your rucksack would follow. Both hands need to be free for this manoeuvre, which requires great dexterity if you are also carrying a mapcase, camera and water bottle.

Most walkers leaving Milngavie are heading for Balmaha on the first day—about 20 miles. But having gone back to restart at Balmore, I covered 15 miles to reach the campsite where we had left the tents up for a second night. As this was Michael's last day, his mission now accomplished, this was as far as I walked. We spent the rest of the afternoon sightseeing, exploring the west side of Loch Lomond by road. Tourists were everywhere, picnicking or simply sitting in their cars looking at the view. When we eventually managed to find a space in a crowded lochside carpark it was not for long. Two drunken youths staggered by, knocking on car windows, pestering the occupants and trying to obtain a lift. We beat a hasty retreat and looked round for a less public place, where we could eat our tea in peace.

As on the previous night, on our return to the site seven new tents had mushroomed in our absence and once again chatter from adjacent tents went on until late. A few feet from my tent were a family with a youngster of about ten years taking his first lessons in camping and walking. Too excited to sleep he was asking endless questions long after midnight. Perhaps one of his first lessons should have been that other campers need to sleep! The site had no noise restrictions and even if it did, with tents as close as this you can still be disturbed by snorers, people coughing, children crying and so on.

Next morning we could get our own back. Throughout my walk I was accustomed to making an early start. Although on arrival I can have my tent up, rucksack unpacked and the kettle boiling in ten minutes, it takes about two hours to break camp in the morning. This includes breakfast, washing and the difficult process of getting everything back into the pack. To leave as early as possible I was usually up between 5 and 5.30am. On a busy site this means trying to do all the chores with the minimum of noise. It's almost guaranteed that attempts at silence will have disastrous consequences. I'd drop the saucepans or tent poles. Every item of surplus of food would be packed in high decibel plastic. Noisiest of all are those efficient and essential items of modern camping—zips. Not just one, but half a dozen or more on inners, sleeping bag, flysheet and the rucksack— all conspiring to wake the entire site with their distinctly audible sound. As Michael wanted to leave by 8am we were up by 6, creeping around taking the tents down as quietly as possible and transporting everything to the barn to do the packing. It was my last chance to stock up with supplies from home. As much food as possible was stuffed into odd corners of the rucksack. Enough to last me to the end. Other campers were just beginning to surface as we enjoyed a final cup of coffee.

### *Unwelcome company*
Michael eventually left at 8.30 and I set off along the road to Drymen. Whenever someone had been with me, I dreaded the time of departure.

Once on my own I quickly adjusted to being alone again, but the actual moment of departure I hated. Saying goodbye was difficult and awkwardly brief. I would just turn my back on whoever had been with me and walk away. I tried to shut my mind to the thought of, in this case, the forthcoming 300 solitary miles.

Drymen was little more than a mile and a half, a distance soon covered on a minor road. After this, five of the eight miles to Balmaha were on forestry tracks. As I walked through the small carpark on the approach to the forest, I passingly noted a single car with a man sitting in it. As it was still quite early on a Sunday morning this struck me as rather odd and a few minutes later I heard footsteps behind me. Determined not to show any sign of nervousness I went up a gear and tried to keep up a steady fast pace whilst resisting the urge to look over my shoulder. My follower slowly caught up until he drew level, when his first words were "My goodness, you're a fast walker. I've been trying to catch you up." My unease deepened. Why, I wondered, was he trying to catch me up. From his dress he was obviously not a walker. No boots. No backpack. Just trainers and casual clothes. He was overly chatty and seemed intent on walking with me. It was a scenario I dreaded, had often envisaged and trusted would never happen, but one which I had also rehearsed many times in my mind. I endeavoured to keep several feet between us and gripped my metal water bottle, full and weighty, in my right hand with the intention of using it on his nose if I should need to protect myself. His endless questions I answered lightly, trying not to show my concern, but at the same time being casually friendly and keeping up a fast pace in the hope that he might tire before I did.

He stuck with me for almost three miles by which time I came to the conclusion that his story—that he was new to walking and was trying out a morning's walk before returning home for Sunday lunch, had a ring of truth about it. He wanted to catch me up he said, because he wanted to talk to a 'proper' walker; to ask questions. Well, this appeared to be true—he had certainly picked my brains on all aspects of walking and backpacking.

Before reaching Balmaha, the West Highland Way has a choice of routes, the high level route ascending Conic Hill and dropping steeply to the shores of Loch Lomond at Balmaha village, or a shorter, gentler route via lanes and roads. I had already decided to 'take the low road'. This was my first day carrying a heavy pack after almost a week of Land Rover transport. My unwanted companion said he was going to the top of Conic Hill. I announced that I proposed going the other way and when we arrived

158

at the point where the paths diverged, I was relieved when he did indeed go the other way. In all my weeks of walking this was the only time when I was really concerned for my safety. Perhaps needlessly, but nevertheless this was one companion I was glad to see depart.

In all the time I walked with this man we encountered no other person, but within a few minutes of turning off I spied a jogger running uphill towards me. A hot and thirsty young woman. As she approached she gasped, "I don't suppose you could spare me some water. I've left my water bottle at home." She was on a regular morning jog of some distance and had realised too late that she had forgotten her water. She drank gratefully from my bottle before jogging off into the forest. I continued my descent arriving at Balmaha conveniently at 11 o'clock, just right for a morning break.

Balmaha is where West Highland Way walkers first make the loch's acquaintance. For three days they will follow its eastern shore for 20 of its 23 miles. Those who struggle to the top of Conic Hill will have been rewarded with a panoramic view of the loch and its islands. From where I sat on at the water's edge, writing postcards, all I could see was one large, wooded island which blocked the view of the rest of the loch. A flotilla of assorted ducks hung around at the water's edge expectantly hoping to share the cake I had just bought at the village stores. When I didn't respond they transferred their allegiance to a more promising group of children.

*Wildlife encounters*

I reached my intended campsite by 1 o'clock. However, it was so crowded I decided in view of the time to push on to the next, even if it meant camping wild. The banks of Loch Lomond are as bonny as the song implies—pleasantly wooded with birch and oak, and with open grassy glades giving everywhere a light, airy feeling. A delightful surprise. I had been expecting oppressive coniferous forest. In places the ground was a carpet of moss, in others, masses of delicate yellow cow-wheat speckled the woodland floor. There were stunning views in every direction—rocky shores, wooded islands and cloud topped mountains, but it was too hazy to take photographs. I had to resist the temptation. I knew I would only be wasting film.

The path runs close to the shore. If you can endure walking on pebbles there is nothing to stop you from doing just that. And if you want company, there is plenty of it. All the beaches were crowded; hundreds of Sunday trippers intent on making the most of the sunshine and water. Power boats and jet skis stormed up and down the loch while youngsters in canoes and rubber dinghies messed about in shallower waters. Toddlers paddled and splashed about with inflatable rings; adults sunbathed and burnt sausages on beach barbecues. A quarter of a mile across the loch the steady roar of traffic on the A82 is a constant reminder that although you are in the Highlands (the southern end of Loch Lomond is their official geographical start), you are not far from civilisation. This was not what I expected of the romantic sounding West Highland Way!

Neither did I expect a close encounter with a 'naked ape' but this intrepid being was wandering round in his birthday suit totally oblivious to my approach. I had spotted him at some distance and assumed that as soon as he saw me he would dash for cover and make himself decent. So with head down, to avoid embarrassing him, I plodded on as if nothing was out of the ordinary. But each time I took a quick look he was still there and did not become aware of my presence until I was just a few yards away. As always I had my camera ready for use. It was usually either in my pocket or in my hand. Unable to think what to say, on the spur of the moment I waved my camera at him and asked "Can I take your photograph?" Whereupon he ran off into the bracken and I missed probably the best photo opportunity of my entire trip. As another female walker observed when I told her of this incident. "The lengths some women will go to just to see a naked man!!"

Much later I heard that there was a man who walked the entire Way in the nude. Had I perhaps encountered his ghost still lingering over a section he'd found particularly memorable? If he was a ghost, he was a very presentable one, (tall, dark and young enough to be my son) and as he disappeared into the bracken called out that he thought he had a safe spot for a bit of sunbathing. What rather worried me for the rest of the Way was that, as any seasoned walker will know, it is not unusual to meet a person one day in shorts and T-shirt and meet the same walker days' later, muffled to the eyebrows in cagoule, woolly hat, gloves and gaiters and walk past without speaking. You just don't recognise them with all their clothes on. I had a dread that I might meet this man on a campsite or in a pub and that I would never recognise him, though he would undoubtably know me. I was puzzled too because, although it was a warm day, it was hazy and overcast with plenty of midges around. Why wasn't he being attacked by midges like the rest of us?

Later I came upon more wildlife, but this time far from naked. A strong odour which I immediately recognised as billy goat pungently advertised the presence of feral goats, and I was confronted by a small herd with long black hair and lethal looking horns. They were browsing happily in the scrubby undergrowth along the foreshore and totally ignored booted intruders.

## *Wild camping*

I had decided to stay at Rowardennan which is the end of the road as far as the motor car is concerned. It lies in the shadow of Ben Lomond and is a focal point for climbers. The hotel there is much favoured by walkers, both as an overnight stop and a watering hole, and the beer garden was overflowing with walkers, climbers, and tourists. Every picnic table was taken; every available patch of grass was strewn with reclining back-packers. Discarded lager cans lay alongside discarded boots. I was about to give it a miss when I was hailed by the man I had walked with from Milngavie. He waved his cup and indicated he had hot water in his flask if I would like a drink. In return I provided the coffee and we sat chatting. I discovered he was Eddy from Kelso and was walking with a friend—or would be the next day. The friend was planning on doing 20 miles a day which Eddy didn't think he could do, so he had left two days earlier to get a head start before his friend arrived.

Eddy was booked in at the Youth Hostel just beyond the hotel. I was going a little further to a permissive wild site provided by the Forestry Commission. These are one-night-only sites and there is no charge but there are no facilities either, so before I left I filled my water bottle from a public tap beside the road. There are several of these permissive sites though their existence is not widely known. Their whereabouts is usually gleaned from other backpackers. The one at Rowardennan was perfectly idyllic; a large, open glade of short grass surrounded by trees. Nearby a clear flowing, eminently drinkable burn emptied itself into the loch. No-one else was there so I had first choice of pitch and opted for a comfortable patch of grass near a tree, with convenient branches for hanging things on. Before anyone else came I took the opportunity of filling my bowl from the burn and having a good wash and then filled other containers for washing up, cleaning teeth and so on.

With time to spare I walked along the loch shore where I found another two tents were pitched just out of earshot. But strangely, no-one else arrived until it was dark. I was already in bed when I heard first German and, shortly after, Dutch voices. Although I couldn't understand a word it was obvious what was going on—it was too dark for them to see what they were doing. There was a lot of continental grumbling, cursing and argument before they settled down for the night. They had no idea that their neighbour was a middle-aged woman and I always felt it was better to remain anonymous and let them assume it was another man. Somehow this gave me a greater sense of security.

For a remote site it was surprisingly noisy. Across the loch traffic roared continuously most of the night. A few yards from my tent the little burn splashed and gurgled over rocks and at daybreak I was woken by the raucous squabbling of seagulls on the beach; an unconventional alarm that at least ensured I was up early. I was away from the site before the other residents were awake.

The only map I now had was Harvey's Walker's Map of the West Highland Way, an excellent strip map with all the information I required — campsites, shops, water, telephone, post offices and even banks. The day before had been an easy 17 miles and none of the route appeared to be very strenuous compared with the Pennine Way. The broad forest tracks from Rowardennan that morning were no more than a comfortable stroll. I came across two men whom I thought were behaving suspiciously. Both wore camouflage outfits and were crouched close together, heads down at the side of the track. I thought I'd disturbed a couple of poachers until I noticed their rucksacks. But they turned out to be two Scots from Dundee, doing nothing more than cowering under their hooded cagoules trying to eat sandwiches and avoid the midges. They were an amiable and likeable pair who were not doing the whole Way as they only had four days. They were going as far as Tyndrum — with diversions to "bag a few Monros" (Peaks over 3,000ft.) on the way. I suspected they might be ex-army as they appeared to be super-fit and very enterprising. At Balmaha they had slept in the marquee which had been used for the wedding reception! I left them still fighting midges but they soon caught up and overtook me on their way to another Monro!

### Rob Roy Country

For those who want an easy life, the broad gentle forest track continues at a high level — a boring path with little of interest. The alternative is a rougher but much more scenic path along the water's edge. I chose the popular and badly eroded lochside path. This is Rob Roy country and a tourist honeypot. Rob Roy is a legendary figure from three centuries back who is buried a few miles away at Balquhidder. Whether he was a hero or a villain depends on your viewpoint. A crag nearby known as Rob Roy's Prison is reputedly where he held his hostages and many day walkers were heading that way. Backpackers, struggling with heat, midges and heavy packs littered the wayside, resting, recovering energy. I found one young fellow with long blond hair and a sweat band leaning on the rail of a bridge as if he couldn't take a step more. He looked absolutely shattered. I felt like saying "Unpack your rucksack and throw half of it out." On man I met reduced the weight in his rucksack by five pounds just by sending home one of two extra jerseys.

I would have loved to take a long break myself; to sit on a rock; enjoy the magical scenery of majestic mountains, summits fading into a blue haze and sunlight shimmering on the loch. But if I stopped for longer than a few minutes I was immediately set upon by marauding midges. I longed to refresh myself with a quick dip, but Scotland's blood-sucking pests made that impossible. The midges, though not a problem while I walked, were at their worst along the shady, tree-lined shore. So I stopped just long enough to gaze in awe at the scenery, to watch birds, look for plants and soak up the atmosphere of the place, then resumed my unhurried wandering along the path.

That day's itinerary included only one notable place—Inversnaid. The waterfall here is significant enough to have attracted the attention of poets. Both William Wordsworth and Gerard Manley Hopkins found inspiration here but on this occasion it was not very spectacular. After weeks of dry weather it had scarcely any water. The surprisingly large Victorian hotel is an essential stopping place for every walker, simply because there is nowhere else to stop. Outside the hotel were picnic tables and piles of boots.Walkers are welcome but are not allowed to trample mud into the carpeted areas. I removed my boots, propped my rucksack against a picnic table to stake my claim to a seat and padded off in red socks nearly as dirty as my boots to order coffee. On the way out I stocked up with chocolate from a vending machine, my strategy being to never miss an opportunity for food. There might not be another chance.

The two Dundee 'poachers' were already sitting bootless at the next table and before I had time to bite into my cheese and tomato sandwiches Kelso Eddy arrived, still alone—his friend having not yet caught up. He joined me and said that lots of walkers had already given up—mainly owing to blisters, bad knees and rucksacks that were too heavy. We concluded that many walkers drop out because they are insufficiently prepared for what they believe will be a short, easy walk. I was finding it relatively easy; after all I had a few miles already under my belt. But the West Highland Way is not to be underestimated, especially by inexperienced first-timers. Heaven knows what some people had in their rucksacks—they were huge and it *is* only a week's walk after all. I was self-consciously aware that many walkers, and surprisingly especially the men, look amazingly clean and smart each morning; T-shirts unsoiled, crease free shorts and a different sweater every day. I could only conclude they carried far more clothes than me. One man in particular was always spotlessly turned out in white, even down to white socks and clean trainers. Never a grass stain on the seat of his pants or the muddy evidence of slipping on a tree root. No sweaty stains under his armpits. Nothing to show he was walking the same path as the rest of us. He could have just stepped out of a car. I couldn't think how he managed it until days later I spotted him trundling a large suitcase on little wheels to the railway station at Tyndrum. He must have been having his many changes of clothing transported by one of the local businesses who offer a daily backpack transfer service.

### Farewell water: Hello rain

When I reached the end of the loch I felt a certain satisfaction at having walked most of its length. However, I had little regret at leaving it behind. Loch Lomond is Britain's largest inland lake and is probably Scotland's most visited one. In a busy weekend it can see as many as 40,000 visitors and having witnessed the crowds on the more accessible southern shores, I can well believe this. The northern end, though, is much quieter. The last few miles were also some of the most hazardous; the path undefined, rough and rocky. It involves tough scrambles over massive rocks. In the heavily wooded areas extra care is needed negotiating the slippery, twisted tangle of exposed roots. Despite the difficult terrain, I spent happy hours botanising, noting several species not encountered before on my walk. But enough was enough. The experience was similar to walking along a canal towpath for several days. It was getting monotonous. It was time for a change and I was looking forward to what was ahead.

As the path began to rise, change it rapidly did! The loch was soon lost to view. I was surrounded by mountains. Moss covered bogs were thick with the red leaves of sundews, tiny glandular carnivorous plants, and the fleshy yellow-green leaves of butterwort and luxuriant patches of golden saxifrage. Tiny, white-flowered eyebrights were scattered like confetti in grassy places. Towards late afternoon the weather began to deteriorate. It was still dry when I reached the backpackers' site near Inverarnan but by the time I had the tent up it was raining. The large, covered shelter with picnic tables and ample washing lines for drying wet gear and tents was a god-send. There were laundry facilities of sorts provided and in a converted outbuilding the farmer's wife ran a small shop. Half a dozen wigwams had already been snapped up by the early birds. I had been beset by a long spell of bad weather at any time I would certainly have opted for one and rather regretted that, in the end, I never had the chance.

There were no other campers that I recognised. Two lads I'd spoken to a few times arrived later in the evening having walked seven miles to my 14. But they didn't stop. They hadn't got up until 11am and were going to carry on walking and camp wild. Few of these West Highland Way walkers started early or made the best use of the day. The evening continued to be miserably wet and the temperature had fallen. To keep warm, I climbed into my sleeping bag and cooked noodle soup in the porch, lying on my stomach, then read until dark. By morning the weather was no better. It was still raining. But I really could not complain. This was my 60th day and only the fifth day of rain. I packed as much as possible inside the tent then grabbed everything else and finished packing in the covered area, strapping the dripping tent on the top of my rucksack.

Soon after leaving I was overtaken by a pick-up truck. The farmer. His mission? To apprehend those backpackers who had decided to camp wild—on his land. These hapless souls were rudely awakened by vigorous thumps on the tent and a demand for payment. While feeling sympathy for them I could see his point. He did offer an excellent site at a reasonable price. It seemed pointless to walk a further mile to camp wild with no facilities, just to save a couple of pounds.

It was an easy morning's walk; pleasant, if damp, through open airy forests of birch with an understorey of heather and bog myrtle; much more attractive than the dark, close planted coniferous forests back home in Wales. Faces were now becoming familiar on this fourth day. Casual exchanges were made as fellow walkers met. At midday the weather dramatically improved. The skies cleared and the sun came out. I stopped to eat bread rolls and cheese on the banks of the River Fillan and surveyed the pitifully scant remains of St. Fillan's Priory and its tiny graveyard. According to legend, St. Fillan had an arm so luminous he was able to write in the dark and when he died his arm was preserved in a casket. Robert the Bruce was said to have taken the empty casket into battle with him and the arm is supposed to have followed of its own accord. A luminous arm would be a great asset in a tent!

By the time I arrived at Tyndrum it was raining again. The campsite was large and boasted a bunkhouse. As my tent and much else were soaked, I decided to treat myself if there were any vacancies. I was in luck. There were, and for the cost of £7 I was given a key and allocated a room with two bunk beds, and just enough room to stand at their side. There were toilets and washbasins in the bunkhouse but the main shower block and laundry were over on the caravan site. There were, I quickly discovered, two disadvantages to the bunkhouse. Firstly, the washbasins all had blocked drains and secondly, because it was a timber building, no cooking was allowed. All meals had to be taken in the adjacent café. Not that I minded. It was not expensive and it made a change. A good range of meals and snacks were served from 7am to 11pm and it was patronised by a steady flow of both walkers and campers. In addition, in another timber building there was a small swimming pool and a shop which sold everything from food to maps and gifts.

I enjoyed a belated second lunch-cum-early-tea, then went to seek out the Big Green Welly Shop. This I had been told was an excellent store which sold everything for the outdoors and there were a couple of items I desperately needed. My undersocks, although not worn out, were completely threadbare. And my gas was almost out. By some strange quirk of fate every time the gas ran out, my margarine ran out too. Both lasted for eleven days. For nine or ten days my rucksack would be getting lighter and lighter, only to be made suddenly heavier again by the addition of a new full cylinder of gas and 250 grams of Flora. The Big Green Welly Shop was as good as it was cracked up to be and I was able to buy all I needed and my next map—the Fort William one, so that I could start planning the next stage of my route. I had a rough idea of where I would go but had not worked out the details.

Tyndrum is only a small village It once owed its prosperity to lead mining but now it relies heavily on tourism and is dominated by huge modern hotels. Travellers have always come this way. In the past, cattle were driven through here to be fattened in England, then in the late nineteenth century, the railways came; two separate lines which do not connect. The West Highland Railway on one side of the road whose high level station served Fort William, and on the other the low level Caledonian Railway which was built to serve Oban. Between the two the A82 carries the main bus and coach links to the north and the Western Isles and this is a convenient stopping off point for coach tours. It seemed to me that half the traffic on the road was either coaches or caravans—and half of those seemed to be foreign. I even saw two dogs holidaying in a camper van— at least that was what it looked like—two Shelties sitting bolt upright in the driver and passenger seat of a smart campervan in the carpark of the Green Welly Shop. Going to the Shetland Islands perhaps?

During the evening I met the two Munro-baggers, now at the end of their trip and having a night of luxury in the caravan of friends who had come to collect them. They reiterated what Kelso Eddy had said, that many walkers had given up and a number were now using the backpack transfer service. With nothing else to do and having abandoned my initial temptation to go for a swim—I didn't think it would be much fun on my own—I whiled away the evening in the café over another pot of tea and a copy of the *Scottish Daily Express*.

Nobody seemed bothered how long I stayed or whether I bought anything. After reading about the rape, violence and scandal in the paper I became quite neurotic and thought "What am I doing wandering round the country by myself?" There were in particular two articles, one about a schoolgirl raped and murdered in a youth hostel in France, and the other about a woman murdered in Bonnybridge the previous Wednesday—August 14th. I began wondering where I had been that day and checked my diary. My suspicions were correct. I was walking through Bonnybridge.

Before dark I went along to the village to phone home, finding as usual that there was a queue. In this case there were two phone boxes, with queues at both. The one was phonecard only in the doorway of a café. In the other, two giggling, skimpily clad girls were squashed, engaged in an animated and lengthy conversation—probably with two equally animated boys. By the time it was my turn, I too had someone waiting. As I only got the answerphone, I gave up and rejoined the queue. My second attempt was still only answered by Michael who was sorry he was unable to take my call and asked me to leave my name and number. I left a somewhat abrupt message saying it was "Me from Tyndrum" and I would phone again in the morning.

### Why am I doing this?

I was still suffering from the effects of reading the newspaper and in the single storey bunkhouse I was so nervous, I closed the window firmly before going to bed. I knew it was faintly ridiculous when I had spent the last two and a half months sleeping in a tent, much of the time out on my own, but the fear was firmly implanted in my mind and I knew I would not sleep easily unless I felt safe and secure.

With less than ten miles to walk next day I did not need to get up early, which was just as well. I did not wake until 8.15, and then it was to a bad headache. I put this down to a combination of sleeping late and being in a hot, stuffy room. The radiators had came on during the night! What I would have liked was a nice hot coffee and a painkiller, but I had promised to phone Michael. I had to get down to the village pretty smartly before he went to work or I'd get the answerphone again.

At times telephoning did become something of a chore, I suppose because it was the one bit of modern technology that I couldn't get away from, and the one thing that restricted me to a fixed time. I took a paracetamol and left about 9.30. Questioned later about the Bonnybridge murder, Michael admitted that he did know about it at the time, having heard the news on the car radio, but had thought it best not to mention it. A wise decision as I would have been even more apprehensive than I already was about walking along the Forth and Clyde Canal alone.

By mid-morning it was pouring with rain—and extremely wet rain too. Sheeting down in stair rods. The path ran alongside the A82 and parallel to the railway line. Traffic on the road was heavy, trains rumbled by at frequent intervals and the skies were leaden. It was so dark and murky that both vehicles and trains had their lights on. For a while I sheltered under a small railway bridge; a narrow tunnel just wide enough to accommodate the footpath. But as the rain showed no sign of abating and I was already soaked, it seemed pointless to hang about getting colder when walking would at least keep me warm. There were literally dozens of walkers in both directions. Mainly day walkers and all looking thoroughly wet and bedraggled. One of them might well have been the naked man from Loch Lomond; I shall never know.

The midges were terrible; a persistent menace. I had bought an excellent little book entitled *The Scottish Midge*. Most informative and I now knew that they were at their worst in low light intensity, the location and weather conditions being of secondary importance. That day they attacked within about 15 seconds of stopping and stuck on my wet face and dripping hair. My headache had not improved, was if anything worse, and my legs felt heavy and lifeless. I had no energy and did not feel like walking at all. If I had been at a more interesting place than Tyndrum I would have had a day off, but I was anxious to get to Fort William and start the next stage.

By lunchtime the rain had eased and I had reached Bridge of Orchy. The name sounds appealing but the place is not. To be fair it probably is in fine weather, but that day it appeared gloomy and desolate. It had nothing to offer—no shop or café, only a Post Office housed in a tin shack near the station and a hotel and bunkhouse. I didn't think the hotel would welcome a soggy, bedraggled backpacker with open arms. I would have given anything for a hot drink, a rest and a leisurely lunch. Outdoors, the midges would not tolerate such luxury. Lashings of midge repellent of both the spray on and roll on variety had little lasting effect. Attending to calls of nature became a nightmare. Combing my wet hair produced a comb black with squashed, drowned corpses. During the whole of my walk I don't think I ever felt so low in spirits. At that moment I would rather have been doing anything, anywhere other than walking the West Highland Way.

A question I was often asked when I returned home was "Did you ever consider giving up?" The answer to that is, "No." Not seriously anyway. There were occasions when I did wonder why on earth I was doing it, but even after a bad day there is always the feeling that things are going to get better and that there is something new and exciting just round the corner. It's rather like reading a really good book. You reach the end of a chapter and even if you are tired and want to go to bed, you have to start the next. You just can't put the book down.

### The menace of the midges

In contrast to the easy contouring path from Tyndrum, the path from Bridge of Orchy breaks free from road and railway and climbs steeply through forestry plantations where purple hummocks of heather and clumps of tall coarse grass grew between the trees. Eventually, conifers gave way to high barren moorland. During the day I had missed several photo opportunities; herds of deer and a large herd of highland cattle with calves, but each time it was far too wet to contemplate getting out the camera. Now, at last, the rain had stopped, the cloud layer was lifting and the entrancing view of Loch Tulla and Inveroran were worth suffering a midge attack to unpack the camera.

It was a misty, grey skyed watercolour scene. The loch, reflecting the clouds, looked like ice. Around the edge grew a dark border of scots pines. Poor, hummocky, boggy wastes, with scrubby bog myrtle bushes and tufts of brown rushes created an air of untouched wilderness. All around rose the mountains—featureless grey shapes, disappearing into the clouds. In this isolated wonderland I was going to camp.

The site was a permissive wild one. I had no idea where it was but had been told to ask at the hotel, one of only a handful of buildings. A sign on the door directed walkers round the back to the Walker's Bar. Here, amongst the usual walker-friendly signs reminding walkers not to 'leave packs blocking doorways' and to 'Hang wet clothes on pegs provided' was one which read 'Please do not remove boots and socks as blistered feet may be offensive.' Another requesting 'No wet clothing in the bar', I didn't notice until I'd been sitting down for ten minutes. This was because having dumped the rucksack and opened the door into the bar, who should I see sitting there already eating a meal, but Eddy and his friend, the one who was going to do

20 miles a day. Having been so depressed and fed up all day this was the most welcome sight and immediately the prospects looked much brighter. I ordered coffee and toasted cheese sandwiches and sat down to talk to them.

The Walker's Bar was small but wonderfully warm and cosy. There were no other customers and the two girls behind the bar did not seem to object to us chatting over coffee for well over an hour. Eddy and his pal were waiting for a taxi! So much for walking 20 miles a day. The friend was already having foot problems and had given up carrying his pack. Now they were waiting to be taxied back to their accommodation and were returning here in the morning. Eddy said they had met a man walking from Land's End to John O'Groats who was about 6 miles ahead. He was expecting to reach Fort William the following day and intended staying there for several days, so there was a chance I might meet up with him.

After Eddy's departure, reluctant to leave the comfort of the bar I ordered more coffee and asked the whereabouts of the wild site. The directions were vague. There were two areas to choose from, both just along the road from the hotel. There was no charge and no facilities, though water was available from a tap outside the hotel. I chose a patch of short grass of no more than a quarter of an acre, beside a bridge over a small river. It would have been idyllic if it wasn't for sharing it with several million midges. Within minutes my green coloured fleece was grey. I have never seen so many midges and I have never put the tent up so fast—and using only one hand too, the other being used ineffectually to try and keep the midges away from my face. Inside the tent I zipped up the porch and set a mosquito coil burning to try and remain midge free and comfortable. The smoke sent thousands into a stupor at the top of the tent pole. For their size, midges have a powerful bite. I don't know how many I received, but the worst were in my hair and at the back of my neck. According to my informative book, there are 36 Scottish species. They mainly feed on sheep and cattle and it was of little consolation to know that only five of these species attack humans.

As no other campers were there and the weather was improving all the time, I braved the midges to look around and take photographs. As there were no 'loos' and there was a lack of trees and screening in the vicinity, suitable locations for this necessary task were in short supply. So I took advantage of the absence of other campers for this and personal ablutions—the latter being much abbreviated, carried out kneeling in the confined area of the porch to combat a midge attack.

As on the previous permissive site, no-one else arrived until late. I was already in bed and lay listening to the commotions outside. All the arrivals were either German or Dutch and I could tell they were having trouble with midges as the word 'midge' seems to be common to all languages. Meaningless strings of incomprehensible language would be frequently punctuated by the word 'midge' and accompanied my much leg slapping and the sound of aerosols as they frantically tried to put up their tents.

## Solitude and spectacular scenery

Next morning, midge-free chores were carried out within the tent before opening up the zip to inspect the weather. Midges floating in the coffee and mixed in the muesli were from the population roosting at the top of the tent pole. When I did pluck up courage to start packing and ventured outside, I found there were now another seven tents on the tiny site. It was a glorious morning. There was a magnificent dramatic sunrise and the rain had cleared the air leaving the mountains in sharp outline and looking near enough to touch.

As I left the still slumbering site, an English couple with a little boy appeared from the other side of the bridge where there were more tents. We set off together, but the boy could not have been more than nine years old and presently I left them behind, soon abandoning the road for a rough track leading into wild and beautiful high country. This was what I had imagined the West Highland Way would be like. The track, a clearly defined old military road, climbed to over 1,000ft. and for the next nine miles the views were spectacular. High, rugged mountains rising to 3,000ft. towered darkly and formidably to the west. To the east the vast open emptiness of Rannoch Moor: an impassable treeless wilderness of water and bog covering 20 square miles: a broad vista of countless lochans, rushing rivers and exposed rock. I enjoyed every minute, absorbing every detail and stopping frequently to identify plants. My most exciting finds were rare blue gentianellas growing on the limestone parapet of Bà Bridge. Less exciting, a set of car keys lay nearby. That must have really made someone's day when they got back to their car after a day's walk!

Apart from the family still visible way behind me, this was the quietest stretch of the Way so far. I met no one until I reached the chair lift at White Corries where a young woman coming the opposite way stopped to talk. She too had been alone all morning and we were both glad to see another face. We discussed the problems, or rather, other peoples' perceived problems, of women walking alone and agreed that in most cases these people are non-walkers.

171

It is ignorance of what is involved that causes them to envisage all sorts of "What if?" scenarios. Their main concern is "Aren't you afraid?" They ask "Don't you worry about sleeping alone at night?" Yet most of Britain is populated by kind, generous, and warmhearted people. The chance of something dreadful happening is about as likely as winning the lottery. You could be mugged on your own doorstep, so why worry about being assaulted in any other place. Women who are themselves walkers are often put off going alone for the same reason. They prefer safety in numbers or the reassuring presence of a male companion. One lady told me she was not afraid to walk alone, but had absolutely no confidence in her map reading abilities and couldn't read a compass! People often told me I was "very brave." I don't think so. I'm just realistic and probably lucky.

After the girl left, I debated whether to stop at the White Corries café which also has a museum. But I had a strong suspicion that you had to take a trip on the chair lift up to the mountain viewpoint to reach the café. It was tempting, but I had taken four hours to walk from Inveroran and with only half of the 18 miles done and the most strenuous yet to come, I decided I could not spare the time. I settled for lunch on a grassy hummock within sight of the Kingshouse Hotel instead.

After the peace and solitude of the morning it was disappointing to find I was back to the noise of traffic. And disconcerting to find this magnificent landscape blighted by an ugly bridge. A huge, brilliant white-painted monstrosity of steel girders which looked from a distance like a marooned ferry. Why ever was such a construction allowed? And why couldn't it be painted in a less obtrusive colour?

At Kingshouse, the flat desolation of Rannoch Moor ends abruptly. The road becomes squeezed between mountains bare of vegetation, great grey-white cliffs of naked rock and scree. In the restricted area of the glen the West Highland Way ran only yards from the dreaded A82. Heavy traffic hurtled past nose to tail on its journey towards the Pass of Glencoe. No-one seemed to take much notice of the 60mph speed limit—except the walkers! Thankfully, this state of affairs was short-lived. At the head of Glencoe, road and traffic continues its frenetic course into the narrowing glen, reaching Kinlochleven after about 20 miles. Those plodding along the West Highland Way veer away from the road to climb steeply up the Devil's Staircase for a quieter, scenic short cut over the hills and reach Kinlochleven after a mere six miles.

The climb up the Devil's Staircase was the most strenuous thing I had encountered since the Southern Uplands. At 1,800ft. it's the highest point of the West Highland Way. Walkers suddenly proliferated as those just out for the day set off from the carpark on the main road and joined the long distance brigade. The path, part of a military road building exercise in 1750, zig-zags up rough and rocky terrain rising about 1,000ft. in a mile and at the top the view is stupendous whichever way you look. To the north are the high mountains of the Nevis Range. Ben Nevis, now for the first time on the skyline, was only one day's walk away.

On the top there was a biting wind, but I needed a breather and rested for a while huddled in the shelter of rocks, boosting the calories from my câche of snacks while feasting my eyes on the scenery. The track was so obvious it was impossible to get lost. I put the map away. My attention could be focused on more interesting things. I decided that this was the best part of the West Highland Way—even better than Rannoch Moor. It was much brighter today and the midges were not such a menace. I had five more miles to go and was able to take my time through truly mountainous scenery. Jagged peaks as far as the eye could see. I was sorry to reach the deep, wooded valley of the River Leven and begin the long descent to Lochleven. The path down a rough track beside massive hydroelectric pipes seemed never ending and took its toll on the knees.

As I entered the village through the dereliction of the aluminium smelter, I could see that Kinlochleven is definitely not the most picturesque of Scotland's towns. But it does have shops and the all important Post Office. What would I have done without them? I topped up my depleted purse, spent some of it in the Co-op and went to find the campsite. There were two. I plumped for the one that was beside the loch and which had a superb view of the Pap of Glencoe. I chose a spot under some birch trees and began tucking into peaches and cakes. After a few days without a shop there is a tendency to crave food. While walking I would think of all the things I was going to buy when I reached one—often unlikely or unsuitable things. Then, when I found a shop, I'd be most disappointed if they didn't have what I wanted. But it was just as much a problem if they did, because I would see other things I fancied too—and buy them all. Then I had to eat it or carry it.

The inner woman catered for, the next priority was the outer woman. After the 'back to basics' routine of the previous night, I needed to wash. Considering this site was one of the most expensive I had used, the unisex shower in a pokey concrete building, open to the elements, was a bit of a let-down. You stepped straight out of a hot shower into fresh air.

While I'd been showering, the people with the little boy I'd seen that morning had arrived and put up their tent close to mine. They were noisy neighbours who seemed to disagree about everything and were constantly shouting at their disobedient son. He spent all his time climbing the tree under which I was camped—swinging monkey-fashion from the branches and generally intruding on my privacy. His parents yelled a lot but never made him get down or called him away.

It was still windy and cold but the skies were clear and it was relatively midge-free. I took advantage of the lovely evening to walk along the loch before phoning home. Life goes on, even when you are miles from home. That night I had a special reason for phoning as it was the day the school examination results were announced. I was naturally anxious to find out how Helen had done though I needn't have worried. She had passed in all ten subjects with excellent grades.

### Through rain and remote glens to Ben Nevis

It was dry next morning to start, but within minutes of leaving it began pouring with rain. I had to stop and put my waterproofs on. Loch Leven is a sea loch and the route of the West Highland Way climbs steeply to a high, U-shaped valley at nearly 1,000ft. with mountains rising 3,000ft. on each side. Through this remote and desolate glen an old cart-track wends its way for some five miles passing from time to time the pitiful ruins of deserted crofts. Old farm implements, including a plough, lay discarded and rusting in the boggy, hummocky wastes. It was difficult to imagine that this glen had once been ploughed and cultivated.

A young woman caught me up. She was walking alone, though she had set out from Milngavie with a friend whom had given up soon after starting. I hadn't seen her at Kinlochleven because she had been at the other campsite and stayed in a wigwam "to have a night away from the midges." All day we were only a few hundred yards apart—sometimes I was ahead, sometimes she was. Our exchanges were brief. It was never possible to hold a proper conversation. There were just too many midges. It was impossible to stop to eat or rest. Essential 'pit stops' were a nightmare. After putting off the dreaded moment as long as possible I eventually accomplished the necessary behind the walls of a ruined croft. Hampered by the additional layers of waterproofs this was no easy task and inevitably as it was still bucketing down, some of my clothing got wet. Oh to be a man! Such a simple feat for them!

The rain was torrential. The stony track was more like the bed of a stream. Water cascaded down the mountainsides as tiny springs became waterfalls. One or two sad-eyed black-faced sheep huddled dejectedly against remnants of walls. No other creatures stirred—except the midges.

My companion later described the West Highland Way as The Ultimate Insect Experience. And she was right. This just about captured the very essence of the walk. If asked what I would remember most about this stage of my route it would not be the scenery, spectacular though it was, nor the weather, for the most part indifferent. It has to be the misery of the midges. I vowed never to walk this Way again and regarded this as one of the least enjoyable bits of Britain.

The only good thing about the day was that after the initial climb from Kinlochleven, walking was fast and easy until the path left the desolation of the glen for the dense greenery of forests. Then it was more hilly. By then the rain was no longer continuous and the sun was beginning to break through. Ahead, Ben Nevis rose impressively high even though the top was shrouded in cloud. Despite the rain it had not been a cold day and as the sun took over it became very humid. Drifts of steaming mist rose from the trees giving it the appearance of a tropical rain forest.

With the arrival of the sun, the midges withdrew. Waterproofs could be discarded. I hung them on the back of the rucksack to dry. A lunch stop was possible at last—taken at a wayside information board, where several other walkers had congregated. My young female acquaintance told me that she couldn't stop as she had a ticket booked on the Fort William to Glasgow coach which left at 6pm. Once she departed she was soon far ahead and I never saw her again. I regarded myself as being very lucky. I would hate to be tied down to such a tight schedule, but lots of walkers seem to be. I knew that Eddy was also planning to leave as soon as he arrived.

For about four miles Ben Nevis dominated the skyline. Then, after a final climb up flights of steps where the hillside was so steep this was the only practical way up, the path emerged from the forest high above Glen Nevis. From here the forest had been felled leaving acres of untidy brashings, but in the process opening up a clear view down Glen Nevis towards Fort William. It was all downhill now to the campsite where I intended staying while I had a day off in Fort William and climbed Ben Nevis. But, according to Michael, thunderstorms were expected next day. As it was already hot and humid this did seem very likely. I sat on a pile of timber, stacked ready for loading beside the track, making up my mind what I should do and decided, in view of the forecast, to abandon Ben Nevis. I would climb that with Michael on the way home—which we did—on a glorious hot day when the temperature at the top was freezing and the wind speed was 50 miles per hour. The summit was in cloud when we reached it but this lifted before we began our descent and we were rewarded with wonderful views.

Having made my decision, there was no need to stay at the Glen Nevis campsite. There was something else I wanted to see—some features known as Parallel Roads, unusual remnants of the ice age. The nearest were at the Glen Roy Nature Reserve, several miles off my route, so I would carry on into Fort William and spend the next day visiting them instead.

On reaching Fort William, the West Highland Way was officially completed. Thereafter I was restricted to the pavement beside a busy main road and felt conspicuously out of place. A busy road junction and traffic lights slowed the traffic to a crawl. I was walking faster than the cars were travelling. I was tired and hot and pounding the pavement was tedious. I felt as if all eyes were on me. I was glad to turn off and arrive at the camp-site—an extensive and expensive caravan city! In exchange for five pounds I was presented with a map of the site. And I needed it to find my way round the network of roads to the vast camping area alongside the River Lochy. Tents were scattered liberally along the field. Mostly huge frame tents that were practically portable hotels. My tent looked tiny and lost in comparison.

I showered in conditions about 200% better than the previous night, but the state of the art laundrette was of little use to me.Two pairs of pants, two pairs of socks, a towel and T- shirt hardly warrant a huge commercial washing machine. I made do with a surreptitious squirt of washing up liquid in a sink labelled 'dishes only.' It was a glorious, sunny evening. There were no sign of midges and it was worth noting in my diary that for the first time in a week I could eat a meal in the open air in comfort!

The summit of Ben Nevis is elusive. There are only about three places from where it can be seen and this was one of them. In the crisp clear evening light, the clouds that had shrouded the summit all day disap-peared leaving Britain's highest mountain majestically bathed in the golden light of the setting sun. Later, just before going to bed, I watched the moon rise over the summit as the last radiant glow of the sun sank below the horizon. What a contrast to the morning. This afternoon's weather had been the best of the entire West Highland Way. A pity it had to come at the end. But would it continue for my day off and the next stage along the Great Glen? Time would tell.

# 12

# Splendid Solitude

## Through the Great Glen

I had now covered over 900 miles. I could not believe I had walked so far. On my return I was frequently asked "Weren't you ever tired?" And in truth, I rarely was. Often I was glad when a day was over—for various reasons: too hot; too wet; too midgey; looking forward to a shower, a meal or company—but seldom because I was exhausted. As soon as the tent was up I would remove my boots, change my socks, make a drink and rest; lying on my sleeping bag in the tent or stretched out on the grass. Within a short time I would be ready for whatever the rest of the day offered. Animal instincts again, like a dog after a long walk. Two hours in his basket and he's ready to go again.

Taking off the rucksack was always a relief. The first eight to ten miles was fine; more than that, especially over demanding terrain and my back and shoulders would start to ache. At one point I had a very sore navel; red and weepy, caused by the hot weather, perspiration and constant pressure from the broad waist band of the rucksack. For two weeks I had a three inch square of plaster stuck on my midriff. After that I made liberal use of baby talc.

The Glen Roy Nature Reserve was a good day's walk off my route, so I decided to use public transport. Having walked for 63 days I had no qualms about doing this. It was after all supposed to be a day off.

It wasn't that far back to Fort William; a 50p. journey and the driver promised to give me directions to the bus station. However, a passenger overhearing my conversation offered to take me personally as she was

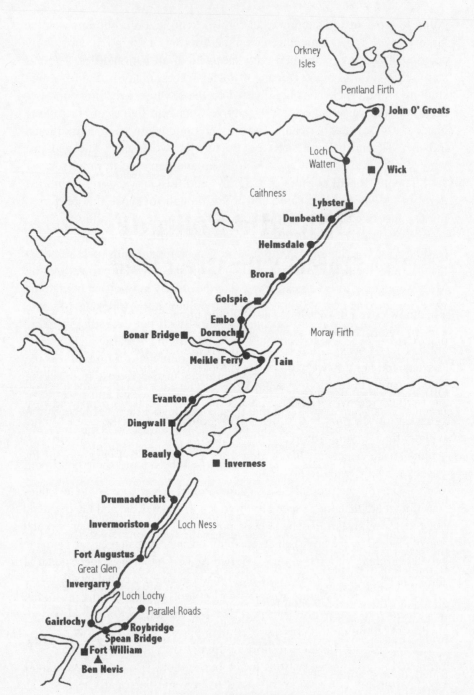

*Fort William to John O'Groats*

going to work at the supermarket right next to it. Fort William was the largest town I had encountered since Buxton. I found it amazingly cosmopolitan. Streets teemed with shoppers of all nationalities. The bus station was just as busy. Dozens of backpackers, many of them foreign students, sat on rucksacks or squatted on the pavement reading copies of their national daily papers. An attractive Canadian Indian girl with long black plaits, soft leather chaps and fringed tunic waited with a traditional indian pack and bed roll, looking for all the world as if she had just walked off a movie set. Coaches drew up and departed in rapid succession, leaving for all corners of Britain—and for Gatwick and Heathrow Airports. A bus to Skye came and went, though for those that preferred rail the Jacobite steam train provides a scenic route via Mallaig.

When it arrived the Inverness coach rapidly filled. Not all who waited could get on. The luggage compartment was crammed with rucksacks, but the driver let me take mine inside when I explained I was not travelling far. Most were going to Inverness; a few like the elderly lady sitting next to me were going to the Fort William Agricultural Show a few miles out of town. I was going eight miles to Spean Bridge, a small but exceedingly lively place where coaches arrived endlessly, disgorging American, Japanese, Italian and French—all heading for the Commando Museum or the Scottish Mill shop. I had to wait 40 minutes in the Tourist Information Office just to pay for a map. There was only one assistant and never have I seen anyone so over-efficient that they could devote their entire attention to finding an American couple bed and breakfast in Glasgow and completely ignore the telephone ringing and a long queue of tourists all waiting to pay for small purchases. Even after booking their hotel, she proceeded with the aid of maps to give them precise route details to and through Glasgow.

I was still five miles from the campsite at Roy Bridge and to avoid a busy main road took a quiet road beside the turbulent River Spean. On the way I passed a graphic road sign which read 'Elderly Cat Crossing'. It depicted a geriatric cat on crutches. I never saw it, though I half expected some scraggy tom to come limping out of the bushes. The road ended at a farm and a footpath continued across fields coming eventually level with Roy Bridge on the opposite side of the river. There was no bridge but the over-efficient Tourist Office assistant had assured me I could cross on stepping stones. If there were stepping stones I never found them—unless she meant a natural dam of rocks, which would certainly not have been passable if the water was of greater volume than it was then. Several youngsters scrambling across on mountain bikes watched disdainfully as I picked my way across trying not to get my boots wet.

### A thunderstorm and parallel roads

It had been hot and humid all day. No sooner had I arrived at the campsite than the heavens opened. It was so sudden I gave little thought to where I pitched, threw the tent up and crawled inside. It was 2 o'clock, oppressive and thundery. The forecast was correct. A man from another tent came to ask if I was OK. He'd seen me queuing in the Information Office and said he would have given me a lift if he'd known I was going to the same site. It rained for over an hour. I drank four cups of coffee and wondered how long it was going to last. I still wanted to see the parallel roads that day if possible and estimated it would take an hour and a half to get there. When the rain began to ease, I thought there was still time.

I took only my waterproofs, camera and a pocketful of snacks. It was road walking all the way but I hadn't realised that it was a long, steady, uphill walk. The rain refused to give up entirely, but it was much too hot to put my cagoule on. I hung it round my shoulders and sheltered under trees during heavier downpours. Thunder rumbled away incessantly in the distance. Over Ben Nevis were great banks of ominous, inky purple clouds, yet to the north the sun was shining from a clear blue sky. For half an hour I walked towards the perfect arc of a magnificent rainbow through a broad glen of unfenced pastures. It was well farmed and even in the rain farmers were busy haymaking. In one field three tractors were at work — frantically baling and hauling round bales in a desperate attempt to beat the weather.

When I reached the Glen Roy viewpoint it was all worthwhile. The parallel roads were an extraordinary sight. It is now known that they were formed when, as the ice melted, glacial lakes overflowed and suddenly dropped in level leaving lines round the mountainside like a tidemark round a bath. Three levels were clearly visible and it was easy to see how, before modern geographical knowledge unravelled their origins, peoples of the past thought up some original ideas of their own. The lines etched into the mountainside, contouring the length of the glen, and matching perfectly on the opposite side of the valley, do look very much like man-made tracks.

The thunderstorm still raged to the south. Later I heard that at its centre it was so violent that window panes had been shattered. My walk back was fast—all downhill. I had time to look more closely at a community of a dozen deserted crofts and the stone memorial cairn of the last clan battle fought in Scotland. Back at the site tent numbers had multiplied and I realised it was Saturday again. The weekend influx had arrived.

During the early hours I was woken by moans and groans from the next tent occupied by two young men. Then, the distressing sounds of vomiting—no doubt the result of over indulgence at the pub. I knew they had been out earlier. On crowded sites there is an almost total lack of privacy, yet people tend to think when they are in their tent they are private. They talk and behave as if they were at home, forgetting that everyone else can unavoidably hear everything. This can be very entertaining, as good as listening to a radio. One of the best comedy shows I heard was put on somewhere in Northumbria by a family of four with a black poodle. It was about dusk. Dad made the evening drinks and took them into the family-size tent. Young Billy, who had been playing ball with the dog all evening, presumably threw the ball to his sister and the dog leapt across the tent to fetch it, knocking over the hot drinks in his travels. Pandemonium broke out, Dad yelling at Billy for throwing the ball, Billy yelling at the dog. Little sister screaming because she's covered in hot tea. Mum blaming Dad for bringing hot drinks into the tent, the kids for playing ball and the dog for behaving like a dog. As far as I could make out all the sleeping bags and the dog were soaked and tea was swilling round the groundsheet. The dog was banished to the car and the two children became suitably subdued while mopping up operations were carried out by torchlight. I doubt any of them gave a thought to the fact that half the campsite was listening in.

### Confined to quarters by torrential rain

After walking 12 miles on what was supposed to be a day off it was nice to know that next day I didn't have far to go to rejoin my original route on the Caledonian Canal, so there was no great rush. I crossed the river and retraced my steps to Spean Bridge. The carpark was already full of coaches and it dawned on me that not only was it Sunday but it was August Bank Holiday weekend. Crowds were flocking to The Mill Shop, full of clan tartans made into everything you can conceivably make tartan. I was tempted into buying several gifts before leaving along the main road to Inverness.

Just after leaving Spean Bridge, on a prominent knoll beside the road stands the Commando Memorial—three soldiers on a stone plinth. It could just as well be called the Commanding Memorial, as in both location and stature it is impressive. It was erected in 1952 in recognition of the services of the commandos who trained in this area during the Second World War. While I was taking photographs a car drew up beside me and two Americans jumped out. Completely ignoring the imposing monument they rushed across the road to capture two scrawny sheep on film. This wasn't the first time I'd seen this happen. Foreigners seem to be fascinated by British sheep.

At precisely the same time as the previous day, it started to rain. I had just arrived at the campsite, on a disused railway line. Quiet and pleasant enough but the ground was hard ballast where grass struggled to provide a thin turf. My tent pegs wobbled precariously, barely in the ground. From the moment it began, the rain was torrential. I spent the next seven hours confined to my tent while it rained unremittingly, the worst and heaviest since Hawes almost a month before. I read, ate, marked my new maps with the route and campsites for the week ahead and became thoroughly bored and physically uncomfortable. My knees and elbows objected to hours of kneeling and lying on my stomach reading. Eventually I could stand it no longer. I had to go for a walk even though it was still raining. There was nothing to do. Yachts passing through the Caledonian Canal provided a small diversion but apart from a small hydroelectric power station there was nothing else. But anything was better than more hours cramped in the tent. That night I lay in bed thinking of the week ahead. The penultimate stage through the Great Glen. My final thoughts were "Would I see Nessie?"

### Red deer and eagles—but where?

The most straightforward route through the Highlands avoiding roads and using a recognised waymarked route seemed to be the Great Glen Cycle Route. Although primarily developed with cyclists in mind, it is also a footpath and uses the network of forestry tracks and sections of the Caledonian Canal towpath to provide an off-road route between Fort William and Inverness, a distance of about 80 miles. It is the perfect solution for walkers heading north. I had no guide to the route. Two attempts to obtain details from Tourist Information Offices had drawn a blank, the relevant leaflet being out of stock and out of print. I would be relying entirely on maps and would not even have the company of other walkers with whom to exchange information.

Throughout the night I was kept awake by the ferocity of the rain. By morning it had been raining continuously for 20 hours and showed no signs of abating. I lay warmly ensconced in my sleeping bag wondering whether to stay put and keep dry or carry on regardless. I still hadn't come to a decision when I finally got up. I didn't hurry over breakfast. My next door neighbours, a couple from Nottingham, spent a good hour chatting as the rain dwindled to a light drizzle and we both began to take our tents down. It was mid-morning when I left. By making the detour to Roy Bridge I had missed the first nine miles of the Caledonian Canal including Neptunes Staircase, the flight of eight locks between Loch Linnhe and Loch Lochy which forms the first, or last, link between the North Sea and Scotland's west coast. Now, I found the cycle route immediately abandoned the towpath for a minor road and then turned onto a forest track.

The weather continued to improve. It was still cloudy overhead, but pleasantly warm and there were glimpses of blue sky. It appeared the rain had gone for good. Cyclists were few. I had expected more and this was a nice surprise. The rough forest tracks are really only recommended for mountain bikes and as noted in the Pennines, none seemed to be fitted with bells. The occasional warning yell seemed to be the exception rather than the rule but I welcomed the opportunity to jump out of the way. It was so quiet I was glad when I saw one, just to know I was not alone.

All along the route are information boards. In the absence of a trail guide I found these invaluable. They gave comprehensive route details, classifying it as either easy, moderate or demanding with a gradient profile and the type of surface to expect. In addition there were historical notes and points of interest and what wildlife to expect. Accordingly I looked out for red deer and golden eagles on the steep hillsides above Loch Lochy but with no success—they were all keeping well out of sight. They must have been somewhere though as at intervals the cycle route took on the appearance of a prison camp. Seven foot high fences, cattle grids and steel gates. Deer fences—though which side they were supposed to keep the deer I couldn't work out.

The path was high with fine views along Loch Lochy and Loch Oich. It was incredibly peaceful. I stopped frequently to note down plants, take photographs and gape awe inspired at the stunning scenery. By the end of the day I had walked 17 long and lonely miles.

### Every nationality but English

Frustratingly, I reached Invergarry on the 'wrong' side of the river to my proposed campsite. To cross required a detour down the valley and back up the other side adding an extra three miles to my journey. However, there was a bonus; an unexpected café on the way. Delicious scones, refreshing tea and fresh milk for next day's breakfast.

The site was at the top of a steep hill. I was directed to a level, grassy area under trees next to an Australian couple. The trees came in handy for hanging up items still damp from the day before and I arranged my soggy socks and waterproofs on suitable branches. The evenings were now noticeably drawing in and getting cooler. Usually I phoned home between 7 and 9 and if the call box necessitated a long trek this was often now done in the dark. It was no longer possible to read or write my diary for any length of time and often I was in bed by 8.30 though I rarely went to sleep. There was generally too much noise until about 11 o'clock. Here, caravans and campervans were still arriving after dark. I almost evacuated as one driver, directed by his wife with the aid of a torch, shunted his caravan backwards and forwards only yards from my tent. They had a fretful child, spent hours getting themselves organised and sounded like a herd of elephants banging around in the van. I consoled myself with the thought that at least my body was getting a long rest.

Since I had been in Scotland, especially now I was getting further north, on most sites the English were in the minority. Instructions for washing machines and so on were often in French and German. And on the roads, with so much continental traffic to cater for, there were permanent road signs in five languages warning motorists to 'Drive on the left'.

Over the weeks I had observed the characteristics of the different nationalities, watching their behaviour both on and off campsites and listening from my tent at night. I knew what to expect when I came into contact with them. The Aussies and Dutch were always the friendliest and the first, or only ones, to engage in conversation and the Australian girl on this site soon came over to talk—surprised to see I was on my own. The Australians and New Zealanders were the easiest to get on with, out-going, generous and full of enthusiasm for life; the Dutch were just as sociable, but in a quieter, more reserved way. They enjoyed everything they did, the younger ones in particular were always laughing and joking. I could easily identify their tents by the tomfoolery and giggling that was going on. They all spoke excellent English and like the French were extremely polite. Not that there were many French on the campsites, they appeared to prefer hotels to the basics of camping. The Germans on the other hand made up about half of the overseas tourists in Scotland, travelling round in luxurious campervans the size of buses—even a huge articulated unit on one site. They rarely spoke to anyone except each other, but between themselves they talked the most and the loudest, sounding to my uneducated ear like vociferous parrots. I sometimes felt like throwing a blanket over their tents at night to silence them. Two Germans on the Pennine Way never spoke more than two words to anyone in three weeks. Belgians and Austrians spoke if they had to, but appeared more reserved and the Italians talked so much to each other they didn't have time or breath left for anyone else. They travelled round in extended family groups with so many children they didn't even notice anyone else. I met no Scandinavians and only one Spaniard—a young man backpacking near John O'Groats who spoke hardly any English. He had camped wild on the cliffs where the mournful howling of seals had convinced him that Scotland still had wolves.

### A cash-flow problem

Before leaving Invergarry, my most immediate concern was to sort out my finances. With considerable alarm I had discovered that my cheque book contained only four more cheques and I had practically no money left in my post office account. I was urgently in need of a Post Office. It was in a tiny shed in a layby with hardly any room for me and my rucksack. With two customers it was packed. I couldn't imagine how they dealt with security. But this was the real Scotland. I was getting a glimpse of everyday living. I wrote a cheque to myself and paid it in hoping it would see me through to the end. For the rest of the way I had to watch my spending. I wrote cheques only when it was for a worthwhile amount and used credit cards where I could. As I had known that hole-in-the-wall facilities would be practically non-existent on my chosen route, I had put the bulk of my money in the post office. Michael was keeping an eye on my bank balance, topping it up when necessary. As credit cards were not acceptable at most smaller campsites, village stores, and in Scotland at many high street shops too, it was essential that I always carried a reasonable amount of cash.

With the finances looking healthier, I left Invergarry in a happier frame of mind and by lucky chance found a Great Glen Cycle Route Leaflet beside the track; slightly damp but otherwise in good condition. This was the leaflet I had tried unsuccessfully to buy and must have been dropped by a passing cyclist. 'Look out for Red Deer and Wood Ants between Invergarry and Oich Bridge,' it said. I saw no deer. But the wood ants were there in their thousands with anthills several feet high spilling down onto the track. It was a quiet and uneventful walk. Light showers were enough to be a nuisance but were not worth putting on a coat for, I saw only two cyclists and the last five miles along the canal were tedious to say the least.

### *I learn how to put on a kilt—and visit the police station*

Arriving at Fort Augustus after hours of my own company I found myself suddenly amongst crowds of mainly overseas visitors. I had plenty of time for sightseeing so went first to find the campsite before looking round. Then I had a big decision—how best to spend my afternoon? For a tiny place Fort Augustus has a lot to offer. The biggest attraction is watching the boats passing through the locks to Loch Ness and the opening of the swing bridge to enable highmasted boats to enter the lock. Americans with camcorders recorded it all to "show the folks back home." It must be the most photographed event in Scotland. The residents must get heartily sick of it. Then there is the 'working' Benedictine Monastery, beautifully sited on the shores of Loch Ness. One of the most famous and well documented sightings of the Monster was seen from there by a monk. Part of the monastery houses the Abbey Heritage Centre, a multi-media exhibition covering the history of the Highlands and its people advertised as 'one of the best tourist experiences in Britain'. In addition, there is the Clansman Centre, a much smaller affair offering a living enactment of life in a Highland Croft. I was also tempted to take the Loch Ness Boat Trip, which left hourly, with the prospect of sighting the monster. In the end, the Clansman Centre won. The two 'Clansman' periodically putting in an appearance outside the door of their reconstructed-inside-another-building croft, looked so authentic in their 'ancient' Highland garb they rather appealed to me. I chose well. It was informative and informal with only a few people being admitted at any one time to the tiny heather-thatched croft. We squatted on a low platform in the dimly lit single room which served for sleeping, cooking and living and the actor-highlander described the primitive living conditions and demonstrated the use of lethal looking weapons, which were passed round for everyone to examine. I was glad I wasn't male and wearing shorts as when the history of the tartan was explained, a 'volunteer' from the audience was required to demonstrate the traditional way to put on a kilt. The most authentic appearance is achieved if the 'volunteer' is a male wearing shorts. The poor guy 'volunteered' was most embarrassed.

At the end of the day it was cold with an autumnal feel in the air. Bedding plant displays were, I noticed, already showing signs of frost damage. That evening I was glad to snuggle into my sleeping bag.

Studying the maps for the remainder of the journey, as yet unplanned, I changed my mind about going to Inverness. I had learnt that the Cycle Way ran out of forest tracks and quiet roads soon after Drumnadrochit. From there, the proposed route was still being negotiated with landowners. There was no advantage in going to Inverness and I had been there before. The most direct route north was from Drumnadrochit to Dingwall and there were several ways this could be achieved. Over recent years road bridges have been constructed over several firths, saving long inland detours to get round them and reducing the milage to John O'Groats. But no-one seemed to know if there were footpaths over them. I asked several cyclists and site wardens but all rather blankly said they had never crossed the bridges or hadn't noticed. So, my first call next morning was to the police station to find out. The officer at the enquiry desk produced a traffic patrol motorcyclist who obviously thought this request very strange. He told me the Moray and Cromarty Bridges were definitely walkable and he was 99% certain the Dornoch Bridge was too, but why on earth did I want to walk to John O'Groats?

### Walking in a trance

Before leaving I dispatched the weekly parcel, packed with gifts, souvenirs and films, bought more maps and stocked up with Scottish Cornish pasties, sweets and chocolate to see me through the morning. It was only eight miles to Invermoriston and I was there by lunchtime. These short days were wonderfully relaxing. By now I was extremely fit and used to walking at a constant speed. I never consciously hurried and never thought about the mechanics of walking at all. Each day was a new adventure, with fresh people to meet and different things to see. I never knew what was round the next corner. I had absolutely no idea what was going on in the world and if it were not for keeping a diary would have had no idea of the date or the day of the week. Likewise, time had lost all meaning. I got up when I awoke, ate when I was hungry, which was frequently, and slept when it got dark. The only fixed time in my day was to make the evening call home. Occasionally time dragged. A long ascent; a hot day; an over-weight pack; can all make a mile seem like ten and an hour like a day. Over the weeks I developed a way of combating this which usually worked. Most important was to resist the temptation to look at my watch every five minutes and, similarly, to avoid looking at the map to see how much further I had to go. I would set my mind on some totally absorbing problem or idea, which was usually the word-for-word writing of this book, in my head. Soon I would enter a trance-like state. When something happened to bring me out of it—the arrival of another person, a stunning view or a major map reading decision—I would find the miles and time had slipped by without noticing. I would have been oblivious to the heat, or rain, and the rucksack had apparently become weightless.

The forest paths were peaceful and empty of humanity, but I had no feeling of loneliness. I still had my 'guardian walkers' and was conscious of their 'presence' more here than at any other time since Somerset. If all else failed and I felt I couldn't carry the pack a step further or would never make it to the top of a steep climb, I called on their assistance. They never let me down. Perhaps it was all in my mind. I don't know. But I was, and still am, quite convinced that someone was looking after me, helping me, and giving me the strength and stamina to get through difficult stages. I had strong feelings that it was my mother. She was familiar with every part of Britain and loved Scotland. I know she would have enjoyed every minute. Had she still been alive she would have been following every step of my journey and I firmly believe that she was with me in spirit.

*Loch Ness Monsters*

From the height of the forest tracks, the views along Loch Ness were breathtaking. I began to get some idea of its true size. At 24 miles it is longer than the width of the English Channel between Dover and Calais, and for most of its length is a mile wide. When a boat appeared it took an interminable time to draw level and pass. The water was smooth and calm. Ideal for Nessie watching. I kept my eyes peeled, but she was keeping out of sight, like the red deer and the golden eagles. The only ripples on the water were the long wakes of boats, which if there were no others in the vicinity, sometimes extended half way across the loch.

Until recently there would have been no views, everything being obscured by trees. Now, many of the mature spruces planted over 60 years ago were being harvested. The trees that remained were larger than anything ever seen in the forests of Wales and beneath them were thick carpets of moss. Where they had been felled, mounds of heather replaced the moss and tall pink spikes of rosebay willow herb colonised the untidy brashings. In the more distant past, before anyone thought of growing conifers commercially, these mountains were clothed with oak, birch and hazel, but during the seventeenth century much of this ancient woodland was cleared and floated down the loch for shipbuilding. More trees were felled to build the Caledonian Canal, mainly to be used as fuel by the workmen, and many more were used for making barrels for the east coast fishing industry. Near Drumnadrochit a stark reminder that oak was once plentiful in these parts lives on in the name of Bark Sheds, where the bark was stripped from oaks for the leather tanning industry.

I spent a happy morning adding more plants to my notebook lists and taking far more photographs than was necessary as the scenery became more spectacular. Photographically I suspected this was all a waste of time, as from my position on the north side of the loch I was always looking directly into the sun. Added to this, a more or less permanent haze and acres of light reflecting water didn't bode well for the results. But I kept taking them anyway—for memories and because I might never pass this way again. People travelling by road never see these uninterrupted, almost aerial views. Driving along the shore-hugging main road, you get no idea of the length of the loch and see very little because there are too many trees in the way. Apart from walkers and cyclists, the only other people privy to these sights are RAF pilots. Both fighters and Hercules use the Great Glen as a flight path—an incredible sight; the fighters fast and low and gone before you hear them; the Hercules slow and majestic, sweeping gracefully over the water—a modern day Loch Ness Monster.

*A hammer for my tent pegs—and where are the Scots?*
The campsite at unpronounceable Rubha Bhan was one of the nicest yet. A long, narrow strip along the shore of the loch with pitches marked out with tree trunks of telegraph pole proportions. The ground is so hard that campers are issued with a metal spike and hammer—the only way to get a tent peg in more than half an inch. The ground must have been solid rock and even with these aids I could still barely get my pegs in enough to hold the tent up.

Arriving at lunchtime there were plenty of vacant pitches, all bare of grass and overcamped. There were several toilet blocks. I always chose to be fairly near these if possible, but on this site there was also a camper's covered area, with picnic tables and a cooking area. I erected my tent opposite this just a few yards from the water's edge. Picnic tables were also provided on about half the pitches, but not mine, so I lugged one over from the next pitch, and had it innocently parked on my patch just in time. Five minutes later, a Dutch couple arrived, set up their tent on the adjacent pitch and pinched the picnic table from another vacant lot. These tables must 'walk' up and down the site all the time.

I spent a thoroughly lazy afternoon reading a book which told me all I needed to know about Loch Ness. I wrote my diary, checked my maps and discovered that I had inadvertently sent one of my new ones home, mistaking it for the redundant Fort William one. I cursed my stupidity; it meant spending more of my precious money on a replacement.

Across the loch, the never-ending vista of hills were purple with heather, now at its best, but never with enough sun to give just that 'lift' to the colours. Tiny wavelets rippled gently onto the shingle beach and a family of mallard hung around hopefully for food. I still hadn't seen the Monster, only the realistic lifesize replica basking on the foreshore near Reception. By late afternoon it had become chilly, there was a fresh breeze and the loch became quite 'choppy'. I adjourned with my books and maps to the camper's shelter. The site was filling up rapidly, mainly with Dutch and Germans. I now had neighbours on each side. The Dutch couple were pleasant and sociable while on the other side an English foursome with a trailer tent were noisy and ignored me completely, even though if I reached out of my tent I could touch theirs. It was so large it took them two hours to erect and filled the entire allocated space, some of their pegs coming over the demarcation logs onto my patch. And all this for an overnight stop! Once again, because it was dark and cold I turned in early but with radios and barbecues all around, it was midnight before I fell asleep.

The odd thing about this part of Scotland was the lack of Scots. Shopkeepers seemed to be from London and the owner of the site was from Nottingham. When I went to hand in my key and collect my £3 deposit before leaving, she was in some distress and anxious to share her troubles. A desperate phone call from her daughter, mother of a three week old baby was the cause. She was sick and too dizzy to get out of bed, her husband had already gone to work and the baby was crying to be fed. She was panicking. Mother was too far away to help and couldn't leave the site anyway and she was panicking too. I could only listen and sympathise and let her get it off her chest. When she calmed down, she showed me a news-paper cutting sent to her by an End-to-End walker a few weeks before; a young woman raising funds for Leukaemia. The girl's feet had been bleeding and bandaged. "What are yours like?" She asked. No-one could believe that my feet were in perfect shape. The last and only blister I had was in Cornwall.

When I managed to get away it was to go only as far as the Post Office and stores at Invermoriston where I found that the postmaster hailed from Wembley! The only noteworthy thing about Invermoriston is Telford's bridge across the River Moriston. Replaced now by a modern bridge, the mighty arches of the nineteenth century bridge, balanced on massive rocks in the centre of the river, are an impressive feat of engineering—and apparently caused Telford a few headaches at the time of construction.

### Raspberries and cycling dogs

I was eating constantly now and set off loaded with provisions on what the cycle route leaflet described as a 'Demanding' climb of over 300 metres to a Victorian viewpoint. Locating the stone seat, which wasn't immediately obvious, and rummaging in my map case for the leaflet, I found it was missing. I knew exactly where I had left it—on the newspaper counter in the Post Office where I had shown it to two girls cycling to Inverness on the main road, unaware that there was a cycle route. Ah! Well! Easy come, easy go. It was a lucky find in the first place and as I was on the last lap it had served its purpose. Perhaps someone else would find and use it.

Along the forest tracks, and indeed throughout most of Scotland, wild raspberries grew in great abundance. Often I supplemented my diet with handfuls of large juicy and wonderfully sweet fruit. Soon I came to Prince Charles' Cave. Not a very auspicious cave; some say just a shelter for estate workers, but a sign assures us this is where Bonnie Prince Charles hid from his pursuers and from where he made his final escape to the safety of the Cameron Clan. Not far away, some of his followers were apprehended and one of them, who looked vaguely like the prince was promptly beheaded and the bloody trophy taken to London where the mistake was realised. By this time of course the prince had vanished, thanks to the sacrifice of his loyal follower.

The Great Glen had all the way provided me with hours of botanical interest. I noted several cotoneasters, patches of orange-flowered fox and cubs normally only seen in gardens, tiny eyebrights, ladies mantle and junipers. All the elderberries were of a red berried variety, an introduced species which naturalises readily and makes an attractive shrub. I never saw any black ones in Scotland. At over 1,000ft. near Bark Sheds I had found the red berried Cowberry, similar to the more common bilberries found in other parts of Britain.

While taking a mid-morning lunchbreak on a large boulder beside the track, a young man went hurtling past on a mountain bike. On his back in a little rucksack was a small dog, probably a cairn terrier. It looked as if it was really enjoying itself, paws on his shoulders, ears blown back, nose in the air. Inwardly kicking myself for not grabbing the camera, I could not believe my eyes when a second cyclist, an attractive young woman, sped by with another dog on her back and an alsatian running behind. She was not travelling quite as fast and I called out and asked if she could stop for me to take a picture. Obligingly she did and told me that the dogs always travelled with them and loved it. Her partner returned to see why she was delayed. "What about the Alsatian?" I asked, "How far does he go?" "Oh! He's not ours," they said, "He just started following us and we can't get rid of him." I thanked them for stopping and they went on their way, the alsatian loping happily behind. About 2 hours and five miles later I met a backpacker coming the oppo-site way with an Alsatian. "Is he yours?" I asked. The backpacker turned out to be German and when he finally understood what I was saying, told me that he had met the cyclists and they had persuaded the dog to walk back with him. He was going to take the dog to the Youth Hostel at Invermoriston in the hope that they would know where he belonged. I had a strong feeling this hound probably did this every day of his life! He was probably quite capable of finding his own way home.

These days through the Great Glen were some of the best of my walk. In places it was hard going but I enjoyed every minute and I will never forget those fabulous views along Loch Ness. The path now was so high it was above the tree line and where forest tracks did not exist, a steep and rugged footpath has been cut. A few miles from Drumnadrochit the official off-road cycle way came to an end on the A82. As I had no intention of risking my neck along a vergeless main road, I found my own way by climbing even higher to an area of moorland where a minor road serving a small farming community lead me the final four miles to Drumnadrochit.

Another town, another campsite. This time at a large equestrian centre with two camping fields. A flat, uninspiring field near the road and a sloping field on the top of a steep bank, with wonderful views. I chose the latter, which at the time was almost empty. It turned out to be the most popular and by evening was packed. No marked out pitches here, tents were barely feet apart. The young couple next to me were New Zealanders on a two year work exchange scheme. They were taking time off to travel throughout Britain and Europe and next day were heading south and going over to Ireland. The boy was a 'Big Truck' fitter, the son of a South Island dairy farmer. With farming in common we got on well, an easy relation-ship rapidly being established. Our tents were next to the adjacent field where two extremely vocal donkeys paraded up and down the fence causing much hilarity amongst the campers with their raucous cries.

In need of provisions yet again, I popped along to the village and spotted a poster advertising Highland Games to be held on the Saturday. I had said all along that if I came across Highland Games anywhere, I would go. It was then Thursday, but this was my chance. I was not going to miss it. I decided straight away to stay until the Sunday. I was overdue for a day off anyway. Discounting the 12 mile day off at Roy Bridge, I had not had a break for 29 days—when I met Ben at Hawes. This was a good place to stop as there was so much to do—Urqhuart Castle, the Loch Ness Monster Exhibition, shops and a good supermarket. There would be plenty to keep me occupied. These would be proper days off; no need to get up early; no need to wear boots; no tent to take down; no rucksack to carry. What bliss!

Towards evening the clouds that had given a grey and overcast day, cleared. The sun came out and there was a brilliant sunset. The forecast was for rain but I wasn't bothered. Nothing was going to dampen my spirits now. This was Day 69. In just over a week I would be nearly there. I was having a wonderful time and the thought of it all coming to an end was almost too much to bear. It was eight weeks since leaving home the second time. During that time I had been completely free—no cooking, housework, washing up, ironing or gardening; no letters, bills, or other people to worry about. No stresses. I had come to realise how little I needed to enjoy life. All my possessions I carried on my back. I could have lived like this forever. But all good things must come to an end. Modern life has its ties and it is difficult to break away from them. In the end it all comes back to money—and I was rapidly running out of that.

### Monster mania

The weather next day was still fine, which was good news. There would be nothing worse than sitting out two days in a tent. I chatted to the New Zealanders over breakfast, and then to an elderly lady in a camper van who had come for the Highland Games. Strictly speaking it is a Highland gathering; a gathering of the clans when traditionally the clansmen show off their skills and strength by competing in the games. This was the gathering of the Macmillan Clan, of which my lady acquaintance was a member. She attended every year, but bemoaned the fact that their tartan had a lot of yellow in it. She didn't like yellow and said it was difficult to find things to wear with it.

I spent the morning at Urquhart Castle, a mile back along the road on a promontory on the shores of Loch Ness. This is Scotland's most visited castle, not least because it is from here that Nessie has been spotted the greatest number of times. The carpark is totally inadequate for the overseas visitors who arrive in their hundreds. Several police officers were trying to keep the traffic moving and directing coaches to parking places. I had the distinct feeling I was the only British person in the melée of mixed nationalities swarming over the ruins like ants on an anthill. The only English speaking people were Australians, Americans and the New Zealand couple who I met again up one of the towers. They had already tooted as they passed me walking along the road.

The noise of strimmers being used by maintenance men on the steep grassy banks of moat and ramparts, added to the babble of many tongues. A lone piper in highland dress 'busked' as each new coach load of visitors disembarked; by his age, an enterprising schoolboy earning extra pocket money.

However hard I tried, I could not get used to the Scottish one pound notes which are still in common daily use. Apparently the Scots objected so strongly to the pound coin that the Bank of Scotland continued to print them, but I kept mistaking them for five pound notes. I bought coffee and a chocolate bar with one before I left the castle and stood with my hand out waiting for my change. "It happens every day of the week." I was told. On other occasions I had handed over a pound note thinking it was a 'fiver' and wondered what the cashier was waiting for.

I intended spending the afternoon visiting the Loch Ness Monster Exhibition. But which should I choose? The 'Official' or the 'Original'. Occupying separate buildings a few hundred yards apart, both were overpriced and enquiries indicated they were both much the same. I went to the 'Official', an audio-visual exhibition of about 45 minutes. Herded round a series of displays in the dark by a hidden 'speaker', it was rather like a school trip, but I enjoyed it and whether you believe there is a monster or not (and they make no claims either way), it is certainly food for thought. On balance I think I came away a believer.

As I was now temporarily a tourist, I did all the touristy things. Photographed the lifesize monster in the puddle-sized 'loch' outside the exhibition, browsed round the many gift shops, one catering almost exclusively in Monster memorabilia—Drumnadrochit's answer to Tyndrum's Big Green Welly shop. They don't call it the Big Green Fluffy Loch Ness Monster Shop-but they could! Americans were snapping up 'authentic' Loch Ness Monster certificates, though I'm not sure what, exactly, they were authenticating. I bought a book on the Highland Clearances to read in the evenings. The fifty pence novel I had bought in a charity shop and started at Land's End was now finished in more ways than one. I had been sending it home in pieces as I read it. Partly to save weight and partly because it had fallen apart.

### Scottish humour

I needed another injection of cash. The postmaster nearly gave me a heart attack when he pushed my withdrawal slip back over the counter saying "Sorry! I'm afraid I can't give it to you." I was about to have a severe bout of panic when he said "Only joking. I used to be a Bank Manager and don't like to see people taking money out of their accounts." A taste of Scottish sense of humour I could have done without.

Later, when I went to stock up with supplies for the weekend, I found the hi-tech business of supermarket shopping all but ground to a halt owing to the endeavours of a local workman. A sign outside the store, a large windowless warehouse, read something like this: 'Due to circumstances beyond our control our power supply has been cut off by a JCB. We hope to be offering a full service by 5pm.' Meanwhile, a barrier of trollies had been placed across the door and if anyone wanted anything, one of the cashiers would pop off round the aisles with a torch, basket and list. I couldn't help wondering if the multinationals back home would do that. I thought not. And nowhere else in Britain have I been in supermarkets where all else stops for personal telephone calls and gossip. It was not unusual to be queuing at a checkout and have to wait while a long discussion was carried on with all the intimacy of a small shop of 40 years ago. The waiting shoppers all avidly listening and even joining in the conversation.

One exchange I overheard while waiting to be served caused much amusement. A customer innocently enquired, "Are you taking part in the Highland Games tomorrow Dougal?" To which came the caustic reply "It was my wedding anniversary last week. I've made my wife miserable for the last 25 years. Why should I take part in the games and drop dead and make her happy?"

That evening the whole site seemed to have been taken over by motorbikes and my new neighbours were Austrians. There were a few backpackers and a whole group of indeterminate continentals in a convoy of eight 2CVs. I was beginning to regret choosing the high level site. By day it was empty. By evening there wasn't room to swing a cat. The low level site, with the exception of a few caravans, remained nearly empty.

## A day at the games

Saturday dawned grey, overcast and cold. The games started in the morning and I was down there waiting at the gate when they opened at ten. Like many shows it was slow to start and didn't really gather pace until lunchtime. Drumnadrochit is only a small town, but the games cover a wide area and are officially the Glenurquhart Highland Gathering and Games. I likened it to a cross between a school sports day and a small local agricultural show. It was all very informal with commentators knowing participants by christian names and making 'off the cuff' comments, understood and amusing only to the locals. Everybody seemed to be taking part; the doctor, the vet, the policeman—but presumably not Dougal in case he dropped dead.

Something was going on all the time—stalls and amusements round the edge of the field, and a fun fair for the youngsters. I was not bored, but for the first time experienced loneliness. It was a case of being lonely in a crowd. No one to talk to, to discuss events with or exchange comments. Everyone had someone—family, friends, acquaintances, children. I had no-one. Early in the day I had seen the Dutch couple from the Loch Ness Campsite. They had recognised me and said hello but soon disappeared in the crowd.

The morning's programme consisted of track events and the local competitors in the Heavy Events. These being putting the shot, throwing the 16lb. Scots Hammer, throwing the 28lb. weight over distance, tossing the caber, and the event I enjoyed most and went back to watch time and time again, throwing the 56lb. weight over the bar. In this event spectators were invited to 'have a go'. To the embarrassment of the locals, and the delight of the crowd, a volunteer, who it was announced was a Canadian paramedic, succeeded in throwing the weight with apparent effortless ease increasingly higher and beating everyone else. As a result, he was invited to take part in the afternoon's open events, but only if he wore a kilt. The rules apparently insist that all entrants must wear the kilt, though this is accompanied by a T-shirt with some incongruous design, trainers and, underneath the kilt, shiny black sports shorts. For the next couple of hours regular requests were made over the tannoy for an extra large kilt for this guy to borrow—he was built like a sumo wrestler.

The Piping Competitions I found disappointing. Each competitor performed on a small platform before two judges for a considerable time, music which included the Piobaireachd, pronounced Pi-broch. This is a theme with variations with no change of key, the variations becoming ever

196

more complicated. I'm sure it was very clever but to the uninitiated and to one from south of the border, it all sounded much the same and not at all tuneful. I listened attentively to the whole of one competitor's performance while he accompanied his piping with a slow march. I tried to appear interested, but when I found the next competitor was playing exactly the same thing and that all the rest were as well, that was enough. I went off to listen to the visiting British Legion Pipe Band instead who were giving a display of marching and music in the arena.

I was fascinated by the antics of pipers tuning their bagpipes. I thought the Welsh harp was difficult to tune, but Scottish bagpipes seemed even worse. The first thing an arriving band or piper does is get as far away as possible from any other piper. Not easy if there are a lot of them. Then they start blowing and turning bits of pipe and making dreadful noises whilst at the same time marching a few paces, turning, and marching back. This goes on for some time until someone decides everyone should get together and see if they are all in tune.

The piping competitions were being taken very seriously by the Scots, but no-one actually looked as if they were enjoying it. The two judges sat in separate cubicles, unable to communicate. One went through the motions of silently playing invisible pipes with every competitor. After each performance no-one spoke, no-one clapped and no-one smiled. The small audience of curious visitors like myself looked bored.

The Highland Dancing displays were also disappointing for the simple reason that they were too far away to be seen. Everything took place in the centre of the arena and spectators had at all times, understandably for safety, to stay outside the ropes. Dancing displays were taking place continuously and were performed by children from a local school of dancing. Some were very young and to my untrained eye appeared to have reached a very high standard. They were immaculately turned out in miniature versions of colourful highland dress. Dutiful mothers hovered about, on hand to make sure their offspring were spick and span with not a hair out of place.

Much local interest was generated by both the road race and hill race. Would any records be broken? The 15 mile race from Inverness to Drumnadrochit, accompanied by a police escort had a record of just over $75^1/_2$ minutes. The hill race, about 2 miles to the summit of a local hill and back, took about 20 minutes. But the event that really caught everyone's imagination was the unscheduled arrival of an Air Ambulance. A call over the PA system earlier had called the duty doctor to the First Aid tent. This had presumably been a life-threatening emergency as, not long after, a helicopter arrived and virtually the whole field of spectators left the roped off arena and flocked with morbid interest to watch it land on the adjacent football pitch. This was slightly strange as a few fields away another heli-copter had been doing 10 minute flights along Loch Ness all afternoon, which the the public had largely ignored.

Altogether, a fascinating though not entirely enjoyable day. The games had not been as action packed and colourful as I expected and in all honesty, they were not something I would bother with again. But they added to my memories of the Great Glen Way—and that I had enjoyed. Next day I would be back to the freedom of the road and heading for my goal—the final miles to John O'Groats.

# 13

# The Final Miles

## Along the Moray Firth

Long distance walking can become as addictive as a drug and after two non-walking days I was beginning to have withdrawal symptoms. I was itching to be on my way, and now I was actually starting to think about the end.

Apart from "How are your feet?", the most frequently asked question was "Don't you find the distance daunting?" And my answer was always the same. "I never think about it". And I rarely did. This was partially intentional in as much as I never let myself think that far ahead. My thoughts were always concentrated on getting to the end of each stage. In practise even this was rarely given much consideration as the aim of most walkers is simply to get to the end of the day. Usually, the only thing in my mind was to reach the next campsite. As the end of a stage neared, I would start a countdown—in three days I will be at the Severn Bridge, or by next week I'll reach the Scottish border. Only once did I ever think of the end, and that was at the half way point, somewhere near Keld. Then, I remember feeling quite dispirited for a while, realising that I had yet to go as far as I had already come. The length in both distance and time was formidable.

Now, with 1,000 miles behind me and about 130 more to do, the end was practically round the corner. I looked forward to getting there, yet I didn't want it to end. I was on the final count down. My arrival date, planned for September 12th, had been brought forward by cutting out Inverness. If Michael came early enough to give me some car support, then the last few days would be long ones and bring the date even further forward. The day I left Drumnadrochit, Sunday September 1st, was my 70th walking day. Theoretically I would reach John O'Groats by the following Sunday.

### *Sunday newspapers have their uses*

Next morning dawned damp and grey. When I crept out of the still slumbering campsite at 7.30, it was already raining. For eight hours it rained copiously. There was no off-road route to Beauly and as the available minor roads would have added considerably to the milage, I decided on a fast 14 mile walk along the main road. By starting early I hoped there would not be much traffic around. In fact it was better than I expected. Traffic was virtually nil, there was a reasonable verge and lovely Glen Gorvich was scenic even in the rain. Craggy moorland, mist-shrouded heather and countless small lochs. A farmer towing a baler behind a Unimog took pity on my soggy state and offered me a lift. It was a genuine offer and kindly meant but I really wanted to see the area I was going through and optimistically hoped the rain would soon stop. I thanked him and he accepted my refusal cheerfully, saying "I know you hikers usually prefer to walk." For the rest of the morning as the rain intensified and I became wetter and wetter, I regretted turning down his offer.

By 1.30 I was at Lovat Bridge on a deserted campsite. A notice pinned on the office door read 'Please Pitch and Pay Later'. In a distant corner of the field were two tents and no vehicles. The static vans were car -less and out of three touring vans only one showed any signs of life. The rain shifted up a gear from continuous heavy to continuous torrential. I dived into the nearest building—a games room with snooker table and darts board. I was soaked. Rain from my sodden hair had run down my neck and wicked its way through my clothes. T-shirt and knickers clung damply to my skin. I was cold and my rucksack was saturated. My drenched waterproofs drained onto the floor making an ever-increasing dark patch in the concrete. I hadn't been so wet since walking on Great Shunner with Ben. I stripped off my wet clothing and taking a chance on not setting fire to the place, unpacked my stove and warmed up with a hot drink. A large map of Scottish tartans and piles of touristy leaflets provided the only entertainment for the next couple of hours.

During the middle of the afternoon, as if someone turned off a tap, the rain suddenly ceased. I put up the tent, changed into dry clothes, and hung all my wet things on a fence. It was only the third time since leaving home that my socks and the insides of my boots were wet. In an unbelievably short space of time the sun was shining and wisps of steam rose as everything began to dry out. When I went into Beauly later to see if I could find any shops open, I bought the thickest Sunday Newspaper I could find. And the *News of the World* came into its own for its only truly useful purpose, stuffing boots, rolling up wet socks, completely carpeting the floor of the tent and providing an absorbent layer between my insulation mat, which was like a soggy sponge, and my sleeping bag. I didn't bother to read it and only kept the crossword puzzle which I cut out to do later.

I couldn't understand why the site was so quiet. It had every possible convenience. I concluded that the end of the tourist season comes early and suddenly this far north. Scottish children I knew had started back to school some time ago, much earlier than the English, and apart from continentals there seemed few British tourists about. I wondered if anyone would turn up for money. I hoped they wouldn't as I was now desperately short of cash and had to watch every penny. The two previous nights had been free. If anyone had come and asked, I would have paid. But nobody did. On most sites, you book in, pay your fee and you are given a label to tie on your tent pole. This has the date of arrival, length of stay and how much you paid. Early in the morning before people are up, someone drives round the site and checks the labels. You can't get away with staying another night for free. At Drumnadrochit, with the sheer turnover in number of campers and the fact that most do only stay one night, I guess they don't expect anyone to book for a second night and don't bother to check. I didn't get away with it here though. Just as I was leaving next day, a man turned up and opened the office and I paid as I left.

### Weightwatchers eat your heart out

My destination was Dingwall. Another day of road walking lay ahead, but first I had an essential purchase to make. I was desperately short of gas. I had been almost out at Drumnadrochit, but the shop there had only large cylinders. The hardware store in Beauly had camping stoves the same as mine in the window and I went in confident of getting a new supply. I could not believe it when they said they only sold complete stoves.

However, I was able to replace the Dornoch map and stock up with extra films and three large cakes. I had reached a stage where I was constantly hungry. I woke up in the night with severe hunger pangs and now actually bought food solely to eat at night—usually chocolate bars and packets of biscuits. A few days before I had caught sight of myself in a mirror after a shower and received a shock. I could see all my ribs and looked like someone out of a concentration camp. I guessed my weight was about nine stone and assumed I was always hungry because I had used up all my body's reserves. But I didn't need to be as frugal from now on. Walking as I was more or less between towns I didn't have to worry about either carrying food or its availability. I could eat more food and more often. During this final week the purchase of several cakes and pasties or pies first thing in the morning became a daily habit. By lunch time they would all be gone. Nevertheless, when I reached John O'Groats I found I actually weighed under nine stone. I had lost two stone in three months.

This particular part of Scotland is well populated. Towns almost merge. There are footpaths even along main roads. So, having had no joy with the gas, I gave up ideas of using tracks and byways to Dingwall and decided it would be much wiser to stay with the main road and try every garage and town I came to. I needn't have bothered. Nowhere had any gas.

It was a gentle, uninspiring walk through a flat landscape cluttered with light industry, warehouses and builders suppliers. The weather was just what a walker would order: dry, not too warm, with breaks in the cloud giving brief glimpses of the sun. I arrived at Dingwall, the largest town since Fort William, at lunchtime. A lively place with ample shops, a traffic free shopping precinct and even a Woolworths. An outdoor adventure shop stocked my gas and the lady who served me was interested to hear I was an End to Ender. She reiterated what had been suggested weeks before, that I MUST visit the Orkneys. I picked up a leaflet advertising an 'All-In' Day Trip for £28 from John O'Groats and promised myself that if the ferry, scheduled to run until September 7th or as long as the weather was fit and there were enough passengers, was still running, I would go.

The town centre was full of uniformed teenagers from the local comprehensive school eating chips. My mouth watered. I was ravenous. I joined the queue of youngsters in the chip shop for my 50p. worth. An unbelievably large portion for the price. Feeling like a big kid myself I bought a chocolate milk shake as well and sat on a bench in the precinct savouring my greasy feast.

With no longer any panic over gas and the rest of the day to cover the last six miles to Evanton, I reverted to minor roads as originally planned. Turning inland, the lane I took gave superb views across the Cromarty Firth to the Black Isle. Way back in the hazy distance were the mountains beyond Loch Ness and, in between, a vast arable patchwork, the warm sunny hues of hundreds of acres of cornfields. The harvest was underway.

Gargantuan combines devoured crops like giant dinosaurs. Palls of smoke rose from fields of burning stubble, presumably of rape as straw burning is banned. Over the silvery expanse of the Firth the new Cromarty Bridge curved across from the Black Isle carrying the A9 and its burden of traffic on its now shortened journey north.

*John O'Groats is on the signs—End to Enders are on the roads*
My road carried nothing more than the occasional tractor and took me to Evanton and the most immaculate campsite I have ever seen. Individual terraced pitches mown to perfection would have been the envy of any groundsman. Each had its own picnic table. No need to filch one here. The price was a little higher than usual, but there was no additional charge for showers and hot water. Usually showers were 20 or 50p. and on a time switch and hot water in the laundry was available by payment in a meter. I always had to make sure I had enough loose change for all these little luxuries. Even the commercial dryer in this laundry was only 20p. for a worthwhile length of time.

As this site too was almost deserted, it appeared that it was indeed the end of the season. There were no other tents until later when two motorcyclists and a cyclist turned up. We were all on adjacent pitches and it developed into an companionable evening. The young man on the bike was having problems with his tent. I watched him struggling for some time and eventually went over to ask if I could be of any assistance. The main hoop was broken. The tent was useless without it and while he managed to do a lash up job using his bike as a frame, I made him a cup of coffee. We shared my picnic table and I learnt that he was a veterinary student at Cambridge whose home was in the Lake District. He was on his way to John O'Groats on the fourth day of a three week cycling tour of Scotland. The two motorcyclists, who came from Yorkshire, joined us and told me they too were End to Enders. They had left John O'Groats that morning but had already done over 600 miles having started from Hull. By the time they returned home would have done over 2,000 miles, a distance they expected to accomplish in 8 days at 300 miles per day. Their routine consisted of sitting on the bike all day and sitting in the pub all night. It was hard work they said—stiff backsides, cold cramped hands, cold feet, cold faces—and they saw very little on the way. I thought my way was far preferable.

At Evanton I was halfway along the Cromarty Firth in the old county of Ross and Cromarty, which under the present boundary system is lumped with Sutherland and Caithness as Highland Region. And today, for the first time, John O'Groats was on the signs. 110 miles from Dingwall. After weeks of totting up the miles, I was now going to be ticking them off until I was down to single figures. As I travelled further north the scenery was changing, with fewer mountains, more moorland and, along the coast, much more agriculture. The few roads there are link the dwindling number of towns. Networks of lanes just do not exist. Footpaths of the field-and-stile type are absent. As in the first 100 miles, where the lack of footpaths in Cornwall gave me no alternative but but to resort to roads, so it was for the last 100 miles. It was a prospect I never relished, but was generally never as bad as expected especially as the roads carried nowhere near the volume of traffic we are accustomed to in the south.

One aspect of road walking that always worried me was the possibility of being offered lifts—which was why my route throughout was planned to keep road walking to a minimum. Where roads were the only option, I relied on my instincts and took basic precautions. Except where there were dangerous bends or no verges, I always walked facing the oncoming traffic. Then, anyone offering a lift must stop on the opposite side of the road well away from you. Usually a firm "No thanks" results in the driver driving on. I also avoided turning round to look at approaching vehicles as this may give the impression you are actually looking for a lift.

Most offers were genuine and well meant and mostly refused on the grounds of a guilty conscience. The occasional one I accepted—for short distances for legitimate reasons—with the excuse that I frequently made up the distance at other times walking backwards and forwards to phone boxes or shops. The most unusual lift was between Evanton and Alness— in a coal lorry. I had already seen the coalman, a young fellow and incredibly clean for a coalman, making deliveries to houses near a callbox I was using. He must have noticed me too because I hadn't gone far along the road when he drew up. "I can take you just a few miles if you like," he offered, "but not far. I'm turning off for another delivery." I hesitated. Traffic was fast and heavy and according to the map I would soon come to a complex roundabout system. Following my instincts that he was a good guy and obviously on a genuine delivery round, I accepted. He hoisted first my rucksack and then me into a spotlessly clean cab and took me about two miles, dropping me at the far side of the busy roundabout, a short distance from Alness; a journey which saved me the worst bit of road walking of the day. He showed no surprise at where I was going and I was already beginning to realise that up here people know that anyone walking along the A9 with a bulky pack can only be going to or coming from John

O'Groats. The question more likely to be asked is not "Where are you going?" but "When did you start" or "When will you get there?"

### A bag lady in fairyland

Every town I come to has its own tantalising bakery. The cakes are nothing like those I'm used to. A breed of their own. I can't name them. I point and say "One of those please." Often butchers and bakers are in the same shop—and the butcher has as wide a range of pies as the baker has cakes. Sometimes huge ones fit for a large family. Three scrumptious, unknown cakes from Alness sustained me over the next few miles through lightly forested countryside. Here, in open glades, cushions of heather were in the full bloom of late summer. There were clear views over the Cromarty Firth where oil rigs were moored off Invergordon and on the far shore, the Black Isle and Cromarty itself. That morning there was a heavy dew. The scene was magical. Everything was cocooned in thousands of cobwebs sparkling with droplets of moisture. The trees were festooned in prolific growths of lichen, hanging down like grey unkempt hair. I stopped in this fairytale wonderland to pick wet bilberries and eat my cakes.

Tain, the town I was heading for I had never even heard of. I had no idea how big it was. So I was agreeably surprised to find it was, for this area, relatively large. A café, which looked down to earth enough to admit a bootshod backpacker, provided a pot of tea and scones and a chance to sit down for half an hour and ease my shoulders. I was conscious of curious, sidelong glances from the waitresses and other customers and got the impression I was regarded as a bit of a freak. I wasn't surprised. I smelt like a bag lady. Of late I had become aware of a distinctly unpleasant odour, which I could account for but was unable to do anything about. I'd tracked it down to a combination of several things. Several items, including my sleeping bag, had not been washed for a long time. My waterproofs, used several time lately and sometimes packed up damp, had begun to take on an aroma all of their own and the shoulder straps of my rucksack, soiled from three months' sweat and use, also emitted a faint, tell-tale pong. In the fresh air none of this was noticeable and well aired overnight, almost disappeared. But after several hours walking the whole rucksack seemed surrounded by its own disagreeable little atmosphere. I tried not to stand too close to people and used copious amounts of deodorant to try and disguise the smell.

For an hour I shopped; replenished the meagre contents of my purse; stocked up with breakfasts and suppers; then made my way to the tiny village of Meikle Ferry two miles out of town. The campsite was practically on the run up to Dornoch Bridge. A linear site with individually marked pitches along a central metalled road. The woman in reception marked my site map with a cross. "You can pitch there," she said. "We get a lot of you these days now that the new bridge is open." Apparently before that, End to Enders had to go inland and cross the head of the Dornoch Firth at Bonar Bridge. "I get on average one walker a week through the main season" she told me and went on to say that one retired man had become quite a regular visitor. He'd stopped there three times and had done it in both directions, twice camping and pushing all his gear in an old pram and the third time staying bed and breakfast. The most unusual End to Enders she'd seen had made the trip with a stage coach and four horses.

It was such a lovely evening I walked down the old road to Meikle Ferry. This was the only means of crossing the Dornoch Firth before the new bridge was built. The pier and ferry point are at the end of a narrow, mile long peninsula which projects right out into the Firth. The tide was out and on the exposed sands seabirds, mainly oystercatchers and curlews, probed amongst mounds of rust-coloured kelp. Flocks of fat, healthy looking sheep grazed the fine sward right to the waterline, assisted by the hundreds of rabbits that were hopping around in the fading evening light. Up the Firth over the mountains beyond Bonar Bridge a striking, stormy looking sunset was developing. As the tide turned and swiftly flooded in over the seaweed strewn sands I sat on rocks watching the sun until it set. Daylight disappeared rapidly and I walked back in the dark.

### Domesticity and domestics

The washing machines at this site were the best value yet—and I had become something of an expert. Every site was different. I was conversant with so many makes and models I could have written a Which survey on campsite washers, tumbledryers and showers. This particular machine gave twenty five minutes of good drying heat for 20p. The worst give ten minutes for 50p. at such a low heat they never get your clothes dry. These were gas machines, the site warden explained, much more efficient than electric. There was no charge for the iron here either and I was astounded to see there was even an upright vacuum cleaner, also free of charge. I could vacuum my tent! I would have liked to have washed my sleeping bag while I had such good equipment, but a prominent sign strictly ordered NO WASHING OF SLEEPING BAGS. There was no excuse for not seeing this—so I didn't dare.

My first impressions of the site being such a nice one was rudely shattered during the night by two incidents. Sometime after midnight a couple three pitches from me began what I can only describe as a "major domestic". For two hours they were at each others' throats and at one time I thought actually came to blows. I could hear every word as they weren't even in the tent. They were chasing each other up and down the site, the woman saying she was going to walk home, wherever that was, and was definitely not sharing a tent with *him*. Eventually she slept in the car. No sooner had all this died down than the couple the other side of me started. They had been out earlier for a meal and in the early hours the woman was violently sick. Next morning they disappeared before anyone else was up.

### Beaches and bombers

Before leaving, I popped in to say goodbye to the site warden. She had been really friendly and it was not her fault I had such rotten neighbours. I was still a little worried about walking over the bridge, but she assured me she walked her dog over regularly. Pedestrians use a narrow cycle lane and it's quite safe. The bridge was opened in 1991 by the Queen Mother, and has the longest span in Europe using the Push and Cast method of construction, whatever that may mean. I thought the draught of passing lorries might be a problem, however traffic was light and I enjoyed the walk. The only pity was the sky was completely overcast with a thick mist obscuring the view both up and down the firth. I was glad I had been able to see it all the previous night though even in poor light, the purple bell heather on the far bank was an absolute picture.

Once over the bridge, I left the main road and took instead a lane running along Dornoch Links, the reclaimed saltmarsh bordering the edge of the Firth. Five peaceful miles unhindered by vehicles. A man strimming his front garden called out to me "Have you come all the way?" meaning, from Land's End. Then added, "Not many of you come this way. Most people use the main road."

The mist had cleared by the time I arrived at the Royal Burgh of Dornoch; the county town when Sutherland was still a county, but little more than a village despite its thirteenth century, much restored cathedral. I did what every tourist was doing. Toured the cathedral, roamed the gift shops, took photographs and bought gimmicky teatowels. Then I took my lunch down to the beach to bask in the sun. Apart from a few golfers on the Royal Dornoch Golf Course, which ran along the back of the beach, it was almost deserted. The passengers from the coaches parked in the town centre don't get as far as the beach.

It was gloriously sunny. Just a few high wispy clouds and a light wind. Empty golden sands stretched endlessly northwards. A calm, almost motionless sea made no more than a feeble ripple on the shore. In the dunes—an idyllic campsite, but as I had come such a short distance I intended going on to the next at Embo. A perfectly lovely day. I was reluctant to leave the beach—and then realised there was nothing to stop me walking to Embo along the sands. It was only three miles but I stopped so many times it took me three hours. Occasionally I sat and simply enjoyed the sights and sounds of the Moray Firth, at other times I poked around looking at shells, seaweeds, watching birds—and hoping to see porpoises. A few days before I'd met a girl who told me she came up to the Moray Firth regularly to watch them. There is a colony of about 130 and the best place to see them is apparently from Cromarty Lighthouse.

My approach to Embo's campsite was unofficial, via the back entrance directly off the beach, and I was staggered by its size. It was without any doubt the largest site I had been on. Acres of static vans, a complex road system, so many toilet blocks I lost count and rows of telephone kiosks. After the best part of half a mile I came to the huge complex of super-market, games rooms, restaurants, bars and swimming pool and made my way to the carpeted reception area to check in. The girl on the reception desk was a bit flummoxed "You do realise it's £8 per tent" she said. "There's a cheaper site at Dornoch." I explained I had just come from there. "Hang on" she said, "I'll ask the manager if I can do a reduction." A few minutes later she came back to say the manager said I could stay for nothing as they did not usually get backpackers. "All our campers come by car." And to top it all, I was told I could use all the facilities and was given passes for the swimming pool, pool table and evening cabaret in the restaurant.

Issued with a detailed site plan and instructed where to pitch, I ended up right back where I started in the sand dunes behind the beach and chose a sheltered spot not a stones throw from the sea. The only other campers were a German family in a luxurious Autohome. I considered going for a swim, but couldn't be bothered. It's not a lot of fun on your own. So I sat on the beach and read instead.

The view across the Moray Firth was crystal clear. Cromarty Lighthouse on the far side of the Dornoch Firth was unmistakable. The sea, a wonderful shade of blue looked more like the Mediterranean than the North Sea. All afternoon the RAF had been really having a ball, taking off from Lossiemouth, flying low over the sea and climbing steeply to disappear into the clouds. A double crack of thunderous sound coincided with their reappearance as they zoomed down from tremendous heights looking as if they would crash into the sea. I thought at the time they were breaking the sound barrier but later discovered that it was gunfire and that there was a potential Iraqi crisis. The planes were out in force getting ready for action.

The wind had increased gradually all day. It was noticeably colder. Cold enough to put on my fleece. A young Australian couple arrived and pitched beside me. I tried to phone home twice to no avail and went down to the tiny harbour to pass the time. The tide was coming in and white-tipped waves whipped up by the strong winds crashed over the rocks. At the seaward end of the harbour the water was easily 15ft. deep, but so clear, the writhing seaweed at the bottom made it appear deceptively shallow. Out across the sea planes screamed and thundered across the sky until well after dark and were still flying when I phoned home again after ten.

## The A9 Alternative

That night was very cold, though I was quite warm enough and slept later than usual until 7am. The ground was white with frost. The Australians were already up and offered me a cup of tea, over which I discovered they were over from Tasmania on a tour of Europe. Then I left to follow the shores of Loch Fleet—a sea loch where a tremendous variety of seabirds were foraging on the vast area of mudflats and kelp exposed by the receding tide. As well as eider ducks, cormorant, shags, curlews, oystercatchers, turnstones and plovers, there were many gulls and ducks I didn't recognise—and somewhere on a low, distant island I could hear seals barking.

Shortly before reaching the head of the loch and the dreaded A9 I was offered a lift. A couple from the site had seen me camping alone and offered to take me to Helmsdale where they were buying a house. This was two days away on foot, so naturally I could not accept—and anyway I would have missed too much on the way. But I had no hesitation in accepting a lift as far as Golspie, as it meant avoiding a particularly hazardous four mile section of the main road. Perhaps it was just as well I wasn't travelling very far, for once within the confines of the car I was again conscious of the rucksack pong and had to apologise for the aroma.

Transported swiftly to Golspie, I collected my morning dose of cakes, pasties and milkshake, then, turning my back on both town and road, took a footpath along the back of the beach. I could see now something I had not fully appreciated from the maps, that the coastline of north-east

Scotland is very low, that there are either shingle banks or sand dunes and miles of firm, people-free sands. Slowly it had dawned on me that I did not need to walk on the A9 as much as I had thought. For many miles it was perfectly possible to walk along the beaches.

Between Golspie and Dunrobin Castle there was a path which initially skirted a private garden. Here I was under the close scrutiny of an unsmiling man who watched from his window and waved his arms furiously if I as much as hesitated at a stile or gate or looked likely to stray from the path. Flowery meadows yellow with ragwort bordered the shore, overlooked by the imposing elegance of Dunrobin Castle. I couldn't help thinking how much of that wealth had been gained at the expense of the evicted Highlanders. The romantic looking castle was the ancestral home of the Countess of Sutherland who with her husband, the Marquess of Stafford, became some of the first landowners to instigate the notorious Highland Clearances of the eighteenth and nineteenth centuries. I would have liked to have payed a visit, especially to the gardens but I really was having to watch my finances now, added to which, at close quarters, my aroma might be offensive to the hundreds of tourists. It was only mid-morning but the carpark was full and passengers were disembarking from at least five coaches. I contented myself with squinting at the gardens through locked gates and stretching my neck to peer over walls.

A local man told me he sometimes walked his dog as far as Brora on the beach. He touched his brow with an old fashioned courtesy seldom seen in England and murmured softly "God be with ye" as he went on his way. Except for the locals, I doubt if many people driving up this east coast realise what they are missing. There is no road access to most of these beaches and they are totally devoid of human life. Rabbits by the dozen reside in the desirable mega-warren of the dunes, their distinctive tracks trailing aimlessly over the sand and well down the beach. Here, prey and predator live side by side. I watched transfixed when, almost under my feet, a stoat ran from the dunes and bounded across the sands to the exposed rocks at the water's edge, where he hunted amongst weed-covered rocks for shell fish.

The sea, once again mill pond calm, barely a ripple reaching the shore, was silent. But it was teeming with wildlife. The air was filled with the cries of many different birds and the mournful dog-like howls of seals. It was almost low tide and large colonies of seals were basking on the sands and showed little inclination to move. And it is no exaggeration to say there were hundreds. I was able to creep slowly closer and closer and then sit down on the sand and watch them, and on more than one occasion counted at least that many. Eventually one, more alert or more nervous than its companions, would get uneasy and take to the water, followed by the rest, humping their ungainly bulk amazingly quickly over the sand. Having reached the safety of a few feet of water, they would turn round and lay with their bellies grounded watching me. A couple of birdwatchers, the only humans I encountered, kindly loaned me their binoculars for a while to get an even closer look and verified my map reading conclusions that I could continue along beaches for most of the way to Helmsdale.

I was so glad that the tide was well out and still going out. Beach walking may have been still possible if it was in, but it would have been nowhere near as interesting. The beaches of northern Scotland must be some of the most superb in Britain. Fine, clean sand and, below the high water mark, firm to walk on. When I told people back home I had spent several days walking along beaches, their first reaction was what hard work it must have been. But it wasn't. It was no worse than the spongy peat of the Pennines. In places I hardly left boot prints and if the going did get too soft I walked along the grass at the back. This was in fact harder going and more hazardous. The grass was long and wiry with no proper path and riddled with rabbit holes—there was a high risk of twisting an ankle.

Occasionally the sand gave way to flatish rocks. Nothing to cause an obstacle to a walker—and the seals thought it was great. Where the rocks offshore were just under water, they were laying on them looking for all the world as if they were floating like little boats. Large numbers of red beaked oystercatchers stood around on the beach doing nothing in particular—until I came along. Then the whole flock would take off *en masse* and land again further along the beach. Cormorants stood with wings outstretched—motionless black statues on partially submerged rocks. I was walking nature's highway, far better than the A9.

### Sutherland—the penultimate county

My stopover was at Brora, a small fishing resort with a handful of shops, golf course, harbour and a whisky distillery. A town with an attractive name but little else to commend it except its elaborate clock tower war memorial. Unusual I thought until I saw similar ones elsewhere and found it was the popular theme for war memorials in these parts. Outside the villages, most houses now were single storey. Many were originally crofts. Their location at regular distances in similar size plots of small fields pointed to the fact that these were some of the former allocated portions of ground. Some still retained stone walls or a small beast house on one end. Others had been modernised, or rebuilt on the same plot and at first glance looked like modern bungalows, until the location and the old stone shed nearby gave the game away. Many lay abandoned, too small to sustain a living or had been amalgamated to make larger viable units. There were dozens of derelict houses which in the affluent South would have been snapped up as holiday homes and perfectly restorable houses were being used as farm buildings or simply neglected.

My campsite was at a croft on a back lane, just off the main road. A small site, with impeccably clean and tidy toilets. A geriatric couple appeared from a caravan immediately I arrived and suggested I pitched next to them for company. Theirs or mine? They were Scots who originated from Brora and returned for holidays. I had standby noodles for tea and, surprisingly, after eating them regularly for three months I was not fed up with them. Old habits die hard. Even when there were shops I still bought them.

Between the croft and the sea was an eighteen hole golf course. With sand dunes all along the coast it is not surprising that even the smallest town has its own golf course. There was no official path across this one. You made a beeline for the sea and watched out for stray balls. During the whole walk I must have walked across a dozen courses. I knew nothing about golf, but I was beginning to work out from which direction balls would be coming and take avoiding action.

I was now in the old county of Sutherland and it was noticeable how from day to day the surnames changed. Each vicinity has its own prominent surname indicating the territories of the old clans. Around Brora everyone is named Sutherland: site owner, shop keepers, garage owner and trade names on vehicles. Over the next day or so this changed to Gunn. Nearly as bad as Wales with all its Jones', Evans' and Davies'.

A cold and frosty morning heralded the start of another exquisite day. Blue sky. Calm sea. Clear horizons. Five miles of pristine sands. I had the beach to myself. Once the sun rose, it quickly became shorts-and-T-shirt weather. Out in the Moray Firth the three platforms of the Beatrice Oil Field were plainly visible. This is Scotland's largest firth, but is nevertheless all part of the North Sea and these oil rigs belong to the nearest of the offshore oil fields. At night when they are illuminated they look very near to the coast.

I was delayed for a while trying to cross a small river. At first sight it didn't look to be a problem. Just another little river wending its way to the sea. But it was wider and deeper than I first thought with a slippery stony bed and fast flowing water. I couldn't chance crossing bare-foot with a rucksack and it was too deep to easily make stepping stones. In any case, it was a sandy beach with few stones. I spent a good half hour fetching and carrying, from some distance, enough stones to make piles high enough to be able to get across without getting my boots too wet.

These days of beach walking were the most memorable of the whole walk. Somewhere, many years ago, I read that you only get one completely perfect day in a lifetime. A whole day of joy and happiness when nothing goes wrong, and nothing and no-one mars the perfection. This may or may not be true, but I do know that these days were the most perfect days of my lifetime and I shall never, ever forget them. And I count myself lucky to have had not one but several. I spent hours pottering along, stopping whenever I felt like it. There were more seals. 60 at least basking on the beach. As many again in the water, howling mournfully. To the south, I could still see back as far as Lossiemouth. The sea, a deep tropical turquoise and smooth as glass, sparkled and glistened in the sunlight. In places, grey rocks were transformed to emerald by a fine grass-like seaweed. Other rocks were boulder-like and pitted; full of holes like a sponge—jurassic sandstone I later found out. Sands stretched endlessly as far as I could see—mile after golden mile. Rabbits hopped around the beach unbothered by my silent progress. A newly dead seal pup lay on the sand not far from the receding tide, its eyes already pecked out by scavenging seagulls. Its mother lay in shallow water a few yards away, howling like a dog on a chain. Did she know it was dead? Was she grieving or calling it to follow her? It was difficult to tell. She was alone with her baby, all the rest of the seals were much further along the beach.

A terribly upper class, plum in the mouth couple walking a dog near Lothbeg Point said "Hello" and told me that I wouldn't be able to get all the way to Helmsdale as there were steep cliffs. I knew about these from the map but thought I might be able to walk below them. This is apparently not possible even at low tide. "Walk along the railway track," they advised. "There are only three trains a day!" This was what one of the Mrs. Sutherlands of Brora had told me. "Locals do it all the time," she said, despite the warning signs threatening £200 fines for trespassing on railway property.

After eight miles I decided reluctantly to find a way across the track before I ran out of beach. The single track line follows the coast and I had already seen both the early morning and the mid-day trains. The next would not be until the evening so it would be completely safe to walk the line, but stepping from sleeper to sleeper on a railway track can be tedious. They never conveniently fit your stride. I decided instead to cut across the fields and make for the A9 at a point where I could see there was a lane which looped off the main road and rejoined it again just outside Helmsdale. It climbed steeply through a community of derelict crofts whose long narrow fields swept down towards the cliffs. If these were the original small allotments of the clearances, it would have been the luck of the draw who got what; who was lucky enough to have a good water supply and who ended up with a barren, rocky strip.

### Stepping it out along the A9

Helmsdale is a tiny fishing port which at one time supported 200 boats with 500 women employed in gutting and salting fish. The main road enters the town over a new bridge but a few hundred yards upstream the old Telford Bridge still spans the River Helmsdale. Nearby the Timespan Heritage Centre re-creates with sound effects and lifesize sets the history of the Highlands. Last entrants were being admitted. I just had time to look round and wished I had more than the remaining hour. There was so much to see: wildlife, Viking invasions, the Highland Clearances, geology, crofting, fishing, gold mining and even the present oil industry. The town as it is today was laid out methodically on a grid system—a new town built to support the herring industry started by the Duke of Sutherland for his displaced tenants. Many houses bear a date—around 1819—and the Sutherland crest, but the people they housed had been evicted from their glens to make way for sheep and the fishing industry was developed as much to make more money for the duke as for the benefit of the people.

I had been warned not too expect much of the campsite, but it was not as bad as I had been led to believe. I had no complaints. A group of Dutch students, cars piled high with bicycles, were already encamped in a circle of silver dome tents, while at the other end of the camping spectrum there was a massive state of the art pantechnicon of an autohome with just about everything fitted, connected or attached. With a generator for heating and lighting, the quantity and quality of the site facilities was not likely to have concerned him. I couldn't find anyone to pay but an absentee landlady, smartly dressed and high heeled, arrived by car towards dark to collect the fees.

By 8.30 it was too dark to read and the temperature was dropping. I went to bed. At home I'm a night bird, rarely in bed before 1 o'clock. Now I was getting nine or ten hours sleep, something I hadn't done for years.

Overnight there was a frost. Begonias growing in an old rowing boat, moored high and dry on a patch of grass in the village, were withered and black. It was Saturday September 6th. In two days' time I would reach John O'Groats. Michael would be setting off during the day and expected to meet me sometime on Sunday. Our only contact now would be on the mobile phone—if and when there was an adequate signal.

Ahead lay 15 miles of tarmac and verges. I had asked in the information office if there was any alternative to the A9. The helpful assistant had obligingly telephoned an off-duty policewoman. Back came the report "Just stick to the verges. They're quite wide in most places. There is no other way."

It is difficult for for those who have never had to do it, to imagine the concentration needed for this type of road walking. The A9, despite being the major road up the east coast is more comparable to a good B road further south. It has no dual carriageway or three lane sections, but does have steep hills and severe bends. On the worst of the bends there are crash barriers and no verges. Walking involves being constantly aware of traffic and, on bends, judging the sound of approaching vehicles to assess whether you have time to get round or should wait 'til it passes. With experience you can estimate this pretty accurately and make a dash for it. If you are caught out by a fast vehicle you pray, run—or jump over the crash barrier. On straighter sections, concentration was still needed as no matter how wide the verge, the draught from passing lorries still almost bowled me over. For safety, I spent much of my time crossing from one side of the road to the other.

I was soon thoroughly browned off with verge walking. They were uneven and awkward to walk on. It was far preferable to walk in the road. It occurred to me that with apparently so many End to Enders they should lay a footpath! Traffic by southern standards was not heavy, but enough to keep me constantly hopping back on the grass. To pass the time I counted and timed vehicles and worked out an average of four a minute; few compared with the unceasing swish, swish of lorries we'd had to contend with on the road from Avonmouth to the Severn Bridge. The bulk of the traffic was caravans and campervans, fish lorries and, for some reason, removal vans. Two Safeways lorries passed me going north in the morning and returned later in the day going south. I'd noticed these on other days. Along with many drivers they tooted and waved as they passed. I supposed they were used to seeing End to Enders on the first or last lap and tooted encouragement.

215

## Caithness—the last county

The A9, which was ultimately going the same place as me, hugged the coastline. The sea was never far away. The scenery superb. Rugged mountains dominate the western horizon, the bare white crags of the highest peaks giving the effect of being snow-covered. Towards the sea, heather-clad moorland leads to steep cliffs, the coastline sweeps as far as the eye can see—and out to sea, always those three prominent oil rigs. Occasionally, where ground is in better heart, there's an isolated croft, the fields yielding a few round bales of hay or grazed by a handful of cattle.

I had crossed the boundary into my final county—Caithness—and soon after hid my rucksack amongst the gorse and heather and left the road to go and see the historic settlement of Badbea. In 1840, 12 families, 80 people in all, were evicted from their glen and forced to start a new life on these steep, inhospitable cliffs overlooking the North Sea. Cottages had to be built quickly to survive the first cruel winter and were crudely built of rough stone with low walls, no chimneys and heather thatch. The rough, rocky ground had to be cultivated without ploughs to grow enough oats to feed the family, and in addition the men had to work for the estate, building boundary walls for which they were paid a shilling a day. High winds, treacherous cliffs, and the steepness of the ground meant that cattle, sheep and even the chickens and children had to be tethered for safety. Broken by such harsh conditions, most of the community emigrated to New Zealand leaving only the old and infirm. Many years later, their descendants returned and using the stone from the houses, erected a tall monument commemorating those that remained. This and the pathetic ruins of those houses are all that is left. It was a sobering experience to see what appalling conditions those poor people had to endure—and such a relatively short time ago.

Back on the road, a number of cyclists hurtled southwards. End to Enders just starting. Cycling it seemed was by far the most popular way of going End to End. The record, I was told, is under two days but most cyclists were happy to aim for something between eight and 11 days.

I ate lunch in the shade of a stone bridge on a redundant section of old road. I'd been having lunch breaks every half hour since 11 o'clock. This was the fourth. I'd phoned Michael at 11. I was supposed to have phoned him when I left Helmsdale, but forgot and didn't remember until my memory was jogged when I passed a call box. At 11 o'clock he still hadn't left home.

216

From such a cold start it became terrifically hot. Most of my water had gone. I was longing to drink the rest, but was diligently rationing it. I knew I needed more fluid and the situation was getting desperate. Habitations were few. There had been nowhere I could ask for a refill. Then, about three miles from Dunbeath, I spotted a woman working in a field beside a croft. Could she fill up my water bottle, I asked—and was immediately offered a cup of tea. "Come in and sit down for a bit" she said. "Drop your rucksack there. It will be alright." There being on the grass beside the road. I was a bit dubious as all my 'valuables'—cheque book, credit cards, camera and so on—were all there for the taking, but she assured me it would be quite safe.

Inside I was shown into a tiny, homely sitting room. Several dogs checked me out. "They're friendly as long as you don't speak to them" I was warned. I took stock of my surroundings. It was like stepping back in time to the post war era. Comfortable, but nothing was new. None of the showy affluence most modern homes exhibit. Clattering cups in the even tinier kitchen, the woman shouted conversationally "I see walkers passing the door all the time and you're the first I've ever spoken to." She was keen to find out what motivated me. Why was I doing it ? How long had it taken me? What did I eat? All the usual questions that people ask. She told me she was the local post lady, delivering not only mail, but bread and news-papers on a 50 mile round. And I was just as interested in her way of life. What were the winters like up here? How did she cope with the lack of shops? "What you've never had you don't miss," was her reply. "I go to my daughter's in Inverness once a year. And sometimes to Aberdeen. I have all I need." I checked the map later. It was 85 miles to Inverness. 200 to Aberdeen.

The croft brought in no income. The land was let to someone trying to run a viable holding. Most holdings were fields of rough pasture, a derelict croft often being used for animals or storage. Several had highland cattle or a few sheep and most managed to produce half a dozen round bales of silage. I passed a sign for a llama farm, but never saw any llamas. Next day I saw a shop selling ostrich eggs—but I never saw any ostriches either. Some crofts, modernised out of all recognition, retained only enough ground for a garden and nearly all had an enormous, neatly stacked pile of peat drying ready for the winter.

The countryside was now practically bereft of trees; a few stunted sycamores. But little else. No oak, ash, beech or holly. Nothing in gardens either. No shrubs, decorative trees or fruit trees. Few vegetables. Field walls, where they existed, were poor efforts built with round stones not ideal for building. Where moorland or forest bordered the road, the scent of heather filled the air. What better way to remember my last county—and complementary to the first and the unforgettable fragrance of Cornwall's bluebells.

Rabbits infested the verges, grazing openly despite the traffic. A gorgeous, pure white one happily hopped around with the rest. A ginger cat was much put out when I walked past just after he'd made a kill. Making sure the rabbit was dead before he left it, he retreated to a safe distance and watched me warily, before returning to retrieve his victim. And, all too often, I came upon the squashed corpses of what I believed were pine martens. Silky furred, brownish cat-like animals which seemed to be as frequent road casualties as squirrels and hedgehogs at home.

## The final 40

Dunbeath at the end of the day was disappointing. A tiny shop sold 'a bit of everything' so at least food was no problem. Other than that, there was nothing. John O'Groats, according to the road sign, was 38 miles. It meant very little. I could not grasp the fact that I had walked so far. When I looked at the map of Britain on the back of an Ordnance Survey map, it seemed incomprehensible that I had walked the whole length. I didn't feel any excitement that I was near the end. Only profound regret that it would soon be all over.

I had promised to ring Michael that evening, but the local phone was out of order despite a fleet of British Telecom vehicles parked nearby—or perhaps because of them! I could find no-one to pay at the campsite, though except for a shower with free hot water, there was little worth paying for. However, next morning, I was apprehended by a man from a run-down looking guest house who spotted me going to the loo and smartly came over for his two quid. My dark green tent was so well camouflaged he hadn't noticed it..

I had a long day ahead; over 20 miles, but over the last few weeks I had been walking much faster; often four miles an hour and, when Michael arrived, I would not have to carry the rucksack. I was able to make contact with him eventually when I found a phone in the next village. To my surprise he was just crossing Bonar Bridge on the Dornoch Firth and was only 55 miles away, having driven through the night. After a bit of quick figuring, I estimated that by the time he arrived I should be just north of Lybster and about to turn off the A9 onto the minor road to Watten. We arranged to meet at that junction.

The overnight temperature had again been close to freezing but the day time temperature soon rose. It was Sunday. Warm and idyllic. There was little traffic about, though I still seemed to spend all my time crossing from one side of the road to the other. At the junction of the A9 with the main road to Thurso, I stopped to admire what must be the most original road sign in the British Isles. A floral one with the names of Thurso and Wick depicted in flowers and two huge arrows marked out in white chippings. Just outside Lybster I met two girls and a cocker spaniel going to Land's End, raising money for some childhood illness which I have since forgotten. We were all delighted to have actually met someone else on the same mission. They took my photograph, me theirs. They were cheerful, bubbly girls, and I had to admire their approach. No maps. No planned route and not much money—just bags of enthusiasm. They had little knowledge of long distance footpaths but were planning on using the West Highland Way. I told them dogs weren't allowed on most of it, but they weren't bothered. They'd carry the dog! Their sole plan was to get there, someway or other, cadging campsites from pubs and farmers and working out a route as they went along. They expected to arrive by the middle of November. They were full of youthful optimism, confident that all would work out all right. No doubt they would have lots of adventures and plenty of stories to tell and a deal more excitement than me, but I preferred my staid, well organised approach. I wished them luck and told them to wave vigorously if they saw a bearded man in a psychedelic blue Land Rover in the next few miles. They left saying, "Don't miss the Camster Cairns. They're brilliant."

As soon as they were gone, I regretted not exchanging names and addresses. I would willingly have given them overnight accommodation if they came down the Offa's Dyke Path and I thought about them many times over the next few weeks. The weather in October was atrocious with snow on the Pennines, and November was not much better. I often wondered if they 'made it'.

### Entombed—and pestered by a kerb-crawler

Lybster is one of several small fishing villages along the eastern Caithness coast. I had lunch in a café just off the main road where the owner, a warm-hearted, courteous Scot wanted to hear all about my journey. What impressed me most about the northern Scots was that they are absolutely genuine and sincere. The whole pace of life is slower. People seemed to have all the time in the world and most of all, have an old fashioned courteousness that is rarely seen these days. It was like turning the clock back by 40 years. On the way home we stopped there again and the man, remembering that I had hoped to go to the Orkneys, asked if I went, and what I thought of them. Whilst preparing our meal and coping calmly and good naturedly with an influx of noisy and demanding lunchtime schoolchildren, he still managed to bring a selection of daily papers to our table and ask if we wanted the radio on. Where else in Britain would you get that service?

Our calculations for meeting could not have been more accurate. As I approached the relevant road junction, the Land Rover drove up and turned in just ahead of me. An excellent piece of co-ordinated timing on both parts. As I had already eaten we did little more than stop to exchange my rucksack for a small day sack and I set off again leaving Michael to take a break. The landscape was one of neglected rushy pasture and ruined crofts. At any point you could easily count a dozen. Later, this gave way to heather moorland and dark coniferous forests. For seven miles the road was arrow straight. Fast for walking—but exceedingly boring.

Michael drove ahead to wait at the Camster Cairns, more correctly the Grey Cairns of Camster. Bronze age burial mounds. Enormous dome-shaped islands of grey rocks surrounded by a sea of boggy peat with board walks providing safe, dry access. To reach the central chamber involved crawling from the tiny cave-like entrance along a low narrow passage about 3ft. high, though the chamber itself, constructed of great slabs of stone, was large enough to stand up in. Fully restored with a small roof-light providing enough light to see, there was no sense of being entombed. Indeed, roomy and draught-free this bronze age stone tent seemed perfect for camping.

More tedious foot-slogging followed along a further length of straight road bordered by extensive peat workings, the plots currently being used for fuel. They were marked out with simple home-made signs with the name of the owner or his croft. Stacks of peat lay drying in readiness for carting home for the winter. Michael drove slowly beside me. Window open. Chatting. There was hardly any traffic and the road was so straight that anything coming could be seen for miles. He had ample time to drive to a passing place if another car put in an appearance. A local farmer drove by, wound his window down and asked me why the Land Rover kept stopping. Was the man with the beard pestering me? "Yes" I replied. "He was my husband. He always pestered me!"

We stayed at Wick that night. And I found out where the Safeways' lorries had been going. Apart from Thurso, Wick is the only town of any size in northern Scotland. By local standards the supermarket was good, but I found the range of products very limited compared with home. The choice of fruit and vegetables was particularly poor. Little can be grown this far north. Everything has to be brought by road. I did a big shop, filling a trolly with tins and bottles. I didn't have to carry them and was not that anxious to take up cooking again. Getting to grips with a tin opener was all I proposed for the next week or two. I also bought twenty identical Lands End to John O'Groats postcards—to send off to the long list of folks promised cards *en route*.

### *Nature has her final fling*

My final day's walk began where I ended the night before. Michael judiciously waited two or three miles ahead, keeping his eyes peeled for vigilante farmers. The countryside was gently undulating. Never much above sea level, but never quite flat. An area of extensive corn growing where the harvest, much later than in the south, was still underway. On ground too poor to cultivate, young forestry plantations replaced fields, and peat and heather were once more dominant.

The Romans, if they had ever made it this far, could not have done a better job of road building. The road was again ruler straight. Occasionally Michael stayed behind in order to photograph me walking ahead. I could see the Land Rover quite literally miles behind, a tiny speck in the distance. Over such rolling country, dangerous hidden dips in the road were common. Approaching vehicles simply disappeared from view. Everywhere is exposed to the elements. No hedges and, except for the vast conifer plantations, no trees. But hundreds of electricity poles. Miles of them. One enterprising, hard-pressed bird in its quest for a nest site, had built a large untidy nest of twigs on the metal stay bracket at the top of a pole.

Massive flagstones standing on edge bounded the fields. They were quarried locally for centuries and, from the tiny harbour at Castletown just along the coast, were exported all over the world. Now the tiny harbour, itself constructed of huge slabs of rock, has a museum and an industrial heritage trail showing the extent of the industry. Flagstones are commonplace in the area. Used for everything, from roofing to building. Back home they would be worth a fortune. A trailer load to take home would have paid for my holiday.

The weather decided it was time to be seasonal. A strong northerly wind whistled theatrically in the miles of power lines. It was bitterly cold. The sky was leaden. It was depressingly gloomy. I wore jumper, fleece and waterproof clothing—and still froze. The waters of Loch Watten were whipped into a frenzy of tempestuous waves giving a good impression of a stormy sea. It was too cold to stop for breaks. I shivered even sitting in the Land Rover. And with a strong headwind practically blowing me over, walking was hard work. But the countdown was on. I was down to single figures.

The last three miles were along a main road. The quiet byways ended near Canisbay, in whose parish the village of John O'Groats lies, and in whose church John O'Groats the man is buried. Most people are surprised to learn that John O'Groats was a real person, a Dutchman by the name of John de Groot. As a young man, in 1496, he and his two brothers were commissioned by the King of Scotland to run a ferry to the Orkney Islands. This they did, charging four pence and thereby giving their name to the fourpenny piece, the groat. Their descendants continued to run the ferry for 250 years ensuring that their name would live on for ever in the community that grew up around the little harbour. We scoured the churchyard in the bitter wind, searching unsuccessfully for his grave. Eventually, numb with cold we gave up, but returned next day after we found out the headstone had been re-erected in the porch.

The weather continued to deteriorate. Drizzle turned to rain. If I had been hoping for the sun to come out and turn into a glorious evening for a perfect photofinish, I was sadly disillusioned. Nature seemed determined to make those final miles as difficult as possible as I battled against the elements to reach my goal. Just after 5 o'clock I rejoined my companion of so many miles, the A9. Having come 285 miles all the way from Edinburgh, it ends unceremoniously in John O'Groats Harbour and, in case you have failed to notice that you have arrived, a prominent sign announces A WELCOME AT THE END OF THE ROAD - JOHN O'Groats. This was the end of my road too. Exactly three months after leaving Land's End, in 79 walking days over an estimated 1,200 miles I had, like the road, arrived. Safe and sound; fit and well. But unceremoniously. It was too damnably cold, wet and windy to even take a finishing photograph.

We hung around in the warmth of a gift shop and hoped the weather might improve. But it looked extremely unlikely. I was much too cold to care anyway. All I wanted was a hot shower and a hot drink. I experienced no feelings of elation or satisfaction. All that would come later—very much later. My feelings on this day were no different to all the others. It was just the end of another day's walk.

Next morning we did a belated photo-finish and I added my name to the End to Enders book in the John O'Groats Hotel. Michael presented me with a poem, written by a friend who throughout had given me tremendous encouragement, boosting my morale and convincing me whenever I had doubts that I could—and would—do it. It bought tears to my eyes. Not only because she had managed to epitomise the entire walk, but because she had taken the trouble to write it at all. I was very touched.

### *I've made it—so what! Where do I go from here?*

At the end of any long walk, people expect a show of excitement. They think you should be jumping for joy. But the reality is quite the opposite. You have a sense of anti-climax. Sadness. You wish it did not have to end. Body and mind are conditioned to spend most of the day walking, always looking ahead. From the moment you reach your goal everything changes. Suddenly the next day is empty. What are you going to do?

From the experience of other long walks, I knew that even after 200 miles you are on a 'high' and I have found it can take a week or more to come down from this. There are withdrawal symptoms. My body has a physical urge to get out and walk. I re-live events and re-run whole sections of the route through my mind like a video. Being indoors is claustrophobic. Sleeping in a bed is uncomfortable. What then would it be like after 1,200 miles ?

I had tried to prepare myself mentally for the after effects. But in addition realised that something was needed to counteract the sudden loss of activity. The solution seemed to be to have a holiday. Michael deserved one. He had been wonderfully supportive throughout and if I had walked the distance, he had driven it—and more. He'd taken me to Land's End. He'd come to John O'Groats. It seemed only logical to make the best use of the journey. For two weeks I was to become what I had scorned for three months—a lazy, car-borne tourist. I would still have the 'buzz' of daily travel; new places and new people and by the time we reached home, would just feel as if I'd returned from holiday. Well! That was the theory.

### *Rewards*

We stayed at John O'Groats for a week. And I fell in love with the place. We searched white-sanded shell beaches for Groatie Buckies—tiny much prized cowrie shells used for making necklaces; walked the cliffs of Duncansby where the five jagged tooth-like sea stacks were comparable to anything Land's End had to offer and watched glorious sunsets from our tent. Across the turbulent Pentland Firth lay the alluring panorama of the Orkneys and the hazardous lighthouse topped reef of the Skerries. We gazed in awe at the tide race streaming from the Atlantic to the North Sea. A current that for five hours races westward at 12 miles an hour, then reverses as the tide flows eastwards for the next seven. I wondered how many End to Enders took the time to see more than the carpark and the celebrated signpost. Not many I suspected. We sat in the carpark one morning watching the comings and goings. A transit van arrived and unloaded cyclists. Almost immediately they left. The van followed. A backpacker arrived—an elderly man, rough bearded and looking a little footsore. No-one met him. He pottered around for a short time, then went to the bus stop and caught the next bus to Wick. A girl, with a considerable back-up team, was given a big send-off on a tractor plastered with posters about BSE and the plight of farmers. All came and went. What did they think of John O'Groats? I doubt they were there long enough to think anything. I could think of nothing worse, after all that time and effort, than arriving with no one to meet you and having to immediately leave.

Perhaps everyone who walks north should celebrate by going to the Orkneys. It was certainly the crowning glory of my journey. When we arrived the ferry was still running, but had broken down. A temporary service was provided by a much smaller vessel, but seeing the squally state of the sea, we didn't fancy that. It was three days before normal services were resumed. By then the weather had improved dramatically and we had an unforgettable day touring the islands. I had only one regret. I wished I had started at the Isles of Scilly. Then I would truly have gone End to End.

### So, you think its all over!

Two weeks later we returned to Wales. But if I thought it was all over, I was mistaken. We live in a close-knit, rural community where everyone knows everyone else's business and where news travels fast. Balloons and posters were stuck on telegraph poles and across our farm gate were more balloons and a yellow plastic banner to welcome me home. I was already booked to give a talk in our village hall and when I did, Helen and Michael made a surprise presentation of an engraved shield—which is now one of my most treasured possessions.

Those first few weeks at home I lived in a dreamworld. My pace of life had slowed down so much I couldn't speed up again. Also, I had increasingly come to realise that the material things of life were an encumbrance. For three months I had lived contentedly with all my needs on my back. I had food, clothes and somewhere to sleep. I did not miss or need all the trappings of modern life. I had not had the bustle and routine of cooking, washing, answering the phone, working and generally managing to do two or three things at once. I had not needed to hurry over anything. Now I had great difficulty adjusting to life in the real world. On my first shopping trip Helen went with me and as I dithered about in the super-market that usually sees me flitting from aisle to aisle flinging items off my list into a trolley, she said "Mum. You've forgotten how to shop."

Despite the holiday, withdrawal symptoms lasted much longer than I ever envisaged. Months rather than weeks. I had achieved a lifetime's ambition—and not many people are privileged to do that. And in doing so I had achieved much more. Self reliance. A confidence in myself which I never knew I had. My whole outlook on life had changed. Agoraphobia was a thing of the past. From being unable to leave the house I had progressed over the years slowly conquering each fear—shops, libraries, theatres, pubs, buses, the list was long. It had been a long struggle. Now I knew I could go anywhere. Do anything. Even the thought of giving a talk to a hall full of people didn't worry me.

There would be no stopping me now. My horizons had been broad-ened. I constantly re-ran the mental video. Another 200 mile walk the following year eased the symptoms temporarily. But it's not enough. I still give talks and each time I do, I relive it all. It was the most wonderful experience I have ever had. I have to do it again. And I say to anyone who has a great ambition—do it. Don't keep putting it off. You only live once. Grab your opportunity and make the most of it. You'll never regret it.

# Bibliography

Books and publications used in planning and walking from Land's End to John O'Groats:

Brown, Hamish *From the Pennines to the Highlands*
Davenport, John N. *A Cestrian Link Walk*
Emery, Gordon *Guide to the Maelor Way*
LDWA Directory of Long Distance paths, Long Distance Walker's
	Handbook
McCloy, Andrew *Land's End to John O'Groats*
Mid-Cheshire Footpath Society, Guide to the South Cheshire Way
Richards, Mark *Through Welsh Border Country*
Wainwright, A. *Pennine Way Companion*

Maps used included:

**The West Country**: Landranger 203, 204, 200, 201, 191,181,182, 172; Outdoor Leisure 9 Exmoor.

**Wales and Cheshire**: Offa's Dyke Association Strip Maps; Landranger 161, 148, 137, 126, 117.

**Peak District and Pennines**: Landranger 118, 98, 91, 86, 80, 74; Outdoor Leisure 24: The Peak District. White Peak. Outdoor Leisure 1: The Peak District. Dark Peak. Outdoor Leisure 21: The South Pennines. Outdoor Leisure 10: Yorkshire Dales. Southern Area.

**Scotland**: Landranger 73, 72, 65, 64, 34, 26, 21, 17, 12; Harvey's West Highland Way; Travel Master 4 Central Scotland and Northumberland; Travel Master 2 Northern Scotland, Orkney and Shetland.

# Equipment

With the exception of my tent, I bought nothing new for the walk. Everything was several years old but good quality and reliable. My Scarpa boots were ten years old and had already done well over a thousand miles. I'd had them resoled in readiness for another thousand confident that they would see me through. My rucksack, a 65 litre Karrimor with a self adjustable back system was several years old and amply large enough for my needs. Anything larger would only have been stuffed with extra clothes and extra weight. The only new item was my tent and this was bought specially for the walk. It was my most expensive piece of equipment. With strict criteria in mind, I looked long and hard at what was available before buying it. First and foremost was the weight; secondly the size and thirdly quality. I chose the Saunders Jetpacker, one of the lightest tents on the market and at 16 inches long when packed, small enough to fit inside my rucksack.

These three items were my most vital pieces of equipment. It was essential that none of them failed, otherwise I would be in trouble. Other items might suffer wear and tear but could be replaced when necessary. Boots, rucksack and tent were paramount to the success of the trip.

## Other equipment included:

Sleeping bag. 3 season
Insulation Mat
Small camp pillow
Survival bag
Colmans gas stove. Lighter and matches
Spare gas cylinder
Compact aluminium cooking pans (half the set)
Small aluminium kettle
Plastic dish
Plastic cup
Set of camp cutlery plus spare knife and
    teaspoon
Comprehensive First Aid kit
Water purifying tablets
Maglite torch
Spare batteries ( which also fit camera)
1 litre Sigg water bottle
Small hand towel
Small toilet bag (sample soap, sample
    toothpaste, toothbrush, two inch sponge)
Deodorant

Sunbloc cream
Midge repellant
Toilet tissue
Role of parcel tape
Whistle
Compass
Penknife
Automatic camera and three spare
    films
Three fun cameras
Personal alarm
Maps (about 4 at any one time)
Mapcase
Notebooks, guidebooks, pen and
pencil
Paperback novel
Personal finances, cheque books etc.
Two campers towels
Collapsible plastic bowl
Lightweight nylon daysack

**Clothing:**
Full waterproofs (Flexothane)
Lightweight gaiters
Three cotton blouses/T shirts
Three changes underwear
Shell pants
Leggings
Windproof cotton walking trousers
Shorts
Swimsuit
Lightweight sweatshirt
Fleece (from mid-Pennines on)
Two pairs thick walking socks
Three pairs undersocks
Lightweight trainers
Sunhat

**Food — 12 days basic rations:**
Packet 200 Candarel tablets
12 individual packets Alpen
12 Pic 'n' mix cheeses
6 Oxo cubes
6 Packets soup
3 Packets Super noodles
3 Packets Instant custard
6 Cake bars
12 Muesli bars
Small jar jam
20 individual coffee
10 Individual cappucino
Instant tea with milk (in plastic bottle)
Sugar — in film canister
Soap powder — in film canister
Dried milk — in film canister

Most of above packed in 2kg Plastic Container for convenience
Additional food bought and carried on a daily basis